# SCOUTING FOR THE BLUECOATS

## Navajos, Apaches, and the U.S. Military, 1873–1911

ROBERT S. MCPHERSON

Robert S. McPherson is Professor of History Emeritus at Utah State University–Blanding Campus and author of numerous books about the history and cultures of the Four Corners Region.

Other books of related interest by the author:
*Stories from the Land: A Navajo Reader about Monument Valley*
    (distributed by University Press of Colorado)
*Navajo Women of Monument Valley: Preservers of the Past*
    (distributed by University Press of Colorado)
*Traditional Navajo Teachings, A Trilogy*
    Volume I: *Sacred Narratives and Ceremonies*
    Volume II: *The Natural World*
    Volume III: *The Earth Surface People*
    (distributed by University Press of Colorado)
*Traders, Agents, and Weavers: Developing the Northern Navajo Region*
    (University of Oklahoma Press)
*Both Sides of the Bullpen: Navajo Trade and Posts of the Upper Four Corners*
    (University of Oklahoma Press)
*Viewing the Ancestors: Perceptions of the Anaasází, Mokwič, and Hisatsinom*
    (University of Oklahoma Press)
*Under the Eagle: Samuel Holiday, Navajo Code Talker*
    (University of Oklahoma Press)
*Dinéjí Na'nitin: Navajo Traditional Teachings and History*
    (University Press of Colorado)
*Navajo Tradition, Mormon Life: The Autobiography and Teachings of Jim Dandy*
    (University of Utah Press)
*Along Navajo Trails: Recollections of a Trader, 1898-1948*
    (Utah State University Press)
*A Navajo Legacy: The Life and Teachings of John Holiday*
    (University of Oklahoma Press)
*Navajo Land, Navajo Culture: The Utah Experience in the Twentieth Century*
    (University of Oklahoma Press)
*The Journey of Navajo Oshley: An Autobiography and Life History*
    (Utah State University Press)
*Sacred Land, Sacred View: Navajo Perceptions of the Four Corners Region*
    (University Press of Colorado)
*The Northern Navajo Frontier, 1860-1900: Expansion through Adversity*
    (University of New Mexico Press)

Copyright ©2022 Robert S. McPherson
Printed in the United States of America
ISBN 978-1-64642-567-9

# CONTENTS

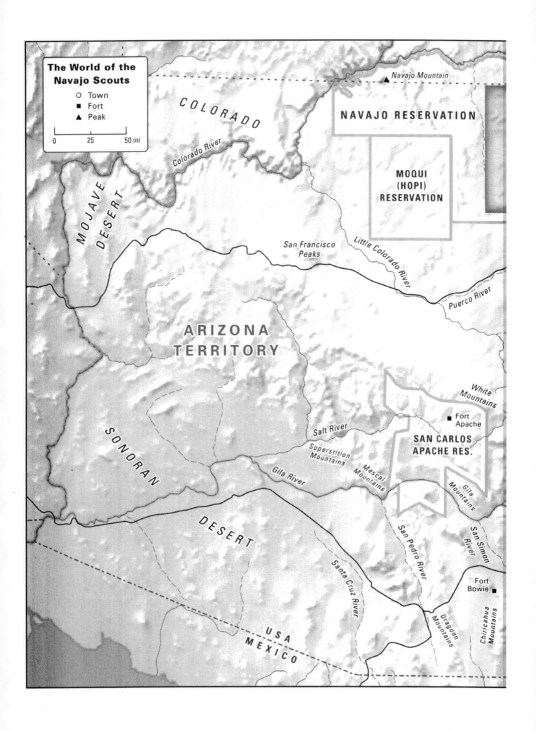

The World of the
Navajo Scouts

○ Town
■ Fort
▲ Peak

0    25    50 mi

COLORADO

Colorado River

NAVAJO RESERVATION

Navajo Mountain

MOQUI
(HOPI)
RESERVATION

MOJAVE DESERT

San Francisco
Peaks

Little Colorado River

Puerco River

ARIZONA
TERRITORY

White
Mountains

Fort
Apache

SAN CARLOS
APACHE RES.

SONORAN

Salt River

Superstition
Mountains

Mescal
Mountains

Gila River

Gila
Mountains

DESERT

San Pedro River

San Simon
River

Santa Cruz River

Fort
Bowie

Dragoon
Mountains

Chiricahua
Mountains

USA
MEXICO

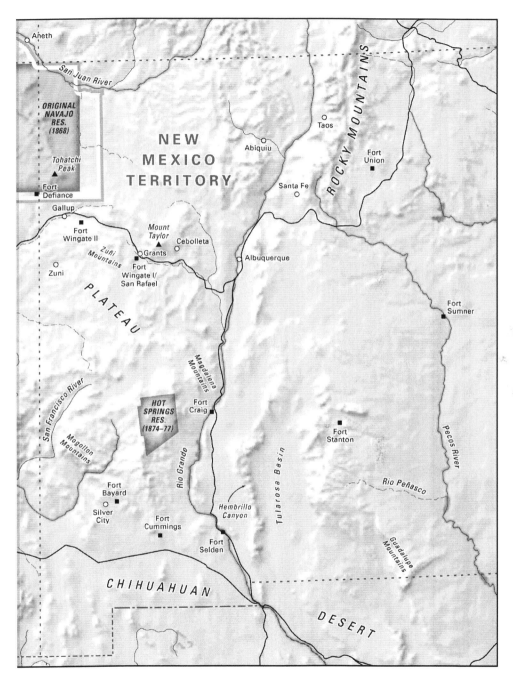

Map by Erin Greb Cartography

v

# INTRODUCTION
# Picking Up the Trail

T he cliché "Winning of the West" suggests the opening of a bright future, a host of opportunities for those who won, but does not hint of those who lost or the price paid. When the layers of time and events are peeled back, a less optimistic picture is revealed with fighting, loss, and heartache coloring both sides of the conflict in somber tones. Certainly, the history of America from start to present has embraced many different hues, particularly in the Indian Wars that started when the Spanish first set foot in America, followed by the English and French settlers, and continuing into the late nineteenth century. One character- istic that is found in many of these confrontations is the exacerbation of intertribal conflicts that existed prior to the white man's arrival but became full-blown during the westward movement. While this is not to denigrate the building of America and its history, it does recognize that the process came at a tremendous cost in life, land, and cultural values. Nowhere is this more evident than in the history of Native Americans—the "losing" side of the "winning." For the best overview of Indians scouting and working against other Indians, see Thomas W. Dunlay's *Wolves for the Blue Soldiers*, which covers the Trans-Mississippi West between 1860 and 1890.[1] Its broad approach places what follows into a more generalized context.

*Scouting for the Bluecoats* examines part of that sizable conflict that oc- curred in a corner of the Southwest, pitting Navajos and Apaches against other groups of Apaches. Yet this is more than just another study in how the U.S. military used its allies to defeat an opponent. The Navajos and Apaches who took up arms against their foe were relatives—some distant, others close to those they fought. Why did they join a common enemy who had recently defeated them both only to place them on unsatisfactory res- ervations? How was a numerically inferior force, so often on the run, able to successfully stymie its pursuers while conducting raids and ambushes that baffled those who had the might of the U.S. military behind them? Finally, what would it take to defeat them? While a number of excellent historians have chronicled the Apache wars, few have spent much time examining the experience of the "auxiliary" forces to learn how they effectively engaged a foe that melted into the landscape only to emerge, sometimes hundreds of miles away, to strike again. For those writers who have recorded the scouting aspect, the Apache scouts have received the most attention. Men like Grenville Goodwin (1907–1940) lived among some of the men who had served as scouts and interviewed them extensively, while others like journalist Charles F. Lummis (1859–1928) and Major John C. Cremony (1815–1879) of the army observed Apache scouts in action. Lieutenant Charles B. Gatewood (1853–1896) was more than an observer, leaving his account of commanding an Apache scout company while also facilitating the surrender of Geronimo.[2] Eve Ball (1890–1984) became a self-taught oral historian who captured a great deal of Apache history from those who knew such luminaries as Cochise, Mangas Coloradas, Victorio, and Geronimo.[3] Aspects of the Apache scouts' stories also emerge in her works. Still, few authors have given serious study to the techniques used and thinking behind the invaluable service these Native Americans provided in defeating those who resisted the proffered reservation life.

In the case of Navajo scouts, who anxiously enlisted to find and fight their Apache "cousins," even less has been written. Military reports of the time often mention the use of these men, giving numbers and some details of skirmishes, but they remained portrayed as effective in tracking the enemy and anxious to engage but generally anonymous. Even in Navajo history written today, little mention is made of the important service rendered by the Navajo scouts—perhaps over five hundred of whom enlisted in the U.S. military. Until recently, there had only been two works dedicated to the topic: a master's thesis entitled "Navajo Scouts, 1873–1895: An Integration of Various Cultural Interpretations of Events" by Robert C. Collman and a short, well-written monograph published as *Navajo Scouts During the Apache Wars* by John Lewis Taylor.[4] Both works center on the traditional approach of using campaign material gleaned from military reports of the time and some brief Navajo testimony obtained in statements made thirty years after the wars' cessation when the scouts were filing for government pensions. This is not a criticism but is mentioned only to point out that these sources are limited in providing the actual scout experience. Other historians have examined, in detail, the military's strategic, operational, and tactical endeavors against the Apaches that led to the Indians' eventual defeat, but for the most part, the Navajo scouts often garner a sentence or two and are then forgotten.[5]

Fortunately, the story of the Navajo scouts was of interest to V. Robert Westover, a man who has worked with Navajo people much of his life and became enamored with the scouts' story in the early 1980s. One of his passions is helping Navajos trace their genealogy. In pursuing that interest, he first stumbled upon the pension files of the Navajo scouts stored in Window Rock, the Navajo Nation's capital, and then broadened his search to the National Archives in Washington, D.C. For three decades, he collected materials dealing with their story, amassing a large filing system with documents of all types and a wonderful collection of photos taken in the 1920s and early 1930s as these old veterans made application for their pension. Always collecting, Bob intended to write the scouts' story, but life remained busy with work and ecclesiastical responsibilities, and so the project became postponed. His main focus of providing genealogical information from his files will soon reach fruition, but being advanced in age, he realized that he needed help in capturing the historical side of this Navajo experience.

I had met Bob in the mid-1980s when I attended Brigham Young University to obtain a doctorate. I had spent the previous six years working both on and off the Navajo reservation, first for the Utah Navajo Development Council and later for the College of Eastern Utah in Blanding. Because of my interest in the Navajo people and since my dissertation was on the Utah Navajo, it was natural that Bob and I became good friends with a common interest. We shared information and enjoyed each other's company, but once I returned to my college duties, life had a way of making my visits to his office infrequent. He retired, and eventually I retired, so we lost touch. Then in 2020, a familiar voice over the phone asked if I would be interested in helping to tell the scouts' story. I readily agreed, Bob opened his files to me, and the process began.

It soon became evident that there was a lot of material to go through, but much was oriented toward genealogy while other sources focused on the Anglo military side of the equation. I was interested in taking a different approach by telling the experience of the scouts, as much as possible, from their perspective. This was difficult because although there is a large body of Navajo oral history collected by anthropologists, linguists, historians, and others in the social sciences, little mention has been made about the scouts. I tried to include much of what I discovered, but there were still gaps. When I went to the Apache side of the Apache-Navajo-military triumvirate, there was a lot more information, much of which clarified and added detail to the Navajo accounts. Since both groups worked together, either alone or in tandem, I have felt justified in using Apache accounts in conjunction with Navajo accounts to get into the fieldcraft of tracking. In related topics, however, the emphasis has been on the Navajo scouts and what they encountered during field operations.

Before leaving the source material drawn upon in writing this book, I have to provide one caveat for the historian and other individuals interested in pursuing some of the sources—especially those found in the last two chapters. Bob explained that when he collected materials during a dozen trips to the National Archives, he was more interested in the information and less concerned about recording where it came from. Consequently, he gathered a lot of documents printed with the National Archives marker but with no identification as to the record group or subclassification that they came from. Because of the nature of the material, I am assuming most of it came from Record Group 75, with its close to 187 million textual pages, of which only 5 million have been digitized. In-house, this is further divided into dozens and dozens of categories. My effort to pinpoint exactly where this material came from proved fruitless. All I can offer is that the information definitely came from the National Archives and that it will probably take a dedicated researcher on-site to get a more specific identification.

What, then, does this study of the Navajo scouts provide? Chapter 1 is pure context—going back to the time when these Athabaskan speakers were united with their Apache "cousins" who speak the same language. Social scientists as well as Navajos and Apaches have shared thoughts on the People's (Diné) origin and subsequent series of divisions among those living in northwestern Canada, Alaska, Siberia, the Southwest, and elsewhere. Even in those earliest centuries before the written word recorded tribal relationships, there is every indication that not all was peaceful and that conflict often lay at the root of the subdivisions that accompanied the Navajo and Apache entrance into the Southwest. There is no doubt there was hostility when Spanish, Mexican, and Anglo chroniclers arrived upon the scene. Internecine warfare was very much a part of Athabaskan interactions. This chapter concludes with elements of both groups incarcerated at Fort Sumner during the 1860s and the friction that ensued when in close proximity to each other.

Chapter 2 examines three different approaches to war—that of the Navajos, Apaches, and U.S. military—as they evolved from older traditions into what was encountered during the 1870s and 1880s. Although Navajos and Apaches shared a number of similarities in their ways of fighting, fundamental cultural differences were at work between the two. The Anglos, on the other hand, came from a dissimilar tradition, took a different approach to seeking a particular desired outcome, and enjoyed a material superiority that did not always comport with the actions in the field. Chapter 3 explains why the Navajo scouts became such an important part of the military structure. Along with those Apaches who agreed to track and fight, these scouts proved invaluable in finding the enemy.

The next three chapters are the heart of the scouting experience, examining the training and fieldcraft of those Apaches fleeing from their reservations, what it took for the Navajo scouts to bring them in, and three personal accounts of what the daily and weekly life of a scout was like when searching for the enemy. In chapter 7 a final evaluation of the scouting experience during the Apache wars follows as an end to the largest involvement of scouts hired by the government at any one time. The diminished number of Navajo men continued with their military associates to quell problems and maintain the peace, but as large-scale Indian issues subsided, there was a movement to shift the Indians' status from short-term enlistee to full-time soldier in a formal military unit. Chapter 8 looks at this phenomenon and the many scouts who turned to law enforcement on the reservation as Navajo police. In both instances, their tracking skills and knowledge of fieldcraft stood them in good stead. The final chapter moves ahead fifteen years after the scouts were disbanded, to the time when the men involved in the Apache wars and other military service sought a government pension to carry them and their spouses through old age. Fortunately, the supervisor over the Eastern Agency located at Crown Point (Pueblo Bonito), worked extremely hard to make sure that these people received what was rightly theirs. Agent Samuel F. Stacher left an excellent record of those still-surviving scouts and fostered the opportunity for those who served to receive a well-earned recompense. The forgotten, for once, had been remembered.

When put in a broader context, it becomes more evident why the scout experience needs to be shared. Take for instance the Navajo code talkers that have become well known for their contribution in the Pacific theater during World War II. Shortly after the government declassified the program in 1968, people became increasingly aware of what these Navajo marines had accomplished. The news spread throughout the United States and beyond, to the point that there has been significant recognition for these men who served as the largest Indian group to use their language in communicating military information on the battlefield. Like the Navajo scouts—due to recruitment techniques, inadequate record-keeping, conditions on and off

the reservation, and the secrecy of the program—there has been no defin-
itive compilation of statistics about those Navajos involved during the war
(1941–45) before being disbanded. Perhaps the estimates given by code
talker Samuel Sandoval, a man who not only served but tried to keep track
of his enlisted comrades, are close. He believes that of the 420 Navajo men
who received code talker training, somewhere between 135 and 145 of
them were in actual combat, with twelve killed in the line of duty.[6]

If this is the case, for comparison purposes with the Navajo scouts,
there were more (estimated over 500 enlisted) who served in a conflict
that lasted more than twice as long (thirteen years—1873–86). They also
lost a comparable number of men and were involved in continual combat
operations once enlisted. While no one would argue that the intensity of
conflict was the same, the scouts fought a wily foe just as determined as
the Japanese. Certainly the deserts and mountains of the Southwest and
Mexico had their own physical challenges, opposite yet comparable, to the
coral atolls and volcanic islands of the Pacific. This is not to detract from
either group, but just to point out that the Navajo scouts have not received
due recognition for the efforts that they made and what they accomplished.

Their story needs to be told. What the reader encounters within the
pages of this book is a group of men who worked under some of the most
trying conditions against a foe skilled in survival, cagey in tactics, and dedicated to preserving Apache freedom at any cost. Both sides believed in
what they did. To a person in the twenty-first century, the Southwest of
the 1870s and 1880s may seem like a time of unmitigated violence and
bloodshed, painted in black and white, good and evil. This position can
certainly be supported, regardless of which of the sides one takes. On the
other hand, the reader will find every hue of emotion and behavior, from
bravery to cowardice, devotion to treachery, and cunning to foolishness.
The life of the scouts and those they pursued was difficult and challenging,
with both sides encountering a kaleidoscope of actions and reactions, all
part of the human experience.

# CHAPTER ONE

# Athabaskan Origins and Conflict

## Roots from the Past

The contrast between the subarctic cold and the blazing desert heat of the Colorado Plateau is stark. These beginning and ending homeland conditions of the Navajos have produced a people who are adaptable and deeply religious. They recognize their place in austere climates that demand an understanding of the land, its creatures, and the role of spirituality in surviving. But for them, it was not just a matter of eking out a bare existence or facing diminishing numbers. No. Their trajectory has taken them to a series of accomplishments—the largest reservation in the continental United States; the largest enrolled population, recently surpassing the Cherokees; the greatest number of Native American language speakers, not including other Athabaskans living in the arctic and subarctic of Canada, Alaska, and Siberia; and the maintenance of one of the richest bodies of traditional oral lore. The Navajos hold a special place in Native American tribal history.

## Northern Origins

How did they get there and at what price? The Navajo people have an important history and prehistory documented through the years by anthropologists, religious leaders, military personnel, historians, and tribal scholars, each with their own slant as to what occurred over the centuries. The story is multifaceted, but as can be best determined now, the earliest identifiable physical remains of the Athabaskan speakers who would one day be known as Navajos are found to the north in subarctic Canada and arctic Alaska and Siberia, where large numbers of these people live today. Perhaps the single best collection of current discussion about their ancestral roots is found in *From the Land of Ever Winter to the American Southwest*, edited by Deni J. Seymour.[1] This collection of sixteen scholars' work from a wide range of disciplines identifies the roots of Athabaskan culture, suggesting where and why the Navajo people migrated to the Southwest. A brief synopsis of this thinking follows.

Language and language change are two of the main connecting links that tie those living in the North to those in the Southwest. There are thirty-two northern Athabaskan-speaking tribes living in the interiors of Alaska and northwestern Canada, while in the United States there are the Tlingits and Hupas on the west coast, the Kiowa-Apache on the Plains, and the Jicarilla, Lipan, Chiricahua, Mescalero, and Western Apache, the latter comprising the Tonto, White Mountain, San Carlos, and Cibecue groups. Add to this the Navajos, who do not consider themselves Apaches but speak Athabaskan. The linguistic differences between these various groups range from small to almost incomprehensible. While all are somewhat intelligible, in some instances there are large linguistic gaps and cultural practices that draw sharp distinctions between various groups. These differences are used by linguistic anthropologists to examine the shift in words, which helps determine when each of the entities separated from a proto-Athabaskan language as well as when more closely related proto-Apache groups subdivided.

One approach used to differentiate when these entities separated is known as glottochronology, a technique that became popular in the 1950s. It is founded in the belief that all languages have a core vocabulary of one hundred words held in common with every culture—water, ax, bow, mother, and so forth. Over a period of one thousand years, 86 percent of these words will be held in common, but 14 percent will change, providing insight as to how long a separation of two groups that share the same language may have been. There are a number of problems based in this assumption, one of the biggest ones being that not all languages change consistently and at the same rate—they are affected by different circumstances. However, glottochronology does provide some ballpark figures such as "the proto-Apacheans split from the Northern Athapaskan group around 1000 AD, reaching the Southwest around 1400 AD, with a later split into what are now recognized as distinct languages."[2] For instance, the Hupas, now living in California, separated from the Navajos about 1,100 years ago; the Kutchin and the Beaver groups, in Canada 890 and 690 years ago respectively, suggesting that the Navajos separated from their ancestral stock roughly 1,000 years ago.[3] The separation of the Navajos from other Athabaskans in the Southwest can also be determined in generalized terms (although the figures given sound far too exact). In 2011 linguist Sally Rice posited that the Navajos parted from the Chiricahua Apaches 203 years ago, the San Carlos and Jicarilla 333 years ago, and the Lipan Apaches 389.[4] Imprecisely precise, these figures provide a generalized approach to approximate Athabaskan group splits.

Anthropologists and archaeologists have garnered other proof that suggests a northern orientation, but they are unsure what route they may have taken in moving south. Three possibilities are popular—the western side of the Rocky Mountains, the eastern side, or down through the middle. While there are now Indian groups who speak this language along the Pacific Northwest Coast and in northern California, and also indications that there were different Apachean peoples out on the Plains until pushed into the Southwest, there is also stunning proof of their existence in Utah. In the desert north of Salt Lake around Promontory Point, caves excavated by archaeologist and anthropologist Julian Steward in 1930 yielded a large collection of 250 moccasins characteristic of the type used by subarctic Athabaskan-speaking peoples. There were also buffalo hides, arrow shafts and points, scrapers, pottery, and other objects that were distinct from the surrounding native peoples. These materials have since provided radiocarbon dates ranging from 1150 AD to predominantly the last half of the 1200s, the time of abandonment of the more local Fremont Indians. Proof of this Promontory Culture of Athabaskan speakers is also found around Utah Lake.[5] All of this raises the possibility that at least some of these people could have continued to the south into what is now the homeland of the Navajo people.

While no one will ever be able to pin down all of their routes and travel experiences, it is important to realize that being on the move in lengthy migration ("big trips") was not just a matter of changing locations, but also a formative period that gave each entity different types of growth and cultural variation. None of this was done in a vacuum. Seymour summarizes a model of what this could have looked like, explaining how each tribal group obtained its own distinctive personality as they hunted and gathered and interacted with others on their way to a new homeland in the Southwest.

> The end result was a movement choreographed on the basis of the actions of neighbors, who drew or repelled Apachean people as raiding

or trading opportunities arose, as the balance of power changed, or as once-powerful groups adjusted their boundaries. Seen in this way, it is not so difficult to comprehend the elusiveness of these early Athabaskans and the distance between colonized residential sites (some areas skipped over entirely), to visualize the diversity of their material and spatial footprints as they moved south, and to understand how such different material culture signatures might develop at the southernmost end of their migration track.[6]

Whether the Athabaskans took a plains, intermontane, or coastal migration route, or a combination, the Navajo and Apache forebears settled eventually in what is now New Mexico and Arizona, where they were influenced by neighboring Puebloan people. There is an ongoing debate as to when the Athabaskans finally arrived—some suggest as early as the 1000s while others push the date to as late as the 1500s. Since they came as hunters and gatherers, they left few remains of their homes and activities that can be definitely dated. Seymour, in 2014, published additional research on the southern mountains of New Mexico, home of the Mescalero Apache, and on Arizona where the Chiricahua Apache lived. In these mountain ranges she found well-preserved platform caches made of stones and various desert plants that were hidden in rock shelters. Pottery, pieces of ceremonial headdresses, and a wand associated with Mountain Spirit (*gaan*) dances, as well as a pictograph depicting their distinctive spirit masks, identified this site as definitely Apache. Plants and other materials evaluated from these sites indicated that some were in use as early as the fourteenth and fifteenth centuries. These new, early dates "provide a basis for re-evaluating long-held views about the end of prehistory and the arrival of ancestral Apachean groups in the heart of the American Southwest."[7]

Dates of the Navajo arrival in the Southwest are also being pushed back to an earlier time than the generally accepted 1500s. For instance, recent excavations north of Farmington, New Mexico, and just south of the Colorado state line have yielded twelve sites with twenty-three radiocarbon dates that predate the 1500s, the earliest going back to the 1300s. Because of this new information "it appears likely that the Navajo were in the Four Corners region by at least 1400 AD. . . . The period of time between the last Anasazi occupation north of the San Juan River and the earliest Navajo sites is now only about a century, suggesting the possibility that future research may establish contemporaneity between the two cultures."[8] This is particularly important since the area producing these early dates is considered by the Navajo people to be the place of emergence from the world beneath and their oldest area of habitation.

The different crosscurrents of Apachean people entering the Southwest, encountering different climates and previously established people, gave rise to their own distinctive cultures.

The Navajos became less mobile, acquired agriculture, fashioned their own style of pottery, built hogans that required either remaining at or returning to their established homes during an annual cycle, and became intimately connected to the landscape for resources and religious beliefs. The Western Apaches established a comparable pattern while the Chiricahua, Mescalero, Plains, and Lipan Apaches were more mobile and dependent on hunting, gathering, and travel for trading and raiding.[9]

## Oral Origins

So goes the story as told by western scholars in various disciplines ranging from anthropology and archaeology to linguistics, art history, and oral history. The various Native American groups offered their own explanations, some of which confirm certain elements of Anglo scholarship, but much of which goes in an opposite direction. Reason: the former is generally based in science and tangible proof, the latter in religion and spirituality. As mentioned previously, the Navajos have one of the richest, most complex philosophical belief systems in North America. Their oral tradition is the basis of a multitiered series of ceremonial practices that heal the sick, answer life questions, and provide guidance for proper behavior down to some of the smallest details. Unique even among the other Athabaskan-speaking peoples, there are shared elements with all, but no other has the depth and intricacy of Navajo beliefs.

Central to Navajo teachings is the "main [corn]stalk of the creation story with its Blessingway ceremony, off of which all other ceremonies in one way or another, refer back to. The importance of the creation story cannot be overemphasized. If one wants to understand the Navajo worldview, there is only one place to start—at its roots. This is why there are so many recorded accounts about these seminal events."[10] However, as soon as a person reads a second and third version of the same story, it will become apparent that although a general outline is shared, they may each vary markedly in scope, emphasis, and detail. Indeed, no two creation stories of the worlds beneath are the same. Each medicine man will tell his account that he learned from his teacher, yet with every raconteur, there will be a different version. Variations abound for other reasons as well:

much can depend on what part of the reservation a person comes from, an individual who is knowledgeable about different ceremonies may tie in or emphasize some aspects and ignore others, and the depth of understanding and age of the narrator can affect vocabulary and extent of insight. Variation from story to story is not a problem for the Navajo people, even when considering fundamental points. Common patterns reveal six motifs found in most versions, which emphasize important elements of Navajo daily and ceremonial life.

In every rendition of the creation story, there were either four or five worlds present, the fourth or fifth being the world humans now live in. The size of each of these worlds was much smaller than the one now inhabited. As the holy people passed through each of them, they obtained the creatures, vegetation, and landforms such as mountains to establish in the next world. By the time they reached this present level, the holy people had gained a lot of experience and the ability to beautify their existence. Placing the six sacred mountains, rivers, and other land formations around the countryside, they were able to blow life into and expand them to their present size. Since everything was created spiritually before it was made physically, each had an inner spirit placed inside. Things like the earth and sky, lightning and thunder, rocks and trees have an inner form, roughly glossed as "animate being that lies within" (*bii'gistíín*), which was present only in spiritual form in the worlds beneath. Each of these animate or inanimate objects had their personalities and teachings embedded internally.

Not all Navajos agree on some of the specifics. Even the place of emergence into this world is disputed, some medicine men insisting it was in the area of Navajo Dam outside of Farmington, New Mexico, while others teach that it was at Fish Lake near Pagosa Springs, Colorado—a distance of sixty miles between the two sites. Regardless of which place it was, both put the Navajos in their Southwest ancestral homeland called Dinétah (Among the People). Many of the initial activities of expanding the land and emplacing geographic forms, the draining of water to the cardinal directions, the introduction to other native groups, and interaction with the holy people began here and then spread to the south and west. The Navajos, with divine assistance, settled upon the land in an ever-widening arc.

There were holy people who emerged with the Navajos into this world and traveled with them throughout the Four Corners area. Each brought blessings and knowledge with them that they shared with the people as they traveled about, but none were more beneficent and helpful than Changing Woman, who is credited with physically creating the first people and starting the Navajo clan system. As the Navajos moved throughout the Southwest, obtained additional clans, interacted and inter-married with other tribes, and followed the teachings of the holy beings, Changing Woman determined it was time to leave her people and join her husband, Sun Bearer, in the West, where he had built a home for her. She told them that she would soon depart, but there were many who did not want her to go, and if she did, they promised to accompany her. Unlike the movement embraced by western scholars of the Navajos moving from north to south, at least some Navajo storytellers suggest the exact oppo-site with the movement of Changing Woman and her people beginning in the south and moving to the north. One version of what happened is told by medicine man Perry Robinson, who provides a more west-north-west version, taking her and her followers into the land of the northern Athabaskans.

> Having lived a challenging life in this world, Changing Woman decided to go with her husband, Sun Bearer, to a home that he built for her in the West. This was the same time that all of the gods moved to their ap-pointed places to remain for the rest of time. In preparation for the long journey to the Pacific Ocean, she selected plants, water, animals, and even some of the people from the Four Sacred Mountains who wanted to remain with her. After gathering an abundancy of the things she needed, she began walking to the west and north, where the sun lies down. Some of the animals that accompanied her were wolves, coyotes, ferrets, buffalo, deer, and other, smaller creatures. Along the way, some of the travel-ers dropped off to remain in areas that they liked. By the time she had reached lands to the north, there were only a few animals and people remaining with her.
>
> Changing Woman with her travelers had reached a place where the climate was really cold and the snow deep. The sunlight became shorter and less intense as the days became darker and colder. The fur on the ani-mals started to modify, many of their coats began to lose their color, their tongue and teeth changed, and their eyes transformed as they looked and hunted for different things. For instance, the coyotes and foxes that are found in our area have different eyes when compared to those located in the north. Ones to the north have blue eyes instead of the yellowish brown of those who stayed behind. Food for these animals also changed. Their songs became different, shifting their behavior and attitude. Now they walked differently and grew bigger or smaller in size, depending on the need and the temperature of the climate. Hunting methods had to be adapted to the new circumstances; the food the animals and people ate

was different, changing their diet and eating habits. This new world and way of life offered new challenges.

The Water People adopted some of these animals back. Many of these holy beings were more numerous than they were in the land of the four sacred mountains. Water was all over the countryside, in rivers, lakes, and in the nearby ocean, so the animals started to eat food from these sources, causing them to swim and dive more and improve their ability to see underwater. For example, some of the bears, like the polar bear, turned into water creatures, whereas the bears that live around here are land people. Their body structure got bigger, they depended heavily on fish, their eyes and mouth changed, even their foot pattern was different. They are now bigger, heavier, and not afraid of anything. The same is true of other animals. Take deer for instance. They are in the same species and family as the caribou, but they each have dissimilar prayers because they have adapted to their own land and act accordingly. Still, they are one and the same animal, but their colors, antlers, feet, and how they walk are different. Caribou are much slower but they swim well, live on land, and travel in herds. Deer, on the other hand, are extremely fast runners and generally do not live in large groups. Change in habitat made a big difference with everything.

At home between the Four Sacred Mountains, the people were becoming lonely and wandering around, missing Changing Woman and the time that the gods were always present. Now the holy people were scattered to the four directions. The humans had received instructions and answers from them, when suddenly they were left alone with no one to lead. They followed the guidance obtained in the past, but it was hard to live a life without the gods always there to assist. The people became increasingly stressed, looking for something that was no longer available to provide answers. They became very unhappy, did not feel good about themselves, and kept asking, "What is going on? What is going on?" as they spiraled into depression. Tears filled their eyes as they cried for no apparent reason. There was no physical pain, but their mind and thoughts kept returning to the uncertainty of the future and what it would be like to live without the gods. Fear encompassed their world and anxiety shaped their decisions and actions as they convinced themselves that even worse things lay ahead in the future. Even after all they had been through with Monster Slayer ridding the earth of its frightening creatures, there were still storms, lightning, and thunder, reminding them of past struggles. The loud clapping of the thunder gods, remembering the fight against the monsters who killed and ate the children, and the hardships of daily life, wore the people down as anxiety grew. Now that the gods were gone, many of these bad things might return. Even though their world had become safer, their minds and inner feelings were getting the best of them. Black clouds scared them as they anticipated the next thunderstorm and changes in weather. Loneliness, depression, and uncertainty gripped their minds, causing them to trudge about aimlessly and cry all of the time.

Leaders and elders gathered together and said, "There are too many people wandering around unhappy. Something is going on that is not good. We need to get Changing Woman and talk to her; maybe she can fix what is wrong. This is one part of life that we do not understand." There was a woman who spoke a lot and was boastful, but she also got to the point quickly. Her name was "Woman Who Talks a Lot" (Asdzą́ą́ Lą́ áníní). Since she was not afraid of speaking up about issues, the leaders selected her to go in search of their elder sister, Changing Woman, and bring her back to fix these problems. Woman Who Talks a Lot found her and reported on the problems of the people and urged her to return. Changing Woman was the one who had helped solve problems and make life better in the past, and now they needed her assistance more than ever.

She started back with many people following her, while others who had originally left with her remained; still others stopped along the way to settle in different locations. The people who stayed in what is today Canada and Alaska are called by the Navajo the Diné Náhódlóonii (The People Who Exist Elsewhere). They speak our language and share some of our teachings and culture. Those that stopped in other places are also related but became involved with different tribes through marriage and so lost their ability to speak the Navajo language. Some remained with Changing Woman and came all the way south to the Havasupai; they speak a language very close to that of Navajo but live in the Grand Canyon area. This splitting off is also seen with the Apache who converse in our language and were at one time part of us. Some of their ceremonies are very similar to what we practice. They used to be Navajos, but they just went farther south. Still, they have preserved a lot of the old ways that we used to practice, including the way they dress. The medicine men who teach about these things—the ceremonies and traveling—always sing about moving to the west and the people who strayed away and joined other tribes. Their knowledge made them holy ones and so when they met other people, they brought their medicine and were accepted as part of those groups. We always sing about different people that we encountered, how we talked to them about medicine, and taught

them about these things. We became their holy ones by sharing this
information. That's my understanding of it.[11]

Robinson's explanation of these events is one of the most complete
accounts of what occurred in the past, and it hints toward the future. The
changes in the animals, plants, and people mark an adaptation to a northern environment, a complete reversal of the anthropological theory of the
Navajos adapting to the American Southwest.

While there is very little discussion of this northern connection in
the Navajo literature, medicine men are well aware of "Diné Who Exist
Elsewhere" (Diné Náhódlóonie) living in the north. One part of the teachings concerning the end of the world tells of when these two groups—
northern and southern Athabaskan speakers—will join together and once
again share their cultures and information. John Holiday, a medicine man
from Monument Valley, recounted when he was vacationing with some
family members in western Canada. They stopped near one of the reservations, and because his back was bothering him, he decided to sit out
some of the touring. He settled down on a nearby bench and waited for
his family to return.

> As I sat there, a couple of men from the Diné Who Exist Elsewhere
> approached. They greeted me with a language I understood. "Hello, my
> dearest. Where are you from?" "My dearest" is how they greet each other.
> "I'm a Navajo from the Navajo Reservation, my homeland," I replied. I
> thought these were some Navajos who were visiting there, too. [After
> introducing himself through clan relationship, he was told] "Well some
> of the same clans live back there within those mountains." [Later the
> two men asked] "Do you know the Blessingway?" "Yes." Then they said,
> "Our people were separated from your people during the Creation. Why?
> We don't know. The Holy Beings held us back and kept us here. We
> heard your people [Navajo] took most of the religious ceremonies like
> Blessingway and others with them. . . . If a Navajo comes here, he will
> have to come to our home, perform a ceremony, and tell our people the
> history of the religion and their beliefs, before he can be released to go."[12]

John was happy to part company once his family arrived.

In addition to these and other stories that discuss the northern migration, there are also stories that speak of the separation and eventual
reacquaintance of the Navajos with the Apaches. In 1928 Aileen O'Bryan
interviewed a Navajo elder and medicine man named Sandoval or Old

*Changing Woman bids farewell to those Athabaskan speakers left behind along her journey through the Southwest as she traveled to subarctic Canada, Alaska, and elsewhere. As a benevolent deity, she helped her people adapt to different environments, giving them spiritual strength for life, as portrayed in the Navajo girls' puberty ceremony and other Blessingway rites. (Drawing by Kelly Pugh)*

Man Buffalo Grass (Tlo'tsi hee) at Mesa Verde National Park.[13] From that series of recordings came a wealth of information about Navajo traditional beliefs, among which is a story of the Navajos meeting the Apaches. Few others have been recorded. While this account is not on a large mythic scale like Robinson's, it does provide insight into how future relations between the two groups would be. A brief synopsis with excerpts follows.

The narrative starts after the holy people had given the Navajos the horse and there were "a great many people in the land," crowding one another. Conflict and quarreling removed peace from their hearts and set the people at odds. The land reflected this tension, filling with thorns and spiked plants while the rocks burned red. Four Navajo chiefs went in search for some of their people who had departed earlier. For two years they moved eastward, sending out scouts to locate those missing. One day one of them came upon tracks and followed them to a water hole. On a number of successive days, scouts went out until campfire smoke, a cornfield, and a village appeared. One of the four scouts drew near to the encampment and heard his language being spoken, so he presented himself to the chief, who welcomed him and directed him to bring his people in to meet with his group. Before departing, the scout participated in the Hailway Ceremony, in which he led his new acquaintances all night long in singing. The two camps joined together, identifying each other through clan relations. For two years they shared activities and helped each other. The scouts had located the people they had been searching for.

As time passed, differences between the two factions arose. Sandoval explained:

> The people who had come last begged the first people to move back with them to the center of the earth [homeland within the four sacred mountains]. But those who had moved to the East said, "Our new country here is good. We have no worry. It makes our whole body sick to think of all of the grief that happened back there. We do not want to return to a country where there is nothing but trouble." Toward the middle of the second summer, being of two different minds, they started to quarrel. The Diné with four chiefs decided to return. They said: "You can stay here forever now. And if we ever see each other again there will be change on the earth," meaning that they would be enemies should they meet again. Then the other people said: "Start out for your home in your own country if you like, but your chiefs will never reach there." So they called to each other bitterly, and they split.[14]

The two groups separated and the prophecy was fulfilled. Lightning struck one of the chiefs, another drowned when crossing a river, the third died from a snake bite, and the last froze to death. Still, as Sandoval described, the Navajos continued to travel, meeting other Apache groups, a number of whom they befriended.

> After a time, some of them [White Mountain Apaches] left and went south to a country where there was much wood. They sent to the people on the plains asking them to join them. They said that they had found a place where there was a lot of wood, but the people of the plains said: "All you ever say or think of is wood, chiz. You will be called Chizgee." Then the people on the mountain said to the Chizgee: "Come up to the mountain where it is cool." But the Chizgee liked their own place, and said: "All the words that you use are of the mountain top. You will be called Dził an'ee (Mountain Top)."[15]

Other Apache groups visited with the Navajos, who had a bountiful harvest of corn at the time. Impressed by the abundance, they named the Navajos "People that Ripen." Sandoval continued: "So that was how the Diné scattered. They moved this way and that, large parties and single families. They joined other tribes or settled by themselves, but many were lost."[16]

An Apache version of this separation was provided by Lieutenant Charles B. Gatewood, who in the 1880s worked extensively with Apache scouts in the military and recorded valuable cultural information in his memoirs. This story, an early version from the Apache people, explains the reason for the split and the enduring attitude of those involved. According to this account, the Apaches were then settled in New Mexico and west Texas. A group of warriors raided their Comanche neighbors in Texas and obtained a large amount of booty that they brought back to their homeland. A furor arose over how the loot should be handled. "Some demanded that these things should be divided among the warriors who composed the raiding party, as nearly equal as possible, while others insisted on the right of each individual's having and holding what he had actually taken into his own possession. The quarrels waxed hotter and hotter, the friends of each side joined the discussions, and friends' friends took part also until the whole nation was embroiled in a political excitement . . . which divided into two factions."[17] Each side refused to relent, with everyone—men, women, and children—taking up arms that led to a bloody battle that ensued for days. The larger group prevailed on the battlefield, with the other fleeing from what would have otherwise been annihilation. Both factions counseled among themselves about what to do and decided that they would remain separate.

> One resolution received unanimous approval of the convention, and that was that the name of "Noo-tah-hah" [formerly what the Athabaskans had called themselves] should be forever discarded and the new appellation "Apache" be adopted. This word means The Man, in capital letters, the superior of all men; and they have striven ever since to demonstrate that the adoption of this name is no idle boast. The victors in this celebrated battle are now called "Navajos," living in northeastern Arizona. The proceedings of this convention were somewhat hastened by the fear that the Navajos might recuperate and follow them and thus embarrass the situation. So it was adjourned in short order and the separation of the tribes accomplished. From that time there was hatred that bred bitter feuds among them.[18]

While this story raises many questions that will not be dealt with here, the fact that Gatewood had a very close association with the Apaches and built that relationship on truthfulness and understanding lends credence to this being an Apache perspective. He was highly respected as a warrior, but more importantly admired for his honesty and desire to help the Apache people as a leader with the scouts and a military officer maintaining reservation peace. Even Geronimo promised protection for him when passing through Apache country. It seems safe to assume that this story is one told by those Apaches he knew and worked with but is confined to a limited number of people and bands.

Dr. Washington Matthews, a physician working for the military in the late 1800s and early 1900s, held a real interest in Navajo history and culture. He studied the ceremonies, recorded aspects of the language, provided detailed oral history, and understood many cultural practices, becoming one of the first Anglo "anthropologists." His early work was based in recording the teachings of medicine men and elders who remembered much of the old days and ways. On the formation of Navajo clans, which he called "gens/gentes," he outlined in 1881–82 the origin of many, listing fourteen Apache clans in addition to fifty-one Navajo clans that had been adopted into the Navajo system.[19] Among those mentioned were Red Rock, White Mountain, People of the Canyon, and Black Water. Each clan had its own origin story, including groups that were adopted into it, and so Apache involvement became recorded through oral history. For example, a large group of Apaches came from the south to the San Juan River, where they met members of the Black Standing Rock clan. The travelers declared, "We come not to visit you, but to join you. We have left the Apaches forever."[20] Another group joined the Black Horizontal Forest clan for similar reasons, while a Navajo woman married an Apache man who was visiting a ceremonial dance, only to return years later with two fair-skinned daughters who started their own clans.[21] Sandoval's story is also mentioned. Navajo clan histories preserved not only the experiences of their own members but the accretion of other peoples during those formative years.

## Early Historic Record

The differences between the oral history of the Navajo people embedded in the mists of time and those of the archaeologist digging in the dirt each have their place in piecing together fragments from the hidden past. The story of the historic Navajos, thanks to written records, becomes increasingly sharper as their narrative moves forward. The first to pick up a pen to discuss the Navajos were the Spanish, who entered the Southwest as early as the 1530s, when Álvar Núñez Cabeza de Vaca traveled through the region after being shipwrecked off the coast of Texas. He drew little distinction between the Indians he encountered. Spanish conquistadors and settlers, as they pushed north from Mexico in the mid to late 1500s and early 1600s, no doubt met and confronted Navajo people who often assisted Pueblo allies in resisting foreign conquest. Unwilling or unable to distinguish between various Native American groups in this early stage of conquest, the Spaniards borrowed the Zuni word for enemy, "*apachú*," and applied it to any Indians offering resistance. While this single term was used throughout the seventeenth century, it became increasingly apparent that there were a number of different Athabaskan-speaking groups that had distinctive cultures and political agendas. Thus, there arose the *Apache del Navajo*, the more northern entity of this Southwest language group. In 1630 Fray Alonso de Benavides in his *Memorial* referred to a specific group called Navajos, which he said meant "great planted fields" since they were noted for being "very great farmers." By the early to mid-1700s, the Navajos were clearly distinguished from the Apaches.[22]

For the next roughly two hundred years (1630–1821), the Spanish became embroiled in a series of treaties and alliances with a multiplicity of Indian nations. All of the Pueblo people along the Rio Grande (Eastern Pueblos), as well as the Hopis, Zunis, and Acomas (Western Pueblos), had their turn at being subjugated, revolting, and being reconquered by their oppressor. Many willingly worked with the Spanish to combat the "wild" or less established Indians such as the Navajos, Apaches, Utes, Comanches, and other nomadic groups that came into the settlements to either trade or raid. Increased mobility with the introduction of the horse; greater food and material resources in the form of sheep, goats, and cattle; magnified war capability through firearms and other metal weapons; the insertion of the Spanish slave trade expanding upon previously existing networks of forced captivity and tribal hostility; the zealous preaching of Catholicism; and the establishment of European thought and values were all part of the advancing horse-gun-settlement frontier.

Each tribe had to decide what was best for its future given previous and contemporary events between friends and foes. Alliances formed, shifted, dissolved, and reformed, but in general terms, the Navajo and Apache tribes found themselves opposing the Spanish and electing to raid their settlements for livestock and booty. Still, there were times when they joined the Europeans as allies and waged war against their neighboring enemies as well as each other. The Spanish, as opportunists, exploited tribal rivalry to relieve pressure exerted upon them and to foist that energy against traditional foes. There was no centralized control with either the Apaches or Navajos, and so as one band of Indians made peace, another one from the same tribe might have waged war against the same group that just developed a new friendship. To track in the written record the fragmented dealings and shifting elements of any group is difficult; still general patterns emerge. Here a brief look at the friction that existed between the Apaches and Navajos provides context for later events in the 1870s and 1880s.

The Navajos, as northern neighbors of the Apaches, considered the Little Colorado as the southern boundary of their homeland but traveled well beyond this river, entering into the territory of the Gila River Apaches (Mimbres/Chiricahua) roughly two hundred miles distant. As early as October 1785, small Navajo groups agreed to support campaigns with the Spanish against these Apaches, serving as scouts and warriors. The Navajos declared war against their cousins and pledged thirty Navajo auxiliaries each month in support of the war waged by Governor Don Juan Bautista de Anza of New Mexico. An interesting incident occurred at the end of the meeting between the Spanish and Navajos, illustrating the power of tribal alliances. "Just as these ceremonies were ending, a Comanche warrior, one of two the Governor had brought with him, stepped into the circle of the council, and exhorted the Navajos to fulfill their agreements or the

Comanches, as the Spanish allies, would exterminate them. Terrified by this representative of their dreaded enemy, the Navajos swore fidelity."[23] The Spanish were elated. A previous alliance between the Navajos and this Apache group was now ruptured. The Spaniards then paid two prominent Navajo leaders to lead their people in attacks and encouraged them to form settlements under the protection and guidance of the colonists. The newly established friendship lasted twenty years.[24]

*The Navajos and Apaches had a long history of raiding Spanish and later Mexican homesteads and settlements for livestock. A major strategy of both Hispanic peoples was to turn one tribe against another by forging alliances, providing material support, and leading expeditions against their enemy. Here, warriors are stealing sheep that are being guided by a young dikohe as part of his training. (Drawing by Kelly Pugh)*

The effectiveness of the Spanish strategy became evident as these fostered hostilities played out. A few excerpts from Spanish reports illustrate what each side encountered. A year after the council adjourned, Comandante-General Don Jacob Ugarte de Loyola wrote, "I have observed with satisfaction that you have already triumphed, not only completing the rupture of the old link which bound the Navajo Indians to the Gilas [Apaches] to attack us, but also succeeding in moving the former to make war on them."[25] What this warfare looked like became apparent in a report in August 1788. Governor Don Fernando de la Concha organized an expedition against the Gila and Mimbres Apaches for which fifty-three Navajos volunteered. Realizing what this would cost him in money and resources, Don Jacob dismissed part of this group but kept a substantial number to serve as guides and spies to locate enemy trails, identify water sources, and attack enemy camps. On September 10, the Spanish force surprised a group of Apaches, killing eighteen warriors and capturing four. Two days later, "several Apaches appeared on the hilltops and one of them recognized Antonio del Navajo [leader] and spoke to him, although at a considerable distance, complaining that he had shown us their territory and saying that all the Apaches were in the gravest consternation on that account, then ending by challenging him and uttering threats. These circumstances are advantageous, as much because of the fear which our knowledge of the area inspires in them as because of the hatred against the Navajos which it has produced."[26]

Fear played out on both sides. The Navajos constructed ten rock towers or fortifications in their encampments to protect the women and children from constant attacks; when the Gila Apaches sent a delegation of eight warriors and two women to sue for peace, the Navajos killed all of the men, although the women escaped; in a three-month period, the Navajos captured seventy-one Apaches, killing all of the adults and enslaving their children; and when the Mescaleros made overtures for peace, the Navajos promised that should they return, the Navajos "will fall upon them and give you [the Spanish] the heads of said Apaches."[27] As the years progressed, hatred became more entrenched.

In 1821 the Spanish officially relinquished control of their holdings in the Americas, granting the Mexican people self-rule. In what would later become the American Southwest, continuing conflict became the problem of this new Mexican government. With fewer resources of men, equipment, and money; with less organizational experience in administering the remnants of a diverse political entity; and not understanding many of the people it ruled, this government brought little improvement to the table. Indeed, for the next twenty-five years many of the policies of the past went by the wayside, encouraging some of the tribes that had been previously friendly to turn against their new ruler. To further complicate issues, the United States fought the Mexican War (1846–48), which fractured many alliances and defeated the Mexican government, which ceded most of the American Southwest to the victors. To many of the Navajos who had never befriended the Spanish or the Mexicans, the American army was an ally and was treated as such. Soon, however, after the Treaty of Guadalupe Hidalgo gave Americans control of the area, the Navajos learned that they had a new "master" to deal with.

Conflict between the Apaches, Navajos, and Americans intensified. By July 1851, inspector general of New Mexico George A. McCall reported that sixteen thousand sheep had been purloined and their shepherds killed. According to McCall, he heard Navajos say at another time "that the only reason for not exterminating the New Mexicans long ago was that it was in their interest to keep them as shepherds." He went on to relate, "Of the eight wild Indian [tribes] that inhabit the mountains and plains of New Mexico and the contiguous country, the Navajos and Apaches are most formidable as enemies and the most troublesome as neighbors."[28] This is not to suggest that the Apaches and Navajos had whitewashed their differences. In some instances, they worked together, but far more often they remained at odds. For instance, in March 1851, the Navajos stole three thousand sheep near Manzana, New Mexico, only to have them returned to their owners by a group of Jicarilla Apache.[29] The feuds between the two tribes continued, leading to further friction. Major Electus Backus from Fort Defiance stated, "The Navajos and Apaches profess to be on friendly terms with each other, yet the Apaches frequently rob the Navajos and there is evidently an unkind feeling between them. The Navajos are afraid of the Apaches—and I am inclined to believe this is the principal reason why the Navajos have moved so far north. They do not like the Apaches for neighbors."[30]

## The Fort Sumner Experience

From the mid-1850s to the mid-1860s, both the Apaches and the Navajos had extensive pressure placed upon them by the United States military and its allies such as the Utes and many Puebloan tribes. At the same time, the two Athabaskan tribes fought each other. Many of the Navajos and some of the Apaches collapsed under the constant conflict and turmoil to the point of surrendering to the American forces. Others, such as the Mogollon, Coyotero, and Mimbres Apaches, while fighting their own battles with the military, united and launched a "very large campaign" against the Navajos. Sandoval, a controversial leader in Navajo history, allied against these same Apache tribes and provided many followers to serve as guides and trackers for U.S. forces. They proved effective, in one instance killing five and wounding three Apaches while recapturing one hundred stolen horses. The brutality of this internecine warfare became apparent when the military inspected the bodies of the dead. "They were stretched upon their backs pierced through with arrows. The fight appears to have been a desperate one; quantities of arrows were found scattered about in all directions, whilst the murdered devils had their heads mashed in with stones."[31] The campaign eventually proved successful, with the Mogollon and Coyotero bands suing for peace and then asking the Americans to get back their enslaved children stolen by Sandoval. The Navajos were slow to give up any of their captives. At the same time, other Apache groups preyed upon the large flocks and other spoils of war the Navajos provided. In 1860 a band of Coyotero warriors killed 44 Navajo men and women, captured 15 children, and obtained 75 horses and cattle; in another fight, 10 men died and 40 women and children were captured.[32]

The pressure to surrender began to pay large dividends. Colonel Kit Carson and other military commanders waged successful campaigns against both the Apaches and Navajos with the end goal of having them moved onto a joint reservation at Fort Sumner, also known as Bosque Redondo, on the Pecos River in eastern New Mexico. By January 1863, there were 248 Apaches there; six months later, 436.[33] The Navajos, in vastly larger numbers, also settled on this desolate land with its alkaline water, scarcity of wood, and poor soil. Eventually, over 8,000 souls, perhaps half of the tribe's total number, lived at Fort Sumner. Their difficult time on the Long Walk, during which the military escorted its captives over four different routes, was just a warm-up for the challenging times they encountered during their four-year incarceration (1864–68). Freezing temperatures killed most annual crops; strange food and an unfamiliar inhospitable land fostered bad health and anxiety; traditional enemies like the Comanches, Utes, and New Mexicans preyed upon these captives; and social issues caused by increased stress developed ripe conditions for witchcraft and other forms of antisocial behavior. During this period, groups both small and large composed of starving, sickened, and frightened Indians, escaped to their homelands. Theirs is a story told another time.

Not surprising, the relationships between the Navajos and Apaches living in close proximity under these circumstances did not change for the better. With a huge numerical advantage, the Navajos commandeered good campsites, planting grounds, and the best resources, which infuriated their Apache neighbors. Historian James L. Haley notes, "Fights erupted constantly, as Agent [Lorenzo] Labadie reported, 'The Apaches defended their fields and gardens, [with] the Navajos endeavoring to destroy them. The commander of the post made use of every means to prevent these abuses, but without effect. They fought; Navajos were confined in the guardhouse; shots were sometimes fired at them by the guard, but all could not prevent them from stealing from the Apaches; in fact, their [Apache] fields were, in some cases, completely destroyed.'"[34] A Navajo raid on a horse herd that contained both government and Apache mounts set in motion a pursuit by the two injured parties that ended in the death of fifty-two Navajos. In another instance, a party of 130 Navajos herding a flock of 5,259 sheep passed near Fort Sumner, which set the mounted military in pursuit. Labadie and thirty of his charges chased after on foot, passed the soldiers, and in thirty-five miles caught the raiding party, killed twelve of its members, and recaptured all of the sheep. When the cavalry element reached the victors, some went in pursuit of those fleeing, but the soldiers' horses were so tired that they gave up. Carleton later commented that the Apaches "did most all of the work . . . in this handsome little battle. These Apaches, who one year ago were our mortal enemies . . . should receive some token of appreciation for their fidelity and gallantry."[35]

By 1864–65, Carleton's experiment of making the Navajos and Apaches into "civilized" Indians settled at "Fair Carletonia" was reaching its numerical height with 450–500 Apaches and 8,300 Navajos.[36] If the commander expected them to homogenize into a new type of Indian, he was sorely mistaken. The two Athabaskan groups, even to outsiders, were culturally different.

> The Apache stalks grim and stoical in his paint and feathers, rarely quitting his shield, lances, bow and quiver full of arrows, imperturbable in countenance, reticent of speech and emotion, and disdainful of work which he leaves to his squaws. Rarely does he smile, and then 'tis in such a sort as though he despised himself for weakness, and even the manner of extending his hand for "tabac" looks more like conferring than asking a favor. The Navajo is all together a different being, his sorrows and joys are loudly expounded. . . . Yet no people of whatever race, exhibits more emotion than the Navajos; every adult meets you with a smile, every child with a laugh.[37]

Differences were even noted in the supply chain. The commissary would not issue corn to the Apaches for fear that they would turn it into a fermented brew called tizwin. Ground flour became the order of the day to avoid drunkenness, while the Navajos received corn for their use. One of the few things that both Indian groups held in common in addition to the deplorable conditions at Fort Sumner was a longing for a freer life in a land they knew. Brigadier General Carleton's no-nonsense policies added

to the discomfort and displeasure to the point that the government relieved him of his command in the fall of 1866. This was not before most of
the Apaches and a number of groups of Navajos deserted the reservation
and returned to their homeland.

The confining elements at Fort Sumner had always been porous, but
on the night of November 3, 1865, the Apaches—some 350 of them—
decided to leave. Actually, there had been small groups departing on the
poorer horses days before, allowing the more capable people with stronger,
faster mounts to leave in larger numbers later. Pursuing soldiers traveled
ninety miles but could never catch them, falling farther and farther behind
the fleeing men (82), women (147), and children (112).[38] Perhaps it was
the two hundred Navajo horses the Apaches appropriated as they left on
their journey, perhaps it was their fragmenting and scattering into smaller
groups, or perhaps it was their familiarity with the land that gave them
success. Even the enlistment of Navajos to scout for those fleeing did not
help. The Apaches made a clean escape, never to return to Bosque Redondo.
Agent Labadie later wrote, "It is my firm opinion that had the Mescalero
Apaches been left alone on the reservation at the Bosque Redondo and not
been associated there with the Navajos, they would have permanently remained. And the Jicarilla Apaches, in that case, would have joined them."[39]

The Navajo incarceration dragged on for roughly another two and a
half years. Even under different military and civilian leadership, circumstances did not improve—sickness, crop failures, a stingy Indian Bureau,
a nation embroiled in a Civil War and its aftermath, and depredations
by neighboring enemies did not make life easy for the Navajos after the
Apaches left. This part of the story has been told elsewhere.[40] On June 1,
1868, the government signed a treaty that released the Navajos from their
confinement at Fort Sumner, allowing them to go to a reservation of approximately one hundred square miles to resume their life within the four
sacred mountains. This piece of their homeland that sits astride a portion
of what is now the dividing line between New Mexico and Arizona soon
began to expand. Through congressional legislation and presidential executive orders, Navajo holdings grew into what is today over 27,000 square
miles. Their journey—whether from the subarctic territory of the north
or into this world from beneath the earth—has led them to be one of the
largest and most successful tribes when compared to many other Native
American groups, including their cousins, the Apaches. The next part of
this story begins in the 1870s and 1880s, following a solid alliance with the
United States military and the formation of the Navajo scouts.

CHAPTER TWO

# Thinking about War

Navajo, Apache, and U.S. Military Approaches, 1870–1886

War is a cultural phenomenon, with each society waging it according to social, religious, and military beliefs. While it is not surprising that the Navajos and the U.S. government had different goals and means of obtaining their objectives, some significant variation also existed between the Navajos and Apaches. Shared similarities, as well as contrary practices about how to achieve success, sprang from their individual belief systems. This chapter examines these cultural approaches—each with its own explanations. Beginning with the Navajos, then the Apaches, and finally the American military, one will understand how they—with their own strengths and weaknesses—brought unique views to the conflict they faced in the mountains and deserts of the Southwest.

## Navajos—Waging a Spiritual War

The Navajos, while grounded in the realities of deadly conflict, approached it as they did many other aspects of life—from a spiritual, religious perspective. Perhaps the best study of purely traditional warfare based on the old way of fighting was written by anthropologist W. W. Hill in *Navaho Warfare* (1936), a nineteen-page monograph.[1] Daily life, from sunrise to sunset, centered in beliefs explained through complex cycles of stories that brought Navajos together, outlined ceremonial performances, healed the sick, protected people from harm, instructed proper behavior, and gave understanding to a spiritual universe. Indeed, the most salient point of this traditional worldview is that, paralleling the physical world, there is a spiritual domain that mutually interacts with those things visible and invisible.

29

Thus, sickness may be caused by offending a power, survival in war is a matter of religious preparation and protection, future and past events with their outcomes can be understood through divination, and an enemy can be defeated as much through supernatural means as physical effort.

The basis for most of the beliefs and practices associated with war-making and manhood in the past came from a lengthy mythology about two young men—Monster Slayer (Naayéé' Neizghání) and Born for Water (Tóbájíshchíní), known as the Twins.[2] These war heroes were born to supernatural parents, Changing Woman (Asdzáá̹n Nádleehí) and Sun Bearer (Jóhonaa'éí) at a time when the world was in its formative stage and inhabited by Navajo-eating monsters. The two boys, who had never met their father, were anxious to leave home, find their second parent, and receive assistance in making the world safe for their people. At first, they needed to be strengthened and toughened for the journey ahead. This task fell to some of the holy people who taught them, through rigorous training, what it would take to physically survive.

Upon leaving their mother, they also received protective amulets, prayers, and songs that guided them through spiritual dangers on a physical journey. As they traveled, evil monsters in different forms—Rocks that Crush, Slashing Reeds, Giant Cacti, and Boiling Sand Dunes—blocked their path and tried to kill them but without success. Spiritual power saved the Twins each time. Finally, they reached Sun Bearer's home only to encounter more tests, this time to gain entrance into his dwelling and later to prove that they were his sons. Most important of all of their powers came through the assistance of the Holy Wind (Níłch'i), a sacred being who guides, warns, protects, and teaches, comparable in function to the Holy Ghost in Christian beliefs. The Twins passed the tests; their father recognized them as his offspring and offered assistance. What did they want? The young men answered quickly—they needed weapons to destroy the monsters inhabiting the earth. At first reticent, Sun Bearer eventually gave them four types of arrows—zigzag lightning, sheet lightning, sunbeam, and rainbow—with instructions for how to kill the evil they soon would face. The brothers returned to earth on a streak of lightning (in other accounts a rainbow) ready to cleanse the world of its dangerous elements, which they did. By the time they had rid the earth of these evil beings, they had become accomplished warriors, but they also suffered from the ill effects of bloodshed, images of war, and spiritual trauma. Only after they disposed of their weapons and had a cleansing ceremony, now called the Enemyway (Anaa'jí or Anaa'jí Ndáá), did their swooning and illness from ghost sickness stop.[3] Now the Twins could return to a life of peace with war and carnage left behind.

This brief synopsis of a very long and detailed story is like a stalk of corn, a metaphor often used in Navajo culture. From it comes many other accounts and teachings that branch out to explain why young men are raised in preparation for war, what needs to be done before they depart, how they should conduct themselves to have the protection necessary to survive, and what is required after their return to remove combat's effects. In other words, this story presents a pattern for life that can be fulfilled in very concrete ways to receive the necessary assistance. Story and ceremony are its basis, but physical trials, as with the Twins, are its tangible counterpart.

As a young Navajo boy moves toward manhood, members of his family ensure he is trained properly. Extended running and rolling in snow to harden the body and inculcate alertness were common Navajo practices to prepare for hardship and provide strength.

A formal recognition ceremony sponsored by a relative or an older man, who preferably had been a warrior, prepared the youth for conflict. This mentor performed a Blessingway ceremony for the initiate before entering a sweat lodge to pray and sing songs of protection. Then the young man started running with people accompanying him, taunting and testing his ability, just as the holy beings had done to the Twins, before he ran back to the sweat lodge to be counseled by a half dozen men. The weapons of a warrior were the same as those used by the Twins. Bows and arrows, clubs, spears, knives, shields, and body armor each had their counterparts to those used by the holy people and were prepared under ritual conditions through songs and prayers that made their users invincible.

By the age of seventeen to twenty, a young man was ready to participate in war. If he wished to become a leader but had not yet had the necessary training, he could approach a medicine man who had this knowledge and accompany him into enemy territory, where they built a sweat lodge in which instruction began. The novice learned "the most important things pertaining to war, the secret names of the enemy, and the songs and prayers which were used before making an attack."[4] For four days, the instructor and student remained, learning the names and prayers, something that could not be done in friendly territory for fear that someone in the family or a relative would die, that an epidemic would occur, or that the enemy would attack. Once the information had been mastered, the young man was ready to organize and lead a war party.

Following the recruitment of warriors who wished to go against the enemy, the men spent three to five days preparing. Songs and prayers first sung by Monster Slayer and now offered in a sweat lodge brought protection and success if performed properly. Offerings of pollen and ntl'iz (four types of sacred crushed stones and shells) ensured the assistance of the Sun and Wind People in providing protection to the travelers. Weapons and equipment were similarly blessed as the men gathered without women for their spiritual preparation. Many warriors wore a close-fitting cap similar to those of everyday use, except that just before engagement with the enemy, the wearer attached a special plume from either an eagle's or owl's tail feathers. "This protected the wearer just like the badge of Saint Christopher."[5] In addition to this, a warrior may have worn a wrist amulet made of bear, mountain lion, eagle, and owl claws to provide strength and power, or a small medicine bundle with the "shake-offs" from a bear, snake, thunder, and cyclone along with a "live" eagle feather. These shake-offs were made from pollen that had been placed on a creature or from a place that was representative of these animals or elements. Once it had been put on the animal or its surrogate and the appropriate prayers said, the medicine man collected the pollen and put it in a medicine pouch to provide protection. All of these elements had strong supernatural powers described in the teachings that spoke of their ability to protect and make the warrior invincible. There is no missing the parallels of offerings, the role of pollen, the power of the eagle, and the idea of carrying a medicine pouch as established by the Twins' pattern. It was their power that was evoked through prayers that established the ability to defeat the enemy as mentioned in this prayer: "Step into the shoes of Monster Slayer. Step into the shoes of him whose lure is the extended bowstring. Step into the shoes of him who lures the enemy to death."[6]

Once the war party stepped into enemy territory, the leader began his chanting and prayers against the foe, inviting others in the party to offer their own songs. They sang for the animals they had come to steal or the revenge they would exact. Strict rules of conduct, the seriousness of the undertaking, good weather conditions like wind and snow to cover tracks and muffle sound, and the ability to put all thoughts of home behind them were part of the mindset. There was even a secret "war talk" used only during hostilities.

> When the warriors entered the enemy's territory, the leader told the men to use certain words other than the usual ones for the animals and objects that they hoped to obtain. This was called "war talk" and "not talking

plainly." The Navaho never practiced this "war talk" in their own territory because it was believed if they did that an attack from the enemy would follow. This restriction lasted from one to three days of the journey. When the leader decided that the appropriate time had arrived, the party lined up in a row facing the enemy's country. At the coming of dawn, the leader began a song in which the rest joined. At a certain part of the song all turned toward their own homes and the taboo against "not talking plainly" was removed.

The leader told the men not to urinate in the brush. He also warned them that should they become separated and wish to communicate with each other, they were to use prearranged calls such as those of the coyote, wolf, whip-poor-will, or screech owl.[7]

This supernatural or spiritual aspect of war continued when the war leader, after his instructions to the group, sent two men from the camp to determine the outcome of future events by "listening." Navajos considered this the most reliable form of divination, although stargazing and hand trembling were also used. With listening, the two men moved about one hundred yards from their group in the direction of the enemy to listen for noises indicating success in their raid. These could include the sounds of livestock, animals running, or a vision of some type that showed them obtaining their goal. On the other hand, if they "heard the cry of a crow, screech owl, hoot owl, wolf, coyote, or any other 'man eating' bird or animal; heard the footsteps or conversation of the enemy, or heard someone shout as if he were hurt (this is believed to predict the death of one of the members of the party), these were considered bad omens and the party would turn back."[8] Through Nílch'i, the Holy Wind, the future was known.

As a war party approached its intended target, scouts moved ahead to detect enemy activity. Just before the attack, which was usually at dawn, the leader, dressed in his war gear including moccasins with protective deity Big Snake painted on their soles, left the group. Alone, he sang songs, offered prayers, and called the enemy by their secret name to again ensure success. "The prayers are like this: he starts with the enemy's head and mentions all the different parts of his body right down to the ground, and ends his prayer in the ground. This is just the same as burying the man."[9] He then returned to his warriors, reported his efforts, and encouraged the men to prepare by painting designs of snakes for power, bear tracks for fierceness and bravery, and human hands to represent "a man." If the leader has performed his part of the ritual successfully and the warriors are prepared spiritually by following practices taught by the Twins and other holy people when they first waged war, then "everyone knows and feels that they will be lucky."[10] A third type of offensive action ideally suited for canyon country was the ambush. This required an extensive knowledge of the terrain, control and planning of those involved in the ambush, and total surprise of the enemy. Small informal ambushes characterized much of the fighting.

The Navajos were not nearly as formal and did not as clearly define defensive tactics. Part of the reason is found in the economic lifestyle they practiced. As hunters and gatherers and later as stockmen and horticulturalists, the carrying capacity of the land encouraged dispersion. Limited grazing areas, the need to use both a summer and winter range for livestock, relatively small areas with enough good soil and plentiful water for crops, and a rugged terrain of desert, canyons, and mountains facilitated a limited political organization of leadership. This system consisted of headmen at the top, a decentralized system of religious practice, camps comprising mostly family and extended family (the outfit), a clan system that was widespread and did not function as a unified entity, and a strong sense of individual loyalty to and dependence on their own kin. When war occurred on a large scale, with a few exceptions, the general populace scattered and hid, at least until arrangements were made for a sizable force to counter the threat. When conflict arose, prearranged smoke signals and messengers, either on horseback or foot, were primary means of notification to bring people together, but it could take a week or more to gather enough warriors for a full-scale attack.[11]

At the conclusion of a battle or at the end of a war, participants faced what is today called post-traumatic stress disorder (PTSD). Navajo culture has a way of handling it. Returning to the story of the Twins, the first enemy they sought to destroy was Big God (Yé'iitsoh), an offspring of Sun Bearer. After successfully killing him with their father's help, the Twins took his scalp and hung it in a tree to prove to the holy people that they indeed had the power to destroy this giant. But shortly after they returned home and told their mother, Changing Woman, what they had done, the Twins began to feel sick, overwhelmed with fainting spells and evil thoughts. She understood what needed to be performed and so prepared medicine made from lightning-struck plants and herbs, sprinkled the men with it, and then shot a spruce and pine arrow over them. The Twins recovered from the harmful effects of the dead.[12] The power to combat what is sometimes called ghost sickness through the Enemyway ceremony was passed on to the Earth Surface People from Monster Slayer and is still in use today. This is a serious undertaking since the purpose of

*Navajo war-making ability depended as much on spiritual preparation as it did the physical act of fighting. From the eagle feathers on a cap to the painted symbols of Monster Slayer on a bow to the "shake-offs" from powerful animals—all supported intense ritual behavior through adherence to songs and prayers that summoned the holy people for protection. (Painting by Robert Bicenti)*

this rite is not to chase away the enemy but to kill these spirits to rid the patient of them.[13] To ensure total healing, the ceremony may be repeated in longer or shorter forms four times over a number of years. In the past, the Enemyway was most frequently used for men returning from war, but women who by mistake came in contact with a scalp or blood from the enemy could also be affected and receive the ceremony.

Even the procuring of the enemy object—scalp, bone, clothing—for the ceremony must be done with caution. When a person travels to get an item of this nature, it is said that "he goes on the warpath." Once it is obtained, it must be treated carefully by limiting exposure and contact with the person who has it. In the old days, it might be tied to a horse's tail or carried on a stick away from the procurer's body. It is then hurried to the place of the ceremony and hidden in a spot away from people until needed. To prevent contamination from the enemy's spirit, blackening (*jint'eesh*) with ash is done to a person to keep the evil away.

Preparation for and conduct of the Enemyway ceremony is filled with symbolic complexity.[14] The rich symbolism embedded within expresses deep cultural values concerning the dead and war. Intensity of activity escalates. Dancing and exchanges are performed, and at one point, preparations to "attack the enemy" become central. Just as Monster Slayer did following his return from war, the blackening of a patient and his wife (or surrogate) is performed to make them invisible to the ghost. The man also receives a sacred name used only during rituals, if he has not already received one. This is kept secret.[15] He next puts on his left shoulder a yucca sash with a pouch attached containing an object from the enemy and an arrowhead, proof of his ability to vanquish the foe. There are also yucca fiber bands tied with slip knots on his soles, ankles, knees, hips, back of each shoulder, palms, ears, and top of head. A specially commissioned man called the "scalp shooter" and "strewer of ashes" selects a place distant from camp to place the enemy scalp or object. He then approaches it with the group observing and fires a rifle or arrows at the enemy. Next the patient and his wife symbolically, without touching the ash-covered object, act out thrusting a crow's bill into the ashes. The scalp shooter intones, "It is dead, it is dead," having sprinkled the enemy object with ashes. As the group leaves the "attack" site and returns to the hogan for concluding ceremonial activities, the participants must be careful never to look back at the scalp. As with so much in the Navajo universe, this final ceremony represents a spiritual conclusion to a physical problem. While every culture—including that of the Apache people—has deep religious concerns and teachings about war, the Navajos take these same ideas and handle them in an intense ceremonial fashion that places them on an equal footing with the physical preparation. From the first affront to the last part of the Enemyway, protection and defeat of the adversary is handled spiritually.

## Apaches—Prowess and Power

The Apaches also had strong spiritual beliefs concerning war but did not take them to the same extent as the Navajos. Rather, they became famous as masters of the physical art of war waged in their homeland and beyond. This fight against enemies was informed by the environment and taught through the traditional beliefs handed down by each generation as a mode of warfare. Often it was a matter of sheer survival as enemy forces placed increasing pressure to limit the Apaches' ability. One of the most concise summaries of the form this fighting took is by Robert N. Watt, *Apache Tactics, 1830–86*, while Grenville Goodwin's *Western Apache Raiding and*

*Warfare* (edited by Keith H. Basso) is a longer explanation informed by actual accounts.[16] Here, a comparison with Navajo practices will set the stage for fighting techniques discussed later.

The mythological basis of the Apaches, as with many Athabaskan-speaking tribes, centers on figures similar to Changing Woman, Sun Bearer, and the Twins of the Navajos. These divine parents are comparable to the Apaches' White Painted Woman and Life Giver (Yusn), with an older son—Killer of Enemies, and his younger brother, Child of the Water, both of whom were born through supernatural means, as were the Twins. In the extensive Navajo teachings about Monster Slayer and Born for Water, the two were born at the same time, with Monster Slayer becoming the most prominent and powerful of the pair. He exuded all of the male qualities necessary to be an effective warrior. Many of the healing ceremonies and those associated with violence, war, and danger featured him as the role model for overcoming evil and harmful elements. For some Apaches, Killer of Enemies played a similar role, while for others it was Child of the Water who exterminated the enemies. In either case, this mythology is not as prominent in the lives of the Apaches. The Navajos' Born for Water assumed second place to his brother and often played a spiritually supportive role, praying and thinking about what was taking place, while Monster Slayer was the man of action. Child of the Water at times followed suit, playing the predominant role, although both had a hand in destroying the evil beings inhabiting the earth.

The Navajos' Twins had a series of adventures, each one filled with teachings that explained aspects of the world and how to heal those who were sick or in need of a psychological and spiritual boost. Complex ceremonial practices make visual their experience and the physical objects that represent things found in the sacred narratives. With them, the person in need reenacts what happened and receives assistance, just as in the myth. A similar pattern was also established with Child of the Water as he assisted Killer of Enemies in ridding the earth of four evil beings—Owl-Man Giant (comparable to the Navajos' Big God), as well as Buffalo, Eagle, and Antelope Monsters.[17] They accomplished this, each time returning to their mother's home, where she greeted them with dancing, applause, and the shrill trilling characteristic of Apache victory dances today. These young men had little fear of ghost sickness and did not teach the accompanying Enemyway ceremony that rid warriors of malevolent spirits. The simplified narratives and practices deemphasize the spiritual ramifications that were of intense concern to the Navajos.

What, then, were the Apache beliefs and practices about war? Extensive preparation in the form of ceremonies and sacred objects that tied into them were of primary concern for the Navajos, while central to Apache success in war was supernatural power (diyin) obtained by a sole individual. At the time of creation, everything—animals and objects, animate and inanimate—received a power that became part of both their spiritual and physical makeup. This power was unique to the being who held it, but it could be shared with someone who knew the songs and prayers that showed respect to that being, making available its power. Controlled power could then be applied to a specific need. Holding the general title of "enemies-against-power" (inda kénhonndi), this invisible supernatural force could heal, protect, and in other ways assist a person in a variety of circumstances that required beyond-human help. Anthropologist Morris E. Opler identified fifty-four creatures or elements that provided such assistance. Size or physical power played only a partial role in determining the amount and type of power. A creature as large as a bear and as small as a centipede could give help once the correct songs and prayers unlocked their forces. Lightning, fog, and a spruce tree stood alongside a wolf, eagle, and grasshopper in rendering aid.[18]

The first to obtain enemies-against-power was Killer of Enemies, who with his brother obtained it from their father, the Sun. The power manifested itself in many forms. For instance, wind power made a person light once a warrior painted wind tracks on the outside of his moccasins. A small tuft of rabbit skin placed inside a moccasin ensured that a man did not wear them out; another power made a person fleet of foot. One kind made an enemy's bow break or made sure he ran out of arrows, while bat power protected a person from being hit. Geronimo and other medicine men availed themselves of a type that foretold the future while star power held sway over guns, and leg songs cured tired limbs. One process repeated four times during travel to enemy country was performed by individuals in a war party, each of whom lassoed a tree, then called out the name of a type of horse he would like to capture. An accompanying medicine man who knew the horse power songs chanted them into success. Arrow songs healed an injured person, regardless of what inflicted the wound.[19]

Asa Daklugie, a warrior intimately familiar with leaders like Juh, Nana, Geronimo, and others during the Apache wars with the U.S. military, gave an excellent explanation of how a warrior obtained enemies-against-power.

> Most medicine men acquire Power when they are adolescents. All boys
> must go alone to the sacred mountains to fast and pray for four days and

nights. They can take no food, water, or weapon. They have a blanket, but nothing else. Many do not obtain the gift. The few who do attain it in various ways, usually do not receive it until the last night of the ordeal. Then the supplicants may hear a voice; they may see a person, an animal or even a tree, plant, or stone that is to be their medicine. It talks to them, telling them what they are to use and how. From that time on, they carry a bit of it in a small buckskin pouch on a thong around their neck. It is their guide and their help all their lives.[20]

Reminiscent of the Plains Indians' vision quest, this Apache practice was an individual undertaking dependent on the initiate as opposed to the group ceremonial protection practices of the Navajos.

There were also times when the medicine power sought out an individual to offer its services. Opler interviewed one man named Chris (no last name) or "In the Middle," whose father had a lengthy experience that changed the course of his life as a man of power. In brief, the father was sleeping by a spring west of the Mescalero reservation when he was awakened by a bear who told him to arise and to get the good things that were in store. The warrior followed the instructions and entered into a rock, where the bear now assumed the form of a man and guided him through a series of experiences in which he met other bears, wolves, geese, and humans, all of whom had their challenges. After meeting men at various levels of power, he went to the highest one, where a holy being handed him a staff and said:

"You'll always have this. It will speak itself. It must never be lost." This man had told him what was best to be done. The power he received, they say, was the power of Bear. And this same man also told him, "All these are yours," and named Goose, Wolf, Lightning, Horse, and many other powers. . . . After this my father knew all the people and their ways and their thoughts, and what was going to be done, and what was going to happen to them. He cured the sick among his own people and even among the whites and Mexicans, and he was known in the Comanche country and by the Navajo people.[21]

Preparation to become a warrior started early but intensified once a boy reached puberty. He became known as a *dikohe*, or a candidate in training, who toughened himself for the adult role of raiding and war. Long-distance runs, plunging into icy water, sleep deprivation, use of a warrior's weapons—knife, bow and arrow, spear, and shield—as well as wrestling,

agility on horseback, rock slinging "wars," and rough-and-tumble play
moved the dikohe to the point where he could accompany seasoned warriors on four raids or war parties. His role was more to serve the men and
observe what they did than it was to actually participate in combat. There
were also restrictions that he followed such as eating limited food, drinking water through a tube, and scratching himself only with a wooden stick
blessed by a medicine man. Successful completion of his tasks on these
four journeys made him eligible to be invited as a full participant.[22]

The art of tracking, a skill that sharpened into adulthood, also began
at an early age. Personal testimony tells of its effectiveness. Daklugie said,
"Maybe a stone will be moved and turned over. Maybe the grass or weeds
will be stepped on and broken off near the ground. But one doing it [track-
ing] could almost tell how long ago it was done."[23] James Kaywaykla noted,
"[The tracker's] sense of smell was much keener than the white man's. If
the Mormons brought fruit—peaches, apples—we could smell that for a
distance, maybe several miles."[24] And Eustace Fatty felt that "trailing was
an art. In soft places we could trail but in the rocks I could not but some
Indians could see it. I don't know how they did it. It was some kind of
Power and they could follow it on the run."[25] These were handy skills for
warpath and hunting.

One of the strictures placed upon the novice during his training period was that he had to use a warpath language that used special
terms for nouns that were employed only during this war time circumstance. Whether warriors after the dikohe stage followed the practice is
not clear. Anthropologists Morris E. Opler and Harry Hoijer identified
seventy-eight such terms in the Chiricahua dialect. The word or phrase
was a type of circumlocution that only the initiated would understand,
even though the words themselves could be translated in everyday Apache.
Some of these terms were easy to connect in the special language once it
had been explained. For instance, when mentioning an old man, the term
used was "knotty joints," chief was "he who is wise for me," ax was "means
by which I customarily chop," and pipe was "that with which I would like
to smoke." There were others not so easy to interpret. Without further
explanation, it might be difficult to understand "a rope has been stretched
between them" to represent a turkey (because a flock walks in single file);
"that which tells a story" for a fire; "he who is moving a hoop along" for a
snake; or "that which I see first" for a hat (referring to what appears first
when someone is seen looking over a hill).[26] While this may seem a both-
ersome way to communicate, it was one more means of achieving self-dis-
cipline and moving the act of war into its own special realm.

A leader of a group of warriors going on a raid selected those men with prowess that he felt would help him be most successful. If he did not hold enemies-against-power, he chose at least one person who did. Once the group had been formed, the warriors individually prepared—making moccasins, pounding mescal cactus into a pulp and forming it into cakes to be eaten with jerky as trail rations, cutting and braiding rawhide ropes to capture horses, and securing a small pouch of corn or cattail pollen to their person for blessings. The Apaches looked upon the act of raiding more as an economic undertaking to obtain horses or supplies than as a blood-letting act of war. The number of participants was relatively small, perhaps eight to ten. A war party seeking revenge, on the other hand, was much larger, depending upon how many warriors an aggrieved leader could muster. For protection, a medicine man with power braided from two to four strands of hide into a sash that was worn by a warrior over his right shoulder slanting down to the left hip. Called the *izze-kloth*, this medicine cord was called upon in battle for supernatural assistance to get out of a tight spot.[27] Those going on the warpath would also paint their face to distinguish them from the enemy. Bernard Second explained that the warriors "looked much alike so it was hard to tell who was who. When Indians went into battle, they unbraided their hair and let it hang free. The Mescaleros painted the lower half of their faces, usually white or yellow. That identified them to each other. Their clothes were similar so they had to make sure from a distance."[28] Eastern Chiricahuas painted a red stripe made of clay across their nose; a single daub of white on each cheek and a line of smaller daubs on the forehead were used by the Mescaleros, while Western Apaches used "freckle-like splashes of white" on their faces.[29] Others painted two white bands across their chest. Some groups wore a red headband or a piece of cloth on their arm to distinguish between friend and foe.

Unlike the Navajos, just before departing, the warriors held a public war dance called by the Chiricahuas an "Angry Dance." Keith Basso summarizes the four phases of this staged farewell event.

> The first phase called "going to war" began shortly after dark. The warriors of each clan were called forth to dance and demonstrate how they would fight the enemy. The second phase was termed "cowhide, picked up" and involved the singing of chants that described the acquisition of property. In the third phase, labelled "invite by touching," women of all ages were encouraged to choose a male partner and engage in social dancing. The warrior performed the fourth and final phase at dawn the

following day when twelve of the bravest and most experienced participants stood in a line and one after the other, sang a song about a personal
success in war. After the last one, the warriors staged mock attacks on
several camps, illustrating how they intended to surprise and defeat the
enemy. This concluded the war dance, and shortly thereafter, the expedition made ready to depart.[30]

For those more reticent to enter into the dance, their name might be called
out and told to join in or else face social ridicule. What should be recognized above all is the emphasis on individual skill and motivation. Navajos
avoided talking about death, did not boast about individual skill, depended
upon ceremonial procedure for protection, and mimicked the pattern established by the Twins.

At the time of departure, the warriors sent two braves ahead to observe
enemy activity while the remainder of the group moved forward to the
foot of a mountain, avoiding open country. When it became necessary to
go cross-country, it was done at night.

> We were very careful not to leave any tracks. Sometimes we used to walk
> just on our toes to leave a small track. And sometimes we kept a man
> out behind to brush over our tracks with some bushes. . . . Every war
> party always had a medicine man along to cure anyone who might get
> wounded or sick. They could cure a man right away. Also, they would be
> able to tell what was going to happen ahead of time, and we would know
> what way the Mexicans were going to act. If Mexican troops were ahead
> of us, and the medicine man said it was all right to go through where
> they were, then we would go. As soon as we started, the medicine man
> would make a big wind so that it would blow brush around and raise so
> much dust that we could not see each other. He would pray. Sometimes
> he would make big hail come down so that it would hit the Mexicans
> and knock them down. This way we could travel past the Mexican troops,
> as they would be all wet, and their things would be washed away, and by
> the time they got ready again we would be a long way past.[31]

Once the raiding or war party was far beyond their pursuers, the leader
let the men relax, repair their moccasins and equipment, slaughter some of
the cattle, and feast upon their captured gain. When they neared home, the
party sent a man to the main camp to tell of the approaching warriors and
to prepare the people to greet the homecoming victors. Upon arrival, the
men distributed among all of those present the materials taken and shared

their stories of victory and revenge. That night, or shortly thereafter, the returning warriors held a victory celebration called "enemies their property dance." Unlike the Navajos' Enemyway ceremony that includes a "squaw dance," there are no religious overtones, no healing properties, and no killing of enemy ghosts that might bother those involved in fighting. Instead, it was an opportunity to tell of deeds, distribute goods, feast upon captured livestock, and relax normally stringent sexual boundaries with women who were not married. The Apaches generally followed a strict moral code of sexual conduct, but in this instance, a certain level of promiscuity became acceptable. Captured materials were shared for sexual favors with a chosen partner. Once the celebration ended, strict morality resumed.

A Mescalero warrior named Chris described what he witnessed at a victory dance.

> One fellow went out and made a big talk. He said, "We have killed all of your enemies. We did it with these," and held up his arrows. He told what brave deeds he did. Then he called on another man. This one was a witness for him. He testified that he saw it and added what he did. Their faces were painted. We saw a great show. . . . Some man who has done something big is the first one out, then the witnesses. This first one does not dance right away. He just walks out there and talks first. There are three or four who talk. Then they yell out and shoot and the big dance commences. Sometimes it lasts until morning. The victory dance is vigorous. They use the knife, then the spear. Some go out there jumping back and forth, sideways, with a blanket, to show what they did in battle. Some use their shield as they did in the fight, and some the spear and other weapons. They call one man and then another to come out and do this dance. Pretty soon they are all strung out there dancing. Some will be dancing and some resting after this. They take turns for the whole night.[32]

From start to finish, from training as a youth through to the victory dance, the prowess of an individual is what the Apaches admired.

## U.S. Military—By the Book

The third culture, that of the Anglo American, in terms of thinking about and conducting war, is far different from that of the Apaches and Navajos. Each group brought its own strengths and weaknesses to the fray, as did the mindset of the U.S. military. By 1870 the Civil War was only four years behind the men and officers serving in the Southwest. It had been the greatest struggle in American history and reflected dramatically in the military worldview. Tactics, technology, and psychology emerging from those battlefields shifted further and further away the long-standing practices of the colonial wars, American Revolution, War of 1812, and Mexican War that had depended on men massing in the open and directing their single-shot muskets at a foe that agreed to fight with similar tactics. The Civil War began with much of the same thing, bringing mass carnage to the struggle—well over 630,000 deaths with a comparable number of wounded experienced the United States' first total war. Recently, this figure has been upgraded to suggest a more likely number was around 750,000 deaths from wounds, disease, and prison camps.[33] Massive destruction of the opposing side, aided by improvements in weaponry, transportation, conscription, communication, and a host of related fields, became part of the formula to defeat a foe—which also included the means of production and efforts from an entire population when necessary. Attrition was the goal, wearing the enemy down to the point of incapacity.

The post–Civil War army in the United States encountered an immediate and severe reduction in force following the cessation of hostilities, with subsequent decreases. The boundaries of the continental United States were established, the South could not rise again, and relations with foreign powers were generally amicable. Consequently, the government reduced its 37,000-man army of 1869 again in 1874 to 27,000. Even with these impossible numbers spread over a vast geographic area, the army's tasks remained fixed. The first two—coastal defense on the Atlantic and Pacific Oceans and maintaining peace in the Reconstruction South—pulled much of the military to centers of large population. The third task of keeping the overland trails open, placating Indians, and protecting settlers, was broad ranging in scope and complexity and more difficult to logistically support.

The army in the Southwest filtered its tasks through two large entities—Division of the Missouri, headquartered in St. Louis, and Division of the Pacific in San Francisco. Geographically, this put the Apache country at the end of both jurisdictions. Departments subdivided the divisions. The Department of the Missouri ranged over Missouri, Kansas, Colorado, and New Mexico while the Department of California, one of two in the Pacific Division, controlled California, Nevada, and Arizona.[34] Again, what this meant for operational integrity is that two departments held responsibility over what would be the New Mexico and Arizona territories.

*Men like these from the 22nd Infantry served as soldiers and troopers throughout the Southwest. Many were foreign-born and relatively uneducated but served faithfully under trying circumstances in the 1870s and 1880s. (Courtesy of Montana Historical Research Center)*

To perform its many tasks across the continental United States, the army formed ten regiments of cavalry but shrank the infantry from forty-five to twenty-five regiments. These numbers rose and fell depending on the funding cycles of Congress, but compared to Civil War manning, the military was a sideshow to the much larger schemes of the Gilded Age. Each cavalry regiment had twelve companies or troops, and each infantry regiment had ten companies. Each was commanded by a colonel and assisted by a lieutenant colonel, while within the cavalry regiment there were three majors, each of whom commanded a battalion; the infantry regiment had one.[35] The reasoning behind this was to give the cavalry more maneuverability with added control. Captains commanded companies with the assistance of a first and second lieutenant. The two platoons within each company served as individual maneuver elements, while four-man squads fought as teams working in support of the platoon, but not as a stand-alone tactical element.[36] On the larger scale, companies were the primary deployable unit that could be detached and sent on independent missions, and it was the company, not the battalion or regiment, that demanded the loyalty of the soldier.

In 1881 the enlisted strength of 120 cavalry companies on paper averaged fifty-eight men, with the infantry companies at forty-one.[37] It was difficult for commanders to muster three-quarters of their soldiers because of desertion, health problems, and extra duties. Part of the issue stemmed from the recruiting process. Half of the soldiers serving in the West came from foreign countries, with Ireland leading at 20 percent and Germany at 12 percent between 1865 and 1874.[38] Most of the officers were native-born Americans.[39] Many of the enlisted men came from impoverished circumstances and had little or no education, and some did not speak much English. Accordingly, the monthly pay for these soldiers was low, with a private earning thirteen dollars and a line sergeant twenty-two. Little wonder that the general desertion rate per year for many units was high. Between 1870 and 1891, there was an army-wide low of 6.2 percent and a high of one-third of the enlisted men in the army that deserted.[40] Over this twenty-year period, it has been estimated that one-third of all enlisted soldiers deserted.

Officers, while receiving higher pay, had their problems too. Promotions were based on seniority, not necessarily on performance, and were slow in coming within such a small force. For example, in 1877 a new second lieutenant might take from twenty-four to twenty-six years to move through the ranks to become a major. That same lieutenant could take from thirty-three to thirty-seven years to get promoted to colonel.[41] This graying of the officer corps meant not only slow promotion, but little upward mobility, few changes, and older men serving in maneuver elements that required the energy and reserves of youth.

The weapons and tactics used in the Civil War gave way to evolving technology that changed the battlefield. By 1873, the 1873 Springfield rifle and carbine replaced earlier models. This single-shot .45/55-caliber breech-loaded rifle fired a metallic rim-fire cartridge, the weapon remaining in service for the next twenty years. Its maximum effective range was accurate to five or six hundred yards and its rate of fire, depending on the skill of the soldier, could be twelve or more shots per minute. The weapon was durable, accurate, and simple to operate. Shorter barrel carbines were easier to control on horseback and so became standard issue to cavalry units.[42]

Repeating rifles, available by this time, were not issued due to their shorter range and the fact that they required more ammunition. Fire discipline and the conservation of ammunition became major concerns, even with men armed with breechloaders. The basic load for most units was fifty rounds per rifleman. If firing twelve rounds per minute, a rifleman in heavy contact could be out of ammunition in four minutes. Soldiers also carried the Colt 1872 .45-caliber army revolver with a six-cylinder capacity. The "Peacemaker's" range was effective for close-quarters fighting but was relatively slow to reload under fire.[43] In the case of both rifles and pistols, there was initially little ammunition for marksmanship training; however, by the 1880s, the men "took great pride in their skill and in the marksman and sharpshooter badges and certificates awarded to soldiers qualifying for them."[44]

In addition to equipment, tactical doctrine also received a facelift. In 1874 Lieutenant Colonel Emory Upton published his influential *Cavalry Tactics: United States Army, Assimilated to the Tactics of Infantry and Artillery.* For the next twenty years, his view of the battlefield determined how engagements would be fought and troops deployed at home and abroad.[45] His overall belief that the cavalry was merely mounted infantry who dismounted to fire their weapons, was a basic tenet of his doctrine. General William Tecumseh Sherman, as the commanding general of the army, favored the development of the cavalry and was highly supportive of this new approach. Improved firearms demanded a change from the shoulder-to-shoulder-by-ranks assault popular ten years before. The dispersal of forces became mandatory, with a five-foot separation between each soldier and a fifteen-yard space between squads. Rather than massing fires through sheer volume, leaders placed more emphasis on selecting a specific target, aiming, and then firing.

The four-man squad or "set of fours" became the fundamental tactical unit for independent employment with the platoon. The squad's horses were a determining factor. Three of the four soldiers dismounted, with the remaining rider taking the horses back from the firing line, preferably to a covered and concealed position away from direct fire and the loud noise of massed weapons. There was even a strap and snap ring on each horse's bridle to keep the animals close together and controlled. Skirmishing could be done either mounted or on foot, the latter being preferred for accurate shooting. An individual could seek cover as long as this did not affect the squad's volume of fire. Odd-numbered skirmishers in each squad fired a round on command and then reloaded as even-numbered skirmishers reloaded and fired on command, then everyone fired at will until told to cease. The two types of fire emitting from the skirmish line were either directly to the front or oblique. One or more squads could be held in reserve

*Training played an important part in maintaining fighting fitness in infantry and cavalry units. Here "D Troop volley fires at 800 yards." The men are shooting the model 1873 .45–.55-caliber Springfield carbine, preferred by cavalrymen because of its short length; logistically, these single-shot rifles conserved ammunition. (Courtesy of LDS Church History Library)*

to the rear for exploitation of a battlefield opportunity or to plug a gap in the line.

The two platoons that composed a company could take individual assignments during a fight. On the conceptually ideal battlefield, company commanders stationed themselves eighty yards behind the skirmishers, with the reserve forces one hundred fifty yards behind the line and centered on the formation. Battalions consisted of not less than two or more than seven companies, with three or four being the normal size. The two basic formations used by the maneuvering companies were the line and the column. Usually one or two companies remained in reserve about three hundred yards behind the skirmish line for situational exploitation.

Command and control on the battlefield were of primary concern. The most obvious form was by an officer in the front. Maneuvering units focused on the direction and speed of the leader of that part of the force, and the men followed. Close to that leader was the guidon, denoting the location of an element and the general vicinity of its command during the ebb and flow of battle. A trumpet controlled soldiers' activities from the beginning of the day to the end. Boots and saddles, assembly, charge, retreat, and so on all rang out over the battlefield, directing the lowest and highest ranked soldier on what his leader wanted.

Particularly important in the 1880s was a Civil War phenomenon that had proved to have great military value—the railroad. Capable of moving massive amounts of men and equipment over long distances, the iron horse became an increasingly important part of operations in the Southwest. The railroad alleviated much of the logistical burden by connecting military installations to civilian supply channels. The Transcontinental Railroad, established by the Union Pacific and Central Pacific and completed in 1869, opened the West to large-scale movement of men and materiel for both military necessity and economic development. Rail lines connected Arizona to California through the Southern Pacific Railroad in 1878 as did the Atchison, Topeka, and Santa Fe Railroad when it made its entrance into New Mexico that same year. Trunk lines and spurs proliferated. The telegraph was a different type of long-distance communication that became an integral part of railroad operations, while the heliograph spanned large open areas, ideal for use in desert-mountain operations. With an average distance of thirty to forty miles on sunny days and a rate of speed of ten words per minute, the military employed the heliograph throughout New Mexico and Arizona.

In order to keep the military's horses fit during extensive field operations, wagon trains or pack mules were necessary to carry enough fodder for the animals and supplies for the men. Unlike Indian ponies that maintained their strength by eating prairie and desert grass, soldiers' mounts required grain; extended campaigns took a heavy toll on horse flesh. Troop I, 9th Cavalry, composed of the famed "buffalo soldiers" (African American) and temporarily stationed at Fort Lewis in the Four Corners area in 1881 and again in 1883, reported that the unit traveled 2,776 miles during that first year of operations.[46] Differing rates of speed of moving elements to an objective required planning and coordination. The estimated speed for horses at a walk was three miles an hour and at a trot six. The length of a day's march varied according to terrain, time of year, and availability of wood and water. An average for many marches of infantry and cavalry indicates a usual distance of about twenty miles. Cavalry could move faster and farther than foot troops for a few successive days, but over a period of weeks, hardened infantry could outdistance horsemen on grain-fed army mounts.

In the 1880s most supplies on tactical operations eventually ended up in horse-or-mule-drawn wagons. Each infantry company required at least one six-mule wagon and each cavalry troop needed three because of the grain to feed the horses. A wagon pulled by mules could travel up to twenty miles per day. If artillery pieces or Gatling guns became part of the mix, an even greater number of wagons and animals were necessary. Depending on the length of the operation and number of people participating, these trains were often slow, large, and cumbersome. Mule pack trains were an option to speed the logistical tail, but the animals could be temperamental and the amount carried on the animal's back was much less than what fit in a wagon. The military often contracted with civilians to handle specially trained mules accustomed to a pack frame. Like the horses, pack mules required grain because they could not subsist solely on grass; they could eat all they could carry in twenty days. The next chapter illustrates how much of this played out in the Apache wars of the 1870s.

In summary, the Navajos and Apaches shared similarities but also had some real differences in their thinking about war, while the Anglo American held very few elements in common with his opponents. The religious and supernatural aspects of war-making were not even considered part of the preparation and conduct of fighting for the Anglo American, while for the Navajos and Apaches, it was perhaps more real than the physical acts of combat. Acquisition of power, carrying objects blessed by a medicine man, exhibiting individual bravery, capturing war trophies, publicly boasting of accomplishments, distributing the spoils of war among community members, and using divination to foresee events were all reflected in the Apache worldview. The Navajos shared some of these practices such as wearing or carrying "medicine" for protection and using divination, but trophies of war such as scalps and objects owned by the dead were shunned, and there was no victory dance at the conclusion of an operation. Power and protection came through group ceremonies performed by a medicine man, the origin of the procedure having been outlined in the sacred narratives. Fear of the dead and the necessity to be cleansed from ghost sickness was handled through the Enemyway, another group ceremony. To members of the U.S. military all of this was irrelevant, even fanciful superstition. Personal accounts from the Native American side attest that this was not so.

# CHAPTER THREE

# Searching for an Answer

## Genesis of the Navajo Scouts

More than twenty years had passed since the United States military had assumed responsibility for quieting the fractious tribal people in the Southwest. By 1870 it had fought major wars with a number of groups of Indians as well as Confederate forces. The federal government had successfully defeated the Navajos and Apaches, placed them on reservations, and hoped for a peaceful opportunity to develop the vast geographical area it had inherited. As hindsight would show, the army was just getting started in subduing hostiles—no easy task, with its soldiers facing some of their toughest opponents in an unforgiving desert environment. At this point in history, they could not do it alone and so fell back on a solution that had been in play since the earliest colonial wars of the nation—recruit Native Americans to work against other Native Americans. More specifically, Navajos and Apaches who knew the land and could find, fix, and fight the enemy became an integral part of the answer. This chapter lays the foundation for understanding their contribution and why they became so necessary in quelling enemy forces. For almost forty years (1873–1911), Navajo scouts continued to play an important role in quieting conflict and assisting the military in various capacities, filling a breach in both war and peace. This organization, in its evolution and devolution, also represents a microcosm of the government's shifting emphasis in working with Native Americans during this period of history. Understanding the land upon which this drama played out, the previous historical experience of the people involved, and their contemporary goals and mindset establish a stage for understanding the approaching conflict.

## Setting the Stage

The Navajo reservation is located primarily on the Colorado Plateau, a high "cold" desert environment. Because of its elevation, cooler temperatures prevail when compared to the Sonoran Desert, characterized as a low, hot desert where summer heat may frequently reach 104 degrees Fahrenheit and occasionally 118 degrees, with winter cold averaging 50 degrees. The Mojave Desert to its northwest and the Chihuahuan desert to its southeast are also considered hot deserts but in some parts have the characteristics of a cold desert where their elevation (2000–5000 feet) increases. All three share a diverse ecology as the land ascends into rugged mountain ranges that reach altitudes over 10,000 feet. And there are many of them—in Arizona there are three dozen mountains or mountain ranges along with eighty-eight named mountain ranges in New Mexico. Some of the better-known ranges within these states that played an important role in the Apache wars were the Superstition, Mescal, Gila, Chiricahua, Dragoon, Mogollon, and Guadalupe. In Mexico, the Sierra Madre served as a favorite haunt. On some of their heights, these mountains have pines, firs, spruce, aspens, and Gambel oaks that thrive on substantial winter snows, giving rise to lakes, streams, and springs supporting abundant wildlife such as deer, cougars, bears, and other large animals. As one descends from the forests into the chaparral thickets and piñon pine on the mountain slopes, one finds rabbits, mule deer, and smaller game, while out on the grassland, pronghorn antelope are found. The desert at the end of this descent specializes in drought-resistant, prickly vegetation such as mesquite, creosote bush, agave, chaparral, and yucca as well as cholla, saguaro, prickly pear, and barrel cactus. Javelinas are one of the few animals adapted to feeding off these pointy plants. There are few major river systems to feed the parched lands, but those that do exist bring welcomed relief to the footsore traveler crossing the desert. In Arizona there courses the Gila, Salt, Santa Cruz, San Pedro, San Francisco, and San Simon, while in New Mexico, the Rio Grande, Puerco, Pecos, Rio Penasco, and part of the Gila River stretch into the desert environment.

The Apaches had adapted well to this challenging terrain. Highly versed in using the plants and animals of the area; knowledgeable as to their location; aware of every spring, seep, and pool of water; adapted to living in the extremes of weather; familiar with various econiches that added variety to an often austere environment; and conscious of hundreds and hundreds of trails that crisscrossed the various land formations, these Indians turned what to others was a barren wasteland into a cornucopia and pharmacopeia waiting to be harvested. As Jasper Kanseah, an Apache fighter, noted, "They knew the country, where to get food and water. They been there before. They can locate water hole. Had plenty deer and eat fruit—cactus fruit is good to eat. They can live on that and wild bananas [yucca fruit], mesquite beans, lots of walnuts too and the red fruit of the prickly pears as well as wild honey and acorns."[1] Paul Blazer, speaking of the mescal (also known as agave or century plant), a cherished food harvested in May and June each year, tells of its processing. "They dried it and kept it. It was their staple food. It is like a cabbage—a big globe above the ground. They chopped off the leaves of the body of the plant, cutting off the head." This was buried in a pit that was heated by fire, covered with dirt and baked, then removed when cooked. "They would work the pulp out of the leaf then dry it. There would be a large center mass that was cut into thin slices and dried. It would keep indefinitely."[2] This same knowledge concerning plants and animals became vital during times of warfare as the Apaches evaded capture or waged offensive operations. Ultimately, it provided a great logistical freedom when compared to what the military had to eat while chasing them.

What was home to the Apaches was the end of the earth to most pursuing soldiers. Nothing brings that point home more clearly than the voice of someone who lived through it. For three years, Clarence B. Chrisman, an enlisted soldier in Company F, 13th Infantry, chased Geronimo and other Apache leaders over some of the most forbidding terrain. He presents a clear image of what that life was like for him and others during those difficult years. Chrisman began by praising his comrades for their fortitude.

> Such soldiers were needed goes without saying, for they had to march hundreds of miles over hot and desolate sandy plains, almost utterly devoid of vegetation and water, and across ranges of mountains that seemed to pierce the very sky itself, often in midwinter through almost impenetrable drifts of snow and sheets of ice. . . . I remember distinctly how the fellows yanked off their shoes, good old heavy regulation government brogans, and began doctoring blisters and sore spots, and that night how we gathered around the campfires, some laughing, some singing, and some, especially the recruits (we had a bunch of raw ones with us) casting furtive glances at the dark woods surrounding us and up at the towering bluff, as though expecting any moment to hear the crack of firearms and the war-whoop of hostile Indians. But most of us gave no thought to such things, and we grouped about the fires exposing

*This formation in the Superstition Mountains, Arizona, is known to the Apaches as Praying Hands. Composed of eroded volcanic remains, this area is typical of the desert environment over which much of the Apache wars were fought—high summer temperatures, little water, and biting desert winds. Some Apaches suggest that the entrance to the lower world is found here and is a place from which dust storms emanate. (Photo by Tony Santiago, Wikimedia Commons)*

ourselves as openly and brazenly as though there were no Indians within a thousand miles.

The territory assigned to the companies of the Thirteenth Infantry was the southwestern part of New Mexico Territory, the birthplace and former habitat of the notorious Geronimo. In guarding this section, our companies were shunted back and forth like the shuttle of a sewing machine. Upon consulting my diary, I find that we marched close to one thousand miles and made some fifty-six camps, sometimes camping at the same place five or six different times. Thus, we became pretty well-acquainted with the territory covered, and became quite expert in the matter of making and breaking camp. When word would come that the hostiles were headed in our direction, detachments consisting of a non-com and five or six men would be sent out to protect the ranches in the vicinity. And there they would be welcomed with open arms and shown every courtesy. At most of these ranches the men would be given at least one meal a day, dinner usually, and surely the cooks must have enjoyed seeing them eat, for never were good meals more appreciated. Along in the spring of 1886, Geronimo headed for his old stomping ground, the Mogollon Mountains. . . . By this time we were thoroughly hardened soldiers and almost every man was either a marksman or a sharpshooter. I am pretty sure that I myself was about the worst shot in the company, as I had never become even a marksman, but even at that I don't think Geronimo would have cared to have me draw a bead on him. Besides shooting at targets, we had by this time had much experience in shooting at moving targets such as deer and antelope. And those old single-fire Springfield rifles, with their long bottle-necked [*sic*] .45 caliber cartridges could certainly send a ball a-whizzing. It was goodbye to anything it happened to hit. Each man carried a web belt of fifty of these death-dealers. And although we scarcely feared a night attack, we nevertheless, when in the immediate vicinity of the hostiles, slept with these belts encircling our waists and the good old trusty Long Tom snuggling beside us at the edge of our blankets. When Geronimo and his followers surrendered at Skeleton Canyon in September, 1886, the curtain fell on the most picturesque and stupendous drama that was ever enacted on the American continent. . . .

On the 16th of September, 1886, we arrived, three companies of us, on the western slope of the Zuni Mountains overlooking Fort Wingate. About 150 of us in all, and the only way you could detect that we were Regular Army soldiers was by examining our arms and equipment. Aside from that, I must say that we looked more like tramps than soldiers. We went out dressed in blue flannel shirts and trousers, with the regulation campaign hats, boots, or shoes. We returned almost literally covered with buckskin, scarcely a patch of blue to be seen, and had on all sorts of hats, boots, or shoes, or what was left of them. Keeping ourselves well shod had been one of our greatest difficulties. One thing we had in plenty was whiskers, for it had been anything but easy to keep well shaved under such conditions. And sunburned?—don't mention it. We were as dark as Mexicans.

Up in those mountains it gets exceedingly cold at night, even in midsummer, and while I was on guard, I could hear the fellows turning and groaning as they tried to keep warm under a blanket or two and find a soft spot on which to rest their weary bones. But the rocks of New Mexico are not noted for being soft. I couldn't help but think, listening to the occasional growl of some poor rookie, about the time some nine months previously, in the dead of winter with snow and ice piled all around me, I had made camp with several other soldiers in that identical spot. We were then on an expedition from Fort Wingate to Fort Craig, New Mexico, and had followed the backbone of the Rockies through snow and ice all the way. . . . Here is what the general [William Tecumseh Sherman] telegraphed to the War Department September 6, 1886, concerning the troops and their marches: "Too much credit cannot be given to the troops for their courage, fortitude, and tireless endurance. Those gratifying results of the campaign, fraught with extreme hardships and difficulties, are due to their most laborious and dangerous service. The Indians have been pursued over two thousand miles in the heart of Arizona and New Mexico, through the most rugged mountain regions. Captain Lawton's command alone has followed the hostiles over sixteen hundred miles, over mountains from 2,000 to 10,000 feet high, and through canyons where every boulder was a fortress." Most vivid of all in my memory are those long grueling marches, often with no water, and sometimes with mighty little to eat—marches that exacted the last ounce of a man's strength, where literally a man had to do or die. For to be left behind on some of those vast stretches of burning sand would have meant certain death; a slow, lingering, horrible death, with the sun flaming above you like a ball of molten brass; and perhaps a few buzzards winging their indolent way across your field of vision, waiting, waiting, patiently waiting.[3]

The land, like the Apaches they hunted, provided challenges on every level of military command.

Certainly one of the biggest challenges in this environment for the soldiers was obtaining and maintaining equipment and supplies. Thousands of trackless square miles pushed the logistical trains into regions and conditions that had not before been encountered, chasing a foe that could meet his own needs on the run. As one experienced army officer wrote in 1891, at the end of the wars in this region, there were some very strong limiting factors to military offensive operations. He compared them to a dog secured by a chain, "within the length of the chain irresistible, beyond it powerless. The chain was its wagon train and supplies."[4] To lengthen the chain limiting the military, a series of forts serving as nodes in a web of primitive roads was an initial answer to providing places of respite and resupply for the soldiers giving chase in the hinterlands. Historian Robert M. Utley pointed out that the basic strategy as explained by officers in 1871 was to "build posts in their [Indian] country . . . demoralizing them more than anything else except money and whiskey."[5] The mere presence of the soldiers allowed for a more timely reaction when trouble occurred, served as a visible deterrent, and offered a capacity to support field operations. Although both the commanding general of the army, William Tecumseh Sherman, and Nelson A. Miles, commander of the Department of the Missouri, agreed on this solution, the army, with only 25,000 men, was stretched too thin to achieve the desired results.

Some of these posts were short-lived while others proved to be well-situated for continuing operations in a shifting environment, as railroads, the telegraph, cattle and mining operations, towns, and other harbingers of civilization made their way into the interior of various regions. Forts such as Bayard, Craig, Cummings, Selden, Stanton, and Union each had their days of service, but in terms of the Navajo scouts, some of whom would be attached to cavalry units at many of these places, Fort Wingate was of primary importance. One can think of it as "home base" where most of these Indians enlisted and had their introduction to working with the U.S. military. Thus, a brief history of Fort Wingate (Shash Bitoo—Bear Springs) is in order.

There were actually two Fort Wingates, both named for Captain Benjamin Wingate of the 5th Infantry, who lost his life at the Battle of Valverde in 1862. The first establishment was located at San Rafael, five miles south of Grants, New Mexico, established by General Edward R. S. Canby in 1862. Soon, General James H. Carleton used it as a springboard for operations during his war against the Navajos. In 1860 the military built another post sixty miles to the west called Fort Fauntleroy near Bear Springs at the headwaters of the Rio Puerco. It was later renamed Fort Lyon and then renamed again as the new Fort Wingate when the older post proved no longer serviceable. This establishment became a primary force in maintaining peace with the Navajos when they returned from Fort Sumner to begin their life on the newly designated reservation in 1868. The nearby town of Gallup (1880) depended heavily on the military for its initial start, but as it grew and the railroad reached both town and post in 1881, the region received a big economic boost. Add to that the Navajo reservation expanding in size and the general settlement of the area due to the rails, and one can see why it played a primary role assisting in the later Apache wars.[6] The majority of the Navajo scouts that enlisted came from this region.

## The Hispanic and Early Anglo Years

The history of Navajos serving as "scouts, spies, and guides" goes back to the Spanish occupation of the Southwest. The best known of those who worked with the enemy of the general Navajo population was a band of Navajos living in the area of Mount Taylor and the Puerco River, now called Cebolleta, New Mexico. As early as 1818, a headman known as Joaquin decided that he would break from the general Navajo population that fought and raided the Spanish settlements, pledging allegiance to help the Euro-Americans against his own people. Those who followed him gave birth to a title that has remained ever since—Enemy Navajos (Diné Anaíí). In the 1830s a leader named Sandoval continued the practice, helping first the Mexicans, then the Americans, to fight the Navajos attacking them. For twenty-five years Sandoval not only scouted out various Navajo bands but also independently waged war against them, capturing women and children to sell in the slave fairs of Abiquiu, Taos, and Santa Fe. He killed most of the men taken prisoner.

A series of broken treaties by both sides led to intensifying punitive expeditions by the American military to subdue their enemies. Sandoval scouted for many of them. Still the soldiers feared that he also was notifying his friends and allies when operations began. This concern of the Enemy Navajo serving as double agents also led to accusations that at times they fomented trouble for their own benefit so that they could capture people and livestock for personal enrichment. Many Navajos hated those that had turned against them. When Sandoval died in 1859, his people lost a strong leader who could have been of real service as the final Navajo war that forced over eight thousand of his people into captivity at Fort Sumner began to heat up. General Carleton, however, ignored their previous service and sent them, just like all the other Navajos he could capture, to Fort Sumner for four years of incarceration and misery.[7]

The boundaries and military control at Fort Sumner were fluid. Groups of Navajos became disenchanted and left for their homelands and better conditions while a lot of others refused to ever enter its confines. Avoiding the Utes and other traditional enemies as well as New Mexicans hunting for slaves and livestock served as an inducement to join those who had already surrendered. To stop the flow of those leaving Fort Sumner and to encourage those who should come in, Carleton enlisted Navajo men given the title of Red Coats to locate and persuade Navajos of the benefits of surrendering. Frank Apache tells of his grandfather's experience when he encountered some Red Coats. Up to this time, he had avoided capture. As he traveled back from Tohatchi Mountain, "he met some Navajo Indians who said they were Red Coats trying to help us to go to Fort Sumner. They said that they had all kinds of things to eat. We went back home to our friends and told them that night that we had met some Red Coats and that they looked like good people. So we moved that night and went as far as Red Lake."[8] The Red Coats brought them and other Navajos into Fort Sumner, then encouraged the grandfather to join them as a scout, which he did. He received a soldier's uniform and later a rifle, then went to work. "I knew where a lot of the Navajos in hiding lived and so whenever we went out, we brought back a bunch of them to the fort. We kept on doing this until we had enough to move them to Fort Sumner. . . . Most of the army men liked me. I don't even know how to talk English, but I sure know how to give hand motions [sign language]. They used to understand very well, so finally they learned a lot from my hand motion. I think that it was a pretty good scheme to be in the army with them."[9]

Navajos had also proven helpful in many duties in and around Fort Sumner, to the point that some officers believed a force of enlisted scouts could be a deterrent to those attacking the Navajos the military was guarding. Captain M. Mullins suggested "that a party of 100 or 200 Navajos, properly armed and organized as a 'police party' to prevent raids being made on this 'reservation,' by Comanches and other hostile Indians [would be helpful]. I respectfully request that I be placed in command of it. I am confident that I could keep its members in a fair state of discipline, and by constantly patrolling and examining the surrounding country, could ensure the safety of life and property on the reservation."[10] Carleton did not agree and failed to pursue the suggestion; however, two weeks later, on July 28, 1866, President Andrew Johnson signed the "Act to Increase and Fix the Military Peace Establishment of the United States." This authorized the War Department to form the United States Indian Scouts, with a membership not to exceed 1,000. Those joining received the same pay as cavalry soldiers and were reimbursed forty cents a day for use of their horse. A year later there were 474 enrolled and by 1877, Indian enlistments had peaked to 600.[11] The order, implemented throughout the West and Southwest, included all Indian tribes who had members wishing to join. Unlike the white soldiers who signed on with a five-year enlistment, the Native Americans were kept for a six-month stint, after which they could reenlist or if the need for their services had decreased, they could be discharged. While the Navajo scouts were not formed until 1873, there was an interim force that served as a prototype, accustoming the Navajos to seeing some of their men in uniform as they served the United States government.

Hard times faced the Navajo people upon returning to their home-lands in 1868, a small part of which had officially been designated as their reservation. In reality, many went back to previously occupied areas, dis-regarding the boundaries and living on lands that abutted Anglo holdings. Poverty stalked the People, encouraging many to pilfer livestock, rob food sources, and fight when necessary. Old patterns of raiding and horse theft were hard to break, and so the borders of the reservation became heated with increasing conflict. Agents such as Captain F. T. Bennett, W. F. M. Arny, and James H. Miller had seen how Navajos employed as a police force could effectively control their people. They requested money to be al-located to make such a unit official and permanent. Bennett was the first to suggest a one-hundred-man organization that would serve as a light cav-alry and receive pay of five dollars and allowances just like regular soldiers, that would be armed with breech-loading carbines for use on horseback, and that would be trained as a military unit. The leader of this horse cavalry, the captain of police, would be paid a comparable amount to what a first sergeant received at forty-five dollars per month.[12]

A snapshot of less than a month's time (May 6–27, 1871) illustrates the problems and attitudes faced by the Navajo "cavalry" and military. Major William Redwood Price wrote to Miller saying that he had recently visited Zuni, where one of the Puebloans had been killed by Navajos; the Zunis retaliated by killing two Navajos, leaving open the possibility of fur-ther conflict. Stolen livestock belonging to white neighbors was also on the list of grievances against the Navajos. Price wondered if he should bring cavalry on the reservation as a show of force. Miller replied the next day, suggesting that two cavalry troops be sent immediately and that these elements be divided into smaller groups and sent to trouble spots. Miller appreciated the different Navajo headmen cooperating with him and the military in searching for stolen goods and livestock as well as identifying the pilfering culprits.[13]

On May 11, Price with one hundred men and seven wagons carrying ten days' supplies set out for Fort Defiance, where they met with all of the principal chiefs. There the major demanded the return of all stolen livestock and surrender of the thieves. That night the Navajos started off for the Chuska Mountains, where the worst offenders had gathered. Price met the chiefs there, but although they retrieved stolen livestock, they also produced no robbers. Frustrated, the officer told them to either turn in some of the bad men or he would hold one of the chiefs as a hostage until it was done. The next morning, the leaders assembled, the cavalry encircled part of the group, and the demands were reiterated. No one moved, and so Price ordered that one of the chiefs be seized and kept as a prisoner. At this, Manuelito stepped forward and offered to be the hostage until there were results, then ordered the Navajos to go in search. In less than an hour, they produced a well-known troublemaker, Juan Martis, who was quickly put in chains. Another culprit fled over the hills but was apprehended by the Navajos; he, too, was placed in chains. They were sent to Fort Defiance and then to Santa Fe to fill their jail sentences. Price was happy, expressing his wish for the government to "organize a sort of police force of from 50 to 100 men under the command of Manuelito to suppress the thievery entirely. I am satisfied it [the operation] has had a very good effect and that there will be less complaints against them [the Navajo]. . . . I believe that an efficient war party of them can be got together against any tribe within a radius of 300 miles of this post." Miller was just as happy. "I can hardly tell how to estimate the good your services at this place has done for me."[14] A few days after Price departed, the Indians brought in a herd of 140 sheep and three burros. A Mexican recognized a horse stolen three years previous, and without discussion, the Navajo turned it over to the man, fearing he might be put in chains. Miller quipped, "Iron has charm."[15] Thus, Navajos policing Navajos worked effectively, and as conditions on the reservation improved—successful harvesting of crops, increased Navajo herds, expansion of reservation boundaries, and the establishment of law and order emanating from a growing number of subagencies and agents—friction began to decrease.

## Early Navajo and Apache Conflict

Navajos working against other Indian groups, especially the Apaches, was another possibility, giving rise to the type of mission undertaken by the Navajo scouts later. In April 1871 Colonel John Green, commander at the Camp Apache Agency for the White Mountain Apaches, contacted Price and asked for assistance in hunting down and subduing some of the Indians that had killed his butler. Price agreed to help, partly because there was an outbreak of sickness at Fort Wingate, and so getting some of the Navajos away from that situation would be beneficial, partly because he understood their effectiveness in the field as scouts. He called for volunteers and was surprised at the reaction. "The Navajos, learning that a scout was contemplated against the Apaches, came in numbers and begged to be allowed to accompany the command. I consented to take five in the morning, the numbers desirous to go had so increased that I ordered rations be carried for ten; when well out on the road [the next morning], I found 15 were running along with the command, who, when interrogated, said they would provide for themselves."[16] He decided to add them to his two companies, E and K, comprising eighty-nine men, and moved on to the agency, only to learn that the Apaches were in mortal fear of the Navajos. Apparently three months before, a group of Navajos had attacked them, killed twenty-two men, and carried off some women and children. Price had to round up the fleeing Indians but left his Navajo helpers at Camp Apache. When he returned in two weeks, he found that they had all left for their own reservation. What cannot be missed is their initial enthusiasm to work against the Apaches, something that the military capitalized on in the future.

The Apaches had their own perspective. In their point-counterpoint relationship with the Navajos, the Apaches held their own, maintaining their freedom and warrior reputation against a foe that far outnumbered them. Anna Price shared a lengthy story, told to her by her father, that illustrates how the Apaches viewed their relationship with the enemy and how this intertribal warfare was perceived. Note the personal attitude and motivation for both life and death and how different it was when compared to that of the Anglo.

This happened when my father was living on the East Fork. Some Navajo came to us to get mescal. They brought sheep hides and blankets to trade. My father and some of his men had gone hunting. These Navajos surrounded them at nighttime and started to fight just as our men were eating their supper of deer meat. Two of our men were killed. Another man shot at the Navajo even though they could not be seen, and managed to kill one. Two days after the hunters returned home, they sent word among all the people to assemble. They made a dance there, a war dance. They used shields made of hide to dance with.

My father talked to the men before they left. "We are going after the Navajo. I don't know why they attacked us. We always treated them right before, but now we might just as well go and see them—fight them all." They started and in two days arrived in the Navajo country. The Navajos had not gone far from where they killed our men on the other side of the White Mountains. Our people surrounded the camp and started the attack before dawn, while the Navajo were still asleep. All of them were killed. They tried to run off, leaving their guns and bows and quivers behind. Our people set fire to their houses and burned them up. They also set fire to the sheep corral.

During the battle my father had talked to the Navajo, "This is what you want. You have asked me to come over to fight you. That is just the way it is. It used to be as if we ate together, but now I have come to fight you." They captured one Navajo boy. He knew of another Navajo camp above this one, so they took him to guide them to it. The same day they arrived there at noon and started to fight immediately. The Navajo in the camp were all killed. A few who were herding sheep in the mountains not far off saved themselves. Thus, they had fought in two places the same day, one in the morning and one at noon. We were lucky and not one of our people was killed. Whenever my father went to war a lot of men always accompanied him, lots of them, just like ants.

They had captured a second man at this Navajo camp who told them, "Some Navajo have been gone on the warpath for a long time. They went against the white people. One man has just returned ahead of the rest and has said the others will be in tomorrow and that they are bringing lots of cattle in two great herds, one in front of the other." Two of our men were sent in search of them. The returning Navajo had sent two of their boys ahead to stop at a spring and prepare some meat for those who were coming behind. Our two men saw these boys, who went ahead and built the fire to prepare the meat. Our men knew that all the Navajo would be eating at that place. They set an ambush for them. It was almost sundown and they placed themselves about the spot where the cooking was going on.

Just about an hour later the cattle came up over the hill. One Navajo was riding in the lead, the chief of the party, I guess. They arrived and our men could see many Navajo gathered together about the fire. They started to eat all in a bunch and our men began to shoot. The Navajo got scared and not one fired a shot. A few of them who were herding the cattle saved themselves, but those who had been eating were slain. One Navajo spoke, " . . . you have killed us all."

My father spoke to his men. "Fifteen of you take those cattle home. We want to fight more. There is another herd of cattle coming. The rest of us will go and fight them again." A Navajo had told them these springs were the only ones in the region and that the second herd would certainly stop there in two days. They stayed only one night at the springs.

The next morning fifteen men took the cattle toward White River. The remainder went on ahead to intercept the Navajo. They kept the boy they had first captured. He wanted to show our men where a spring came

*Navajo and Apache warfare increased in bitterness as each rivaled to outdo the other. Stealing livestock, conducting ambushes, and fomenting raids fueled brushfire wars that encouraged the Navajos to assist the U.S. military in working against their common enemy. (Drawing by Kelly Pugh)*

out between two adjoining hills. At the foot of the one to the west was a little spring. When our men arrived there, the Navajo were bringing in their cattle at the same time and the two parties ran into each other. They saw the cattle coming and so formed a semicircle about the spring so that the Navajo might drive the cattle right into them. There was a bluff on one side and at its foot the spring. It was just like a corral and they had only to arrange themselves on one side because nothing could escape on the side of the bluff. A few were on top of the bluff.

The Navajo arrived and started to water. There were a lot of them. Just then, one of our men started to shoot. They were cut off on one side by the bluff and not one of them escaped—all were killed. At the end of the fight, two Navajo were still alive, one of them having had his side shot away, and the other shot through the leg. They both were sitting there and talked even though shot down. The one wounded in the leg said, "I have killed your men many times and left their bodies for the coyotes. But now you have done the same to me."

All our men gathered about them and my father, being chief, talked to the Navajo. "You have asked for me and for this fight. We used to be friends just as if we lived in the same camp. I don't know why you want to fight my people, so I fight you. The cattle herd ahead of you has been taken down to White River for me; the herd you were bringing home I'm going to take to my home also. You have done well for me and brought lots of cattle from the warpath. You can just sit there and tell your people. I want you to tell them about me. But you who are shot in the leg, side, arm, I am going to kill you." So he killed one, and the one was left, the one who still sat there, said, "If any of you have some mescal, I wish you would give it to me. I want it. Then I will eat it up. Maybe that will bring me home to tell my people about you. I have had a hard time from your people. Give me some water." "Here," he said, "this will take you home to tell your people about us." Then the Navajo said, "All right, take your cattle home and I will talk to my people about you and also you tell your people about me. Put me in the shade. You have killed me. Put me in the shade of that pine." So they did. My father told him, "When you get home, tell your people about me and call my name. Tell them I am the one who got your cattle."

The fifteen men who took the first herd home got there first. The second bunch had been gone seven days when they got home with the cattle. They killed the Navajo boy when they left the spring. My father had said when he started to war, "My heart is moving within me just as the sun moves overhead. That is the way the killing of my relative makes me feel." When a man gets mad, his heart beats fast and hard. This is what he meant.[17]

## Beginning the Navajo Scouts

In July 1872 Major General Oliver O. Howard agreed to experiment with a formal Navajo police organization. Manuelito, the last headman to surrender at Fort Sumner, had now surfaced as a major leader of the peacetime Navajos and had agreed to lead the newly established force. Thomas V. Keam, a trader and interpreter for the Navajos and Hopis, received instructions to work with Manuelito, recruit one hundred men from different Navajo bands, and guide them in recovering stolen stock and patrolling the reservation borderlands. Manuelito requested that the Navajo policemen be "dressed in United States uniforms for then every Indian would know them and every white man would respect them. . . [and have them receive] the same pay as soldiers; then they would be proud and obey their leader and there would be no more trouble from the Navajos."[18] Each of the thirteen bands provided seven to eight men to enlist in the Navajo Mounted Cavalry. Observers were enthusiastic about the results. Agent W. F. Hall felt that the different band leaders involved were "proud of their position and very energetic and determined in the discharge of their duties" and later he said, "I most earnestly recommend that the Government afford every facility for the most complete organization, equipment maintenance, and reasonable compensation of these faithful, hardworking and efficient men in the belief that such a course will conduce to the best interests of the Government, the Indians, and the settlers of the surrounding country."[19]

Indeed, perhaps it was their efficiency in quelling problems that caused, within thirteen months of their founding, for them to be disbanded. Now, there was no apparent need for their services. Still, there was no lack of appreciation. W. F. M. Arny, although he had a somewhat checkered career as the Navajos' agent, enthusiastically endorsed their efforts and sought not to have the group dissolved. In his mind, "the police force embraces some of the principal chiefs, and the relations of others, who are proud of their position, and very energetic and determined in the discharge of their duties, which they would not be if their pay was to cease."[20] Officially this first Navajo police force ended in 1873, but many of the agents felt a continuing need for an internal force to control unruly elements on the reservation. Soon the funding agency became the Office of Indian Affairs, later known as the Bureau of Indian Affairs, instead of the War Department. Some agencies had their own force that coordinated with those controlled by the tribe's agent. Still, the government in the 1870s and 1880s needed scouts who could work beyond their own tribe's borders against those who fought the government.

The official start of the Navajo scouts occurred on January 23, 1873, when the War Department authorized the District of New Mexico to enlist fifty scouts for duty. Conflict with the Apaches had steadily increased, and so—given the general animosity felt between the two tribes, familiarity with the region and desert operations, the Navajos' ability to track, and the desire many young men felt to get off the reservation and engage in some type of warfare—recruitment came fairly easily. At times, there were too many trying to join, and so the army became increasingly selective. A scout's pay was comparable to that of a white soldier's set at thirteen dollars a month, while forty cents a day reimbursed each individual that used his own horse. This was cost-effective since the Indian mounts could eat local grasses and desert plants while those of the cavalry required hay and oats provided by a logistical chain of wagons following the troops. Smaller trains meant faster movement. Not until General George Crook traded heavy dependence on wagons for mules with pack frames, called aparejos, did logistical support start to slim. Although mules required being fed with oats and hay, their ability to go over rough terrain was a leap ahead in mobility. Crook also decreased the amount of equipment the soldiers

*Pictured in its most basic form is the winning combination for the Apache wars. General Crook (center), who rewrote the military's rules for desert operations, employed pack mules instead of supply trains and emphasized the employment of Navajo and Apache scouts as trackers and fighters. Alchise (right) served as a faithful White Mountain Apache sergeant who tirelessly campaigned against Chiricahua bands that left the reservation. (Courtesy of Wikimedia Commons)*

packed, lightened loads on the animals, and exploited their ability to move cross-country where wagons could not venture, placing pressure on those pursued. As one of Geronimo's men noted, "Troops generally carry their ammunition and supplies in wagons, therefore they follow the flat country. It was only when General George Crook chased the Indians with a column supplied by mule pack trains that the Apaches had a hard time staying out of reach."[21]

Navajo scouts also traveled light. Once enlisted, they received a full blue soldier's uniform, campaign hat, and "a canvas-covered leather cartridge belt with loops to hold fifty .45–70 cartridges required for the issued 1873 Springfield Trapdoor rifle or the Springfield Trapdoor carbine [.45–.55 caliber]."[22] Once in the field, most Navajos shed their uniform for traditional clothing, allowing more freedom of movement. As mentioned previously, care was taken to distinguish friend from foe through some designated article of clothing that could be recognized at a distance. Both the Navajos and the Apaches had been raised from youth to be long-distance runners and learned how to traverse the uneven terrain they encountered. The more freedom the scouts had to move to their own rhythm—whether on horseback or foot—the more level the playing field, making encounters with the enemy more likely.

The military organized the scouts into companies of twenty-five men each, while a regular infantry company or cavalry troop could have an authorized strength of 50 to 100 men. For instance, in 1881 the average number of enlisted men in an infantry company was 41 and in a troop, 58.[23] A captain provided leadership assisted by a first and second lieutenant and a first sergeant along with lower enlisted ranks as noncommissioned officers (NCO) in these line units. In the smaller scout companies, there was one officer and an NCO or a civilian chief of scouts. Occasionally a full company of scouts might be deployed as a single unit with a much larger military force, but more often the men were parceled out to smaller maneuver elements working to locate the enemy. Indeed, the primary role of the military during the Apache campaigns was to find, fix, and either capture or destroy those they were pursuing. The scouts participated in all three phases, but their real expertise was in the finding while assisting with the rest.

The first detachment of Navajo scouts began on March 1, 1873, and continued until 1880. There followed a break until 1882, when the detachment was reorganized and made into Company B, which remained in service until at least 1890. At the same time, there were other detachments assigned to specific military units performing duty throughout the

Southwest, including New Mexico and Arizona as well as Colorado. There is no firm number for how many of these detachments were employed. During the Apache campaign (1885–86), including the surrender of Geronimo, there were three Navajo scout companies—A, B, and C, or as the Navajos referred to them, First, Second, and Third, that were in service from May to October 1886. This was an outgrowth of General Crook's emphasis on having Apaches and Navajos be the prime movers in locating the enemy and assisting the military as needed in the fight.

Crook, perhaps one of the most successful officers to work with Indian scouts and auxiliaries, framed what a successful relationship between the Indians and army looked like. Advising a junior officer who was working with Apache scouts, he said:

> The first principle is to show them that we trust them . . . they are quick to note any lack of confidence. . . . They appreciate the situation, and understand thoroughly what is expected of them, and know how to best do their work. They understand this business better than we do, and to direct them in details will merely disgust them and make them "time-servers." They will work in your presence, and when away from you, loaf. The only directions which can be given them, with any probability of good results, is to explain to them what you expect of them, and let them do their work in their own way, holding them responsible that it is done. . . . They know better how to obtain the information which is needed—namely the presence of the renegades—than we do, and should be allowed to use their own methods in getting it. . . . We cannot expect them to act automatically as drilled soldiers do. Their best quality is their individuality, and as soon as this is destroyed their efficiency goes with it. . . . The question is how to get the most valuable service, and hence the caution sought to be conveyed in this letter, which is based on long experience in the use of Indian scouts and auxiliaries.[24]

A final look at the big picture concerning this period of the last wars against the Indian helps put the detailed discussion of what happened with the Navajo scouts in perspective. The United States military, while very much aware of what was happening in the West and Southwest, never devised a clear strategy for the unconventional warfare it was engaged in, although in modeling itself on European tactics and thinking, there were a number of practices that went beyond this model. Engaging in winter campaigns when Indians were less mobile, attacking encampments filled with noncombatants, waging a total war to remove resources and support

*These two Navajo scouts, photographed by Ben Wittick, served in the 1886 campaign against Geronimo. They are dressed and equipped in typical fashion—knee-length moccasins made from deer and cowhide, white muslin or cotton pants that extend to the calf, shirts of calico, and the 1873 Springfield Trapdoor carbine. This breech-loading rifle with a shortened 22-inch barrel could fire between eight and fifteen rounds per minute, depending on the skill of the shooter. (Courtesy of Palace of the Governors Photo Archive, New Mexico History Museum, Neg. #015708)*

systems, and maintaining constant pressure on the enemy were some of the goals and techniques adopted and adapted to fighting Native Americans. On the Indians' side, their goals were to preserve offensive capability, protect family and resources, fight at a time and place of their choosing, and escape when conditions were not favorable. In order for the military to be effective, it needed to concentrate enough power to deal a winning blow against its enemy. By 1880 General Sherman felt that the railroads had expanded sufficiently to allow this to happen, but much of the Apache wars were waged in deserts and mountains where the railroad had not yet ventured. Still, between 1880 and 1891, the number of military posts in the West declined from 111 to 62 as part of this consolidation, reorganization, and recognition that the military was no longer needed to fight Indians.[25]

But until this time of defeat for Native American forces, the army faced the issue of finding and capturing these will-o'-the-wisp warriors and concentrating them on reservations. It could be argued that there were no more skilled opponents in a more formidable terrain than the Apaches. Navajo and Apache scouts were primarily the only ones who could find the enemy on their own terms. Very few engagements occurred without them. They were the ones who knew the land, its resources, hiding places, and familiar haunts of those they chased. It also required skilled army officers to lead them. As historian Robert M. Utley recognized:

> Exclusive or even major use of Indians as combat forces entailed grave risks. They were kinsmen, racial if not tribal, of the people being hunted, and one could never be fully certain of their reliability. Good leadership offset much of the gamble. Crook chose his scout officers with great care. Young men of ambition, dedication, sensitivity, and above all rapport with their men offered the best prospects. These officers, remarked one perceptive observer, were less "Indian fighters" than "Indian thinkers." Indian scouts and fighting auxiliaries compiled an almost uniform record of faithfulness.[26]

Perhaps no other American military commander was a bigger advocate for Indian scouts and employed them more effectively than General Crook. Not only did he use warriors from other tribes, but he also had a large contingent of Apache scouts that he used against the Apaches he pursued. The men he chose were skilled and dedicated, and it brought results. Apache opponents noted how the tenor of the chase and combat shifted when kinsmen pursued kinsmen. Psychologically, it also had a large impact. As Crook explained in 1886:

To polish a diamond, there is nothing like its own dust. . . . It is the same with these fellows [scouts]. Nothing breaks them up like turning their own people against them. They don't fear the white soldiers, whom they easily surpass in the peculiar style of warfare which they force upon us, but put upon their trail an enemy of their own blood, an enemy as tireless, as foxy, and as stealthy and familiar with the country as they themselves, and it breaks them all up. It is not merely a question of catching them better with Indians, but of a broader and more enduring aim—their disintegration.[27]

In the following chapters, the effectiveness of the scouts is highlighted. Their employment by the military, some personal experiences, and relationships with the Apaches with whom they worked or pursued are discussed. Above all, their dedication is apparent. In a sense, they are unsung heroes. More has been written about the Apache scouts than the Navajo scouts. Indeed, relatively little was recorded about them as with many other aspects of daily, undramatic frontier soldiering of the time. Yet many of the officers who worked with them valued their efforts and insight, as expressed in after-action reports and enlisted evaluations. They were tough men in a tough terrain fighting a tough enemy.

CHAPTER FOUR

# The Apache Wars, 1873–1886

## Apache Fieldcraft and Individual Tactics

T|he Apache wars (1873–86), the last of the significant military conflicts between Native Americans and Anglos in the continental United States, represent the end of over 250 years of strife. Although the Apache experience is at the close of this chain of events, it was also one of the most difficult of all of the tribes to subdue. The circumstances surrounding this conclusion have been studied extensively in a variety of ways. For instance, those readers interested in the day-to-day operations—the comings and goings of military units and Apache reactions—should read Donald E. Worcester's *The Apaches: Eagles of the Southwest*, James L. Haley's *Apaches: A History and Culture Portrait*, or Dan L. Thrapp's *The Conquest of Apacheria*, all excellent works detailing political and social aspects as well as the many protracted campaigns that finally brought these Indians under total federal control.[1] Other secondary sources build upon different experiences from both the army's and Apache leaders' perspectives.[2] There are also works that outline the valuable service rendered by the "buffalo soldiers," Black military units that worked alongside their white counterparts to capture their elusive foe.[3] Other aspects to consider are the relations of Apaches with Mexicans on the border of Mexico, their ability to use the international boundary for refuge, various cultural practices within the different tribal groups, the effects of new technology and tactical innovation introduced in this post–Civil War era, and the economic development of the Southwest in spite of the resistance. The list goes on.

Here a different approach is taken. When one turns to this conflict's primary sources—those written at the time or the interviews and autobiographies of participants collected later—one finds threading throughout the gritty details of just how difficult life was for all those involved. Every discussion underscores how wily the Apaches were, how difficult soldiers found it chasing their will-o'-the-wisp adversaries, and why General George Crook, in particular, depended so heavily on Indian scouts and mule train mobility. Indeed, finding, fixing, and fighting the enemy summarizes the goal and frustration of these primarily small-scale conflicts. It is the fine-grain detail of how these participants fought this war as outlined through personal accounts that this and the next two chapters turn. The first one looks at Apache training of the individual and the techniques used on a small scale to baffle the enemy that made them so difficult to run to ground. The next examines scouting techniques and experience that made pursuit possible, as illustrated by specific incidents, while the third chapter provides three daily accounts of individuals caught in the throes of war.

In 1976 John Keegan published his landmark work *The Face of Battle: A Study of Agincourt, Waterloo, and the Somme.*[4] The author analyzed three different engagements (1415, 1815, and 1916 respectively) spread over a span of five hundred years but fought in the same geographical area. Keegan examined the effects of war on the participants, painting a picture of the combat elements men shared in conflict. Rather than follow the larger strategic developments that led to the struggles, he centered on the individual experience and factors that produced the results for both winning and losing sides. These elements encountered personally, yet held in common by many, provided the fuel for his analysis. This approach became a model for understanding the experience or "face" of battle.

Here, the "face of scouting and battle" is discussed as it relates to the Apache wars. It is in the details that one comes to understand what made the undertaking so formidable. Particular attention is paid to four different groups. In keeping with the theme of this book, the role of the Navajo scouts is discussed as much as possible. Unfortunately, although there were more than five hundred scouts enlisted and serving in these wars, there was little recorded about their experience, while the Apache scouts, who served beside them in the field, had much of what they did preserved in interviews, field reports, and autobiographies. There were obvious differences between the two native groups—Apache scouts had the advantage and sometimes disadvantage of sharing family ties, Apache thought processes, similar cultural values, and greater familiarity with the terrain and where those fleeing might go. Still, Navajo and Apache scouts often worked side by side and encountered similar circumstances when facing the third group—those Apaches fleeing from or fighting against them. Finally, there was the U.S. military with its western way of thinking and conduct of warfare. Each of these four groups brought its own skills to the battle and a unique perspective, but understanding the training and capability of an elusive foe reinforces why scouting and fighting was so difficult. That is the purpose of this chapter.

## Apache Training for Combat

Before a young Apache man was formally allowed to participate in battle, he prepared to become one of the most successful light infantrymen the United States has ever fielded. Physical fitness was high on the priority list for those at the tender age of nine and ten or older. Running long distance, often much of it uphill, with a mouth full of water that had to be spit out at the end; simulating combat with blunt arrows, slings, and clubs; wrestling, close quarter fighting, and racing on foot and horseback; eating and sleeping little; plunging into icy winter waters or traveling long distances under the blazing summer sun; hunting and stalking game, hiding and camouflaging the body, as well as remaining still for hours—were all part of training for manhood responsibilities. But it was not just the young men. James Kaywaykla, an Apache who lived through these wars and knew Victorio, Nana, Geronimo, and other fighters, shared his experience.

> The little girls in the band received the same training as the boys. Each day all practiced with bow and arrows, sling and spears. Each was taught to mount an unsaddled horse without help. We caught the mane, dug our toes into the foreleg, and swung ourselves astride the animal. Then we had to become able to leap astride the horse without a handhold. That was difficult but we learned by running down a slope for the takeoff. At first, we threw ourselves face down across the back of the Spanish pony and wriggled into a sitting position. I think it may have been three months before I could perform the feat on level ground.[5]

This type of training and preparation was necessary. A few examples reinforce why. Palmer Valor told of a raid for horses into Mexico and concluded his account by saying, "Now it was seven nights and days since we had had a real sleep, and that is the way we used to do when we were on the warpath or on a raid. A man had to be mean and smart so that he would never be caught by the enemy."[6] Long-distance travel played another important part. Geronimo said that he and his warriors regularly traveled fourteen hours a day covering forty-five miles, while Jason Betzinez stated that warriors traveled cross-country seventy-five miles a day. Britton Davis, a leader of a scout detachment, on one occasion "ascertained that the hostiles traveled ninety miles without a halt for any purpose and did not make camp until they reached the Mexican border."[7] In each instance, this was done with the warriors carrying their equipment needed for operations.

Starting with individual gear, some items were indispensable and common to all. Traversing the landscape required sturdy footwear, the Apache moccasin being especially adapted for this environment. All Apache men knew how to make them, carried the equipment and hide for repairs, and understood where to get materials if they ran short. For example, thick cowhide soles were most desirable, while the upper part of the moccasin was fashioned from deer hide. Both types of leather were readily available. Raiders might butcher a cow and then receive enough leather for each person to fashion one pair of soles to replace those they had worn out.[8] Kaywaykla explained just how versatile this footwear was to use.

> The tanning of a hide is a slow and difficult process. Much buckskin is required for one pair of moccasins. The footgear was long and could be drawn up for warmth; or it could be folded below the knee for protection against thorns and rocks. In those folds we carried our valuable possessions, valuable primarily in the sense of usefulness. Sometimes these included extra cowhide sole, for soles wore out quickly and had to be replaced. We carried the end of thorns of a mescal plant with fiber attached for sewing the soles to the uppers. The soles were tanned with the hair left on, and they protected beyond the toes and terminated in a circular flap with a metal button sewed to the center. This piece turned back over the toes for additional protection. Because we frequently had to abandon our horses to scale cliffs, the moccasin was our most important article of dress.[9]

Another piece of indispensable gear, besides moccasins and knife, was the bow and arrow. Even when a warrior was well equipped with one of the best rifles and Colt revolvers of the time, he still carried a mulberry bow strung with deer sinew. Trained as a youth who spent many hours practicing accuracy, a man found different occasions where his skill was put to use. This silent weapon facilitated the killing of sentries or a fight at night so that the user's position would not be revealed. For this same reason, it was effective in killing game without scaring other animals away. The weapon was so light and out of the way when strapped across the back that it was not an encumbrance. Finally, they were reliable in close combat when ammunition for rifles and pistols ran low.[10] With sufficient metal to tip the arrows, enough time to dry the wood for a bow, and the knowledge of how to cure and form the materials, a warrior could replace one if it got broken or lost, whereas more sophisticated weapons had to be obtained through trade or raid.

## Desert Logistics

Ideally, every Apache had with him or her a small pouch of emergency rations. The literature is full of examples where Indian camps were surprised, attacked, and destroyed, leaving the inhabitants to flee on their own with bare essentials. People were scattered, possibly wounded, and separated for a lengthy period of time with no one available to assist the more helpless. Predesignated gathering or rallying points were emplaced to collect those who survived, but in the meantime, a person might be on their own. Kaywaykla understood this. "I, too, had a food bag, a small one containing mesquite bean meal. For months no Apache child had been without his emergency rations, nor had he slept without an admonition not to remove it, and not to abandon his blanket in case of attack. My food bag had never left me, day or night."[11]

Food that had not already been obtained could be collected on the march. The men hunted and the women gathered plants, roots, bulbs, seeds, and nuts, all in their season. Daklugie recalled how deer were killed in the late fall when the meat was best, while mescal was harvested in the spring and baked, then processed. Piñon nuts in the fall provided a lot of protein and could be easily stored. As the men hunted, women and children shook or knocked the nuts off of tree branches or collected them from the ground. An easier way to get them was from pack rats. "We began our harvest of piñon nuts by finding trails of pack rats and tracking them to their dens. The nests were sometimes two and a half feet high, and about that in diameter. Sometimes we got as many as two gallons or more of the tiny nuts from one cache. The rats never carried a faulty piñon to their hoard."[12] Knowing edible plants helped many Apache when deprived of various other foods.

Nature also provided medicine. The environment provided a pharmacopeia with dozens and dozens of plants that met specific needs. One example here will suffice. Lieutenant Britton Davis recalled when one of his men, Big Dave, in a group of Apache scouts, approached an enemy encampment in the Sierra Madre Mountains and came under fire. A bullet smashed into his arm, rendering it useless. When the scouts returned to their camp, the accompanying surgeon felt that the only course of action was to amputate, which Dave and others refused.

> Procuring some green twigs about the thickness of the lead in a pencil and some three inches long, they bent them into two circles, each the size of a dollar. These they wrapped around and through with narrow strips of cloth until the hole in the center was about the size of a dime. One of these circles they put over the hole made by the bullet when it entered and the other where the bullet had come out. Before doing this, they accepted the aid of our surgeon to the extent of removing the small pieces of splintered bone, which Dave stood stoically without anesthetics.
>
> The small circles in place, a poultice was made of green sprigs of snake root, and bound over the wounds. This dressing was removed and renewed daily for two or three days while Dave remained in camp with us. One care of the wound that particularly struck our surgeon was that no water was allowed to touch it. This, he said, was a knowledge he would have supposed the Indians not to possess. He was still intent that Dave's arm would stiffen and he would have little or no use of it; but when I saw Dave at Fort Apache three months later, he had recovered the use of his arm and of all the fingers of that hand except two, and these he said would recover.[13]

Medicine Apache-style had saved the arm.

One of the biggest factors in success or failure of any military operation in this environment—regardless of which side—was the lack of water, and both sides knew it. Apache familiarity with the vast territory they ranged in both the southwestern United States and Mexico, gave them a large advantage over their non-Apache foe. Yet even they suffered from insufficient water when on the run or were deprived of its use when the enemy occupied the source. Limited water could prove to be both an advantage and disadvantage. Known sources made some movements predictable; denying that resource was also part of a strategy to bring an enemy to bear. Man and beast depended on it for survival. As James Kaywaykla pointed out, "After twelve days a man eats what he can get, whether he be red or white. One thing White Eyes never learned—to detect the presence of water underground. Many perished, when by digging two or three feet they could have obtained water."[14] Jason Betzinez agrees, pointing out that the Apaches moved mostly in the mountains because they knew of the waterholes and springs that were present. He noted that often the enemy would go to a dry streambed lined with green cottonwoods and dig in some low places expecting to find water, but it was down too far. But in the mountains, especially in a rock basin at the foot of a dry waterfall, he could scoop the sand out and find enough water to keep him and others alive.[15]

Yet even the Apaches suffered from thirst. Geronimo could find food easily, killing cattle whenever he needed meat, but he suffered greatly from lack of water. One time he had no water for two days and nights, almost killing his horses. General Crook understood the type of logistical pressure this placed on his enemies and so stationed scouts at watering holes and likely crossing places where they could be detected.[16] Not surprising, a number of fights centered around the control of water holes. For example, Captain—later Major—John Cremony, a company commander in the 2nd Regiment California Volunteer Cavalry, witnessed a protracted fight over a waterhole. The unit had just been on a long march across the desert and was focused on reaching a spring located in a canyon defile. Expecting no attack, the leader, Captain Roberts, had proceeded two-thirds of the way into the canyon when firing from both sides erupted thirty to forty yards away. "On either side the rocks afforded natural and almost unassailable defenses. Every tree concealed an armed warrior, and each warrior boasted his rifle, six-shooter and knife. A better armed host could scarcely be imagined. From behind every type of shelter came the angry, hissing missiles with not a soul to be seen. Quickly, vigorously, and bravely did his men respond, but to what effect? They were expending ammunition for no purpose; their foes were invisible; there was no way to escalade those impregnable fortresses." The troops withdrew to the mouth of the canyon, reorganized, sent out skirmishers, and covered their advance with howitzer fire. Cremony commented: "In this manner the troops again marched forward. Water was indispensable for the continuance of life. Unless they could reach the springs, they must perish. A march of forty miles under an Arizonian sun, and over wide alkaline plains, with their blinding dust and thirst-provoking effects, had already been effected, and it would be impossible to march back again without serious loss of life, and untold suffering, without taking in the seeming disgrace of being defeated by seven times their force of Apaches."[17] Although the rifle fire was ineffective, the howitzer shells were not, creating significant casualties (one Apache claiming sixty-three) before the Indians had to abandon their positions. The necessity of water for both sides had cost lives.

There were also more passive ways of denying the enemy this precious resource. Lieutenant Charles Gatewood, with eighteen scouts and eighty buffalo soldiers, chased Chihuahua's Apaches through the desert heat, destroying their horses, exhausting the men, and forcing them into territory that had increasingly scarce water. In two days, the cavalry traveled seventy miles, pushing men and mounts to the limit. When they reached their desired destination where they could obtain spring water, Gatewood reported, "We found a tank of clear and cool water, but . . . a coyote had been killed and disemboweled in it, and it had been otherwise disgustingly poisoned."[18] At other times, Mother Nature played a role in providing water that appeared to be fine but was naturally laced with alkali that loosened the bowels and cramped the stomach. Some soldiers, even though aware of the consequences, drank some only to later regret it.

Caching was an important principle that aided the Apaches in this mobile warfare. Planning ahead, storing what was needed, and replenishing supplies whenever possible provided flexibility as to where tribal members could flee when in trouble. Kaywaykla described where these food and materiel supplies were kept. "We harvested food as we went [south], and stored surpluses in caches, preferably in caves near a water supply. We also left cooking utensils because pottery breaks easily. And we stored blankets, bales of calico, and other commodities taken from smugglers who were constantly going back and forth in caravans. If our people were forced to flee, they used these reserves."[19] Jason Betzinez recalled that after a group of warriors had returned from a successful raid and were loaded with booty, the entire group decided to move northwest to further their success. They went on foot, leaving all of their horses in that area because of abundant grass. Before doing so, "We concealed in caves our saddles and loot which the men had brought back from the earlier raid, as well as our camp gear which we could not carry on our backs."[20] Thus the necessities of life were available in a variety of places.

## Physical and Spiritual Communication

Communication was an important part of field operations for both sides, each one having a number of different groups or elements spread over a large geographical area. For the Apaches, smoke and mirrors filled much of their need. Smoke signals, stereotypically tied to Indians in general, alerted the observer to a number of bits of information, but unlike what is seen in movies, it did not work like a poor man's morse code with different sizes of puffs spelling out specific information. They were, however, deliberate attempts to notify others of certain situations. Green wood and branches produced enough smoke so that it could be seen for a long distance. Apaches often mention that when building a normal cooking fire or one for warmth, dry wood was used because it concealed one's location, while green wood was good for communication. Betzinez believed that his people built signal fires on mountaintops to only indicate that there was something wrong and that others should come there to investigate. Using cover and concealment, those coming to help approached cautiously, fearing an enemy ambush.[21]

Cremony, on the other hand, told of a time he was bivouacked with his group, when a sergeant awakened him and pointed to lights moving in three of the cardinal directions and eventually the fourth. Unsure of what it meant, he watched other lights, now identified to be torches, join the group and grow in number. Eventually they all came together and moved off to the east. Baffled by the sight, it took Cremony a year before an Apache explained what he had seen.

> He said that, as the Apaches are a dispersed and perpetually wandering race, it is impossible for one detachment to know where others might be at any time; but that when a great body of them was needed for a joint undertaking, they made smoke signals of a certain character by day and signals of fire by night. That, on the occasion of which I write, the nature of the country prohibited fire signals from being seen except for short distances, so runners were hurried through the district bearing torches, which indicated that the aid of all within sight was required.[22]

The Navajos used a similar system up through the time of the Long Walk. Wolfkiller remembered that when he was a young boy, dispersed Navajo groups used smoke signals to indicate both that there was a problem and that they needed to get together to discuss what action they should take against the military invasion.[23]

Mirrors served both the military and those they chased. The army's heliograph system spelled out through long and short flashes for the alphabet the morse code, rendering very specific information. Continual sunny days, visibility over long distances, ease of employment, and flexibility were qualities that endeared many commanders to this equipment. Indeed, by the end of the Apache campaign, when General Nelson A. Miles assumed command, he depended heavily on the heliograph. According to scout leader Britton Davis, this commander garrisoned all of the water holes and ranches where he anticipated Geronimo might appear and maintained

twenty-five to thirty signal points that could flash information instanta-
neously in this fluid environment.[24]

The Apaches were quick to learn. People guarding a camp or preparing
for a fight used pieces of mirror to flash warning signals. None knew morse
code, and so it was employed in a more general sense or by a predesignated
number of flashes to indicate an agreed-upon meaning. One problem with
this system for the Apaches is that friend and foe could see the same signal,
making it important to use it judiciously and attempt to shield it from
known enemy locations.[25] Still, it had greater flexibility than the telegraph,
which the Apaches understood was an important form of communication.
To frustrate their enemy, they went along the line, removed the wire, and
then discarded it. The location of the break was obvious to those wishing
to reestablish contact, and so the Apaches developed a more frustrating
practice. "In the past, the wire had been cut and miles of it thrown into
deep canyons. Men had gone out with new wire and repaired the lines.
Geronimo was determined that word should not reach the cavalry at San
Carlos, but was at a loss to prevent it. Grandfather sent the boys up the
trees to cut the wire, tie the ends to the limbs with buckskin thongs, and
thus conceal the breaks. They did this in many places—wherever they
found the wire attached to a tree. His method was effective."[26]

Smoke signals, fires, and mirror flashes were physical means of trans-
mitting information, but there was another kind—spiritual/supernatural—
that was equally effective for the Apaches, yet unexplainable to their Anglo
enemies. Divination is a result of understanding a power obtained by an
individual through a close connection to a spiritual being. As discussed
previously, power can come from a number of sources including plants, animals, or inanimate (according to the Anglo classification system) objects
given to an individual as a special gift. A two-way relationship results that
is based on respect and understanding; a person might have a specific but
limited gift while another might have a far-reaching ability to see into
the future. For example, James Kaywaykla witnessed this power within his
own family.

> Grandfather Nana's Power was to locate and capture ammunition trains.
> The value of his medicine can hardly be exaggerated, for while rifles
> can be used indefinitely, ammunition is soon exhausted, and the supply
> must be replenished frequently. Nana could obtain it when all others
> failed. He also had Power over rattlesnakes, but I never saw him touch
> one. . . . Grandmother's Power was that of healing wounds. Mother's
> was in avoiding them. In all the skirmishes in which she fought beside

my father, and later with Kaytennae, she never got a scratch. These great gifts had been given the women after they had been tested on the Sacred Mountain. Though Power was bestowed for the benefit of the tribe, there were those who used theirs for evil; and these we regarded as witches.[27]

Others controlled weather. One Apache scout wanting to hide his group's movement called up a covering wind. According to John Rope, another scout named Flattened Penis said, "'We don't want anyone to see us coming back over this open ground,' so he made a wind. He knew medicine for wind and prayed for it. Right in the middle of the mesa, a big wind came up and there was so much wind we could hardly see each other."[28] There are many instances where Navajo medicine men, through prayer, also controlled the weather.

Lozen, an Apache medicine woman and also stalwart fighter who helped the men, was highly revered for her ability to locate the enemy. Many times, with outstretched hands while slowly rotating, she sang this prayer: "Upon this earth on which we live, Ussen [Yusn] has power. This power is mine for locating the enemy. I search for that enemy which only Ussen the great can show me."[29] When finished, she would know the position of approaching fighters pursuing her Warm Springs Apache band. Kaywaykla described it like this: "When Victorio wished to know the location of the enemy, Lozen stood with outstretched arms, palms up, and prayed to Ussen. As she turned slowly, following the sun, her hands tingled and the palms changed color when they pointed toward the foe. The intensity of the sensation indicated the approximate distance of the enemy. The closer the adversary, the more vivid the feeling. Time after time I have seen her stand thus to ascertain the direction and proximity of the pursuers."[30]

Respect for the use of this power was absolutely critical. This fundamental quality lies at the foundation of why an answer is received and how successful the petitioner will be. Apache John Rope described an experience he and twenty other scouts had while attempting to locate enemy tracks. The trail had gone cold.

The first night we left, we stopped and made camp. We had a medicine man with us so we were going to find out if we would see the Chiricahuas or find their tracks. The medicine man sat on the opposite side with the other seven men to help him sing. Now he said, "No one must laugh while we are singing—if they do, it will be no good." When they started to sing, we with eagle feathers, closed our eyes and listened to the song. Our feathers commenced to get big and strong in our hands and started

*Lozen, an Apache woman, was welcomed by the men on their warring expeditions and was well known for her ability to use divination such as hand trembling, as depicted here. Navajos, Apaches, and many other Native American tribes had various spiritual means to foretell the future, examine the past, or understand current circumstances even though not present. (Drawing by Kelly Pugh)*

to move our arms from side to side. It was not we who moved our arms, but the feathers. Then one of the men singing laughed a little. Right away the eagle feathers and our arms dropped straight down to the ground. The medicine man said, "You make fun while we are singing—now we won't know about the Chiricahuas."[31]

This experience and other Apache examples are similar to those had by Navajos who employed three forms of divination—listening, hand trembling, and stargazing or crystal gazing—with similar results.[32]

Sometimes there was no visible performance but a prophetic event occurred anyway. Jason Betzinez told of sitting around a fire eating beef when Geronimo dropped his knife and told the men that the people he had left in camp had been captured and were in the grasp of the U.S. military. Their campsite was 120 miles away. Everyone there believed him, he asked what they wanted to do, and all agreed to go back to where they had left their relatives. Since they had in tow some Mexican women as captives, it took three days to cover the distance and find that what had been predicted was a reality. Geronimo soon made another prophecy.

"Tomorrow afternoon as we march along the north side of the mountains, we will see a man standing on a hill to our left. He will howl to us and tell us that the troops have captured our base camp." We marched quite early the next morning, straight west through a wide forest of oaks and pines. About the middle of the afternoon, we heard a howl from a hilltop to our left. There stood an Apache calling to us. He came down through the rocks to tell us that the main camp, now fifteen miles distant, was in the hands of U.S. troops. General Crook with some cavalry and Indian scouts had taken all the rest of the Apaches into custody.[33]

Lest the reader question the veracity of these accounts, a final one, provided by Lieutenant Britton Davis working with his troop of scouts, is offered. For six weeks, Davis had been waiting near the Mexican border with his scouts for the arrival of Geronimo. Each day he sent parties out in different directions to locate where the war leader might be, but they were without luck. He opted to use a medicine man to determine his rival's location. Although somewhat flippant in his tongue-in-cheek explanation, referring to him as the "Reverend Doctor," who "uttered incantations," his description and explanation ring true.

Preparations for the offices of the Reverend Doctor were elaborate. First a brush hut was built on a plot of ground a little remote from the camp, so that he might be undisturbed. The hut was covered with canvas from the pack trains, only a small opening being left. With his pouch of "medicine" the Doctor entered the hut and the opening closed.

There he remained all that day and into the night, uttering incantations and from time to time burning a pungent powder, the odor of which we could smell a dozen yards away. Toward nine or ten o'clock he came out of the hut; but the incantations were not yet finished. From his right hand depended a thin buckskin thong to the end of which was attached a small, flat piece of wood with a hole in it [bullroarer]. Twirling this around his head it gave out a shrill, whistling noise, not unlike the call of a nightbird.

Around and around his hut he went, then around the camp and through it, north to south, east to west, swinging his call and uttering incantations. The scouts, squatting in a circle, awaited his decision. The camp and all points of the compass properly incanted, he stopped at the scouts' campfire, threw on it his pungent powder, and raising his face to the stars in a singsong chant made many gestures with his waving arms; then suddenly he ceased and, bathed in sweat, tottering a little with weakness, announced that he had found Geronimo. Entering the circle of scouts, he prolonged the suspense for several minutes while he gazed at the stars and mumbled a final incantation. Then he announced that Geronimo was three days away, riding on a white mule, and bringing a great many horses.

I was sending daily three or four scouts to patrol south and west along the border as we were not sure at just what point Geronimo might come in. Some four or five days after the Reverend Doctor's prophecy, the patrol came in with the report that Geronimo was nearing the border and would arrive that afternoon; also, that he was riding a white pony.[34]

Davis closed this account with a series of rhetorical questions about how the medicine man knew these things that the head of scouts could not answer. He did, however, close the door on the possibility of someone sharing information with the medicine man or any other type of prior knowledge. It happened and only an answer concerning the supernatural could explain how.

## Maintaining Security

One important aspect of Apache fieldcraft was security. This took a number of different forms that were both active and passive measures. Camouflage to avoid detection was an individual and group responsibility taken to a high degree of success. There are countless stories about how warriors appeared seemingly out of nowhere to kill or capture their prey. Cremony explained how it was done.

> Let it be understood that the Apache has as perfect a knowledge of the assimilation of colors as the most experienced Paris *modiste*. By means of his acumen in this respect, he can conceal his swart body amidst the green grass, behind brown shrubs, or gray rocks with so much address and judgment that any but the experienced would pass by him without detection at the distance of three or four yards. Sometimes they will envelop themselves in a gray blanket, and by an artistic sprinkling of earth, will so resemble a granite boulder as to be passed within near range without suspicion. At others, they will cover their persons with freshly gathered grass, and lying prostrate, appear as a natural portion of a field. Again, they will plant themselves among the yuccas, and so closely imitate the appearance of that plant as to pass for one of its species. These exact imitations of natural objects which are continually present to the traveler, tend to disarm suspicion; yet, I would not advise the wayfarer to examine each suspected bush, tree or rock, but simply to maintain a cautious system of marching—never, for a moment, relaxing his watchfulness, and invariably keeping his weapons ready for immediate use.[35]

Application of what Cremony observed is found in the account of Kaywaykla: "Grandmother kept two young boys on the cliff as lookouts. They rubbed clay into their breech clouts, tied bunches of grass or feathers on their heads, and took their places on the ledges above us. Their bodies blended so nicely with the rock that unless one moved, it was almost impossible to locate him."[36] Another example of effective camouflage occurred when a Mexican officer with a companion walked across a two-mile-long field that was totally barren except for its foot-high grass. When he reached the midpoint, an Apache rose up, seized his arms, removed his weapon, and surrounded him with twelve other Apaches. Fortunately, they were friendly, but the lieutenant learned his lesson about the effectiveness of camouflage.[37]

Cremony offered a final, personal incident that he had with an Apache named Quick Killer.

> While crossing an extensive prairie, dotted here and there by a few shrubs and diminutive bushes, Quick Killer volunteered, while resting at noon, to show me with what dexterity an Apache could conceal himself, even where no special opportunity existed for such concealment. The offer was readily accepted, and we proceeded a short distance until we came to a small bush, hardly sufficient to hide a hare. Taking his stand behind this bush, he said: "Turn your back and wait until I give the signal." This proposition did not exactly suit my ideas of Apache character, and I said: "No, I will walk forward until you tell me to stop." This was agreed upon, and quietly drawing my pistol, keeping a furtive glance over my shoulder, I advanced, but had not gone ten steps, when Quick Killer hailed me to stop and find him. I returned to the bush, went around it three or four times, looked in every direction—there was no possible covert in sight; the prairie was smooth and unbroken, and it seemed as if the earth had opened and swallowed up the man. Being unable to discover him, I called and bade him come forth, when, to my extreme surprise, he arose laughing and rejoiced, within two feet of the position I then occupied. With incredible activity and skill, he had completely buried himself under the thick grama grass, within six feet of the bush, and had covered himself with such dexterity that one might have trodden upon him without discovering his person. I took no pains to conceal my astonishment and admiration, which delighted him exceedingly, and he informed me that their children were practiced regularly in this game of "hide and seek," until they became perfect adepts.[38]

Even the scouts, when leaving on a mission, rubbed dirt into their headbands and pants to dull the color and provide a certain amount of camouflage.[39]

Application of this camouflage expertise could also be found on the offensive. Again, Cremony pointed to a time when he and a companion named Richard Purdy shared the responsibility of guard duty for their encampment. Well aware that they would be watching on a moonless night but one with abundant starlight, Cremony and his partner noted the location of every bush and shrub in their sector and agreed that rather than walking their post, they would observe in the prone behind some concealment. All went well on their first watch, but during their second, Cremony noted that a bush had slightly changed its position. Further observation confirmed that it was moving, so the officer fired at the base of the shrub. "The shot was followed by the yells of some fifteen Apaches, who had approached within thirty paces of our camp by covering their heads with grass and crawling upon their bellies. Our comrades jumped to their feet and commenced shooting at the Indians, who discharged one volley into our camp and left us masters of the field."[40]

A desired goal for the military when chasing Apaches was to surprise them in an encampment so that the women, children, and old people could be captured, the warriors would be distracted by protecting them, and supplies, equipment, and horse herds would be rendered useless. The Apaches are most often pictured in the desert, but they actually consider themselves mountain people. Cool summer weather, good hunting, plentiful wood, clear mountain streams, rich grasslands, and long-range observation were appealing as opposed to a hot desert environment in the summer. Kaywaykla said, "We were essentially a mountain people moving from one chain to another, following the ridges as best we could. If there were no mountains, we took cover in arroyos, but survival on the desert and plains was much more difficult. . . . I doubt that any people ever excelled us as mountain climbers. Scaling walls was taken for granted. When closely pursued we killed our horses and scaled cliffs no enemy could climb."[41]

One technique used while staying in the mountains was to have the horses secured at a site a couple miles downriver after the packs had been unloaded and then carried on people's backs up the side of the mountain where they camped. This helped prevent the highly visible animal tracks leading to the people. Another way to avoid capture was to put the noncombatants in a secure place to observe, and then have the men go to more distant surveillance points to detect enemy movement and scout terrain, later returning to the temporary camp, picking up the women and children, and moving to a final resting place under cover of encroaching darkness.[42]

One standard operating procedure for the Apaches when being pursued was the splitting off into small groups from the main party over time. Charles Gatewood, as a chief of scouts, described this technique when following the tracks of a large group of warriors. The scouts would start on a major trail headed in a specific direction, but by the time they caught up to what they believed would be the entire body of enemy soldiers, all they might find was fifteen or twenty broken down horses and no warriors. He noted:

Some fifteen miles back on the "wagon road" [large trail], perhaps they began, one by one, leaving the main body, and going to some place of rendezvous agreed upon, which may be to any point of the compass from the place where the last disappears; or they may intend to break up into small parties and act separately; or—who could tell what a body of Chiricahuas would be likely to do? . . . When [I] asked the scouts as to the enemy location, the answer was "no sabe," with a shrug of the shoulders. . . . Then mortification set in all around, for we had obliterated the main trail with our horses and pack mules. There was nothing to do, however, but to march back and follow the greatest number of hostiles which could be found to go in any one general direction.

Now this never happened, so far as I know, with White Mountain [scouts] in advance. On several occasions, they gave dire notice that this trick was being played, and while the column either halted or marched slowly ahead, they followed the several tracks nearest, and from signs and indications and their own judgment, soon announced the direction the main body would take. In every instance, they were right.[43]

The Apaches made breaking camp with its children and livestock a well-practiced science. Kaywaykla explained:

If any people knows how to be quiet it is the Apache. If anybody can control his children and his women, and his horses and dogs, it is the Apache. But the cattle! We got everything ready to move in less than ten minutes. Not a dog barked. Not a baby cried. We tied children's feet together under the bellies of the horses. We tied small children to adults. And we started. At first we moved slowly, very slowly. We had to, because of the cattle. But after we got out of hearing we put boys with lances to keep the cattle moving, and we made time. By morning we were far north of that spring—maybe twenty miles.[44]

Herding sheep, especially when stolen, was also ingeniously engineered for speed and control. One army officer observed of the Apache:

When the rascals have time to make their arrangements, the sheep are formed in a parallelogram, the width of which never exceeds thirty feet, with a length sufficient to accommodate the flock. The strongest sheep are then selected and their horns lashed together in couples, and these couples are ranged along either side of the main flock, forming a sort of animal fence which prevents the enclosed livestock from wandering, especially while running at night. Along each side of the mass are stationed a string of Apaches on foot, who preserve regular distances, and animate

*Tracking the enemy could lead to success in battle or an ambush and defeat. In July 1882, these soldiers and scouts followed a group of fleeing Apaches, which eventually resulted in the Battle of Big Dry Wash. Five companies of soldiers surrounded an Apache camp under Na-tio-tish, surprised its occupants, and either wounded or killed every warrior. (Courtesy of Wikimedia Commons)*

the sheep to maintain a regular rate of speed. Immediately in front, a small body of select warriors and keen runners lead the way, while the main body of Indians follow in the rear to push forward and urge on the plunder. In this manner, the Apache will run a flock of twenty thousand sheep from fifty to seventy miles in one day, gradually lessening the distance, until they deem themselves tolerably safe from pursuit. They have been known to accomplish the distance of fourteen to fifteen hundred miles in this described manner.[45]

The military situation on the ground forced the small bands of Apaches to constantly be on the move once off the reservation. Security in movement was a necessity, with women, children, and elders being vulnerable targets as well as being an important support system for the men that needed to be protected. Once they broke camp and began to travel, the warriors provided all-around security with an advanced guard to serve as point element, left and right flankers, and a rearguard. Terrain dictated distances between those providing security for the main body, but each element served as early warning of enemy activity and initial covering of defensive fire as the camp fled in the opposite direction. Other security elements would join the fray. The flexibility in this formation was that as the situation dictated responsibilities on the battlefield, the point element either could maintain its position in defending the group or could instead become a flank element as the direction of the main body changed.

Two other techniques also helped prevent an enemy surprise. The first was avoiding what are called lines of drift. Animals and humans alike often select the path of least resistance when traversing difficult terrain. Lines of drift indicate this natural flow of travel, making encounters more likely. Avoiding these natural pathways provides greater security. "Apaches on the warpath, especially when accompanied by women and children, move high up in the mountain ranges whenever they can. This way they can see troops approaching and they avoid many combats by following routes that the soldiers dislike. Troops generally carry their ammunition and supplies by wagon, therefore they follow the flat country. It was only when General George Crook chased the Indians with a column supplied by mule trains that the Apaches had a hard time staying out of reach."[46]

The second technique was to always have at least one rally point so that if a camp was attacked, if the group were broken up during movement, or if for some other reason people got separated, everyone knew ahead of time where all should reconvene. Usually this was a clearly identifiable location, familiar to everyone, providing defensible positions and good observation of approaching elements, and located far enough away to evade the enemy if detected. Terrain dictated distance and accessibility, but some rally points could have been fifty miles away. Still, standard procedure in each situation would be to scatter and later regroup. This made finding those fleeing difficult, prevented large numbers of a party from being successfully engaged, avoided noncombatants being captured wholesale, allowed those escaping to regroup to retaliate, and gave flexibility to the leaders to collect all of those who had been badly injured and needed assistance. Fight or flight of those in contact were the two main options once a group became compromised.

There were times when the security plan failed. For instance, Victorio led a group of approximately thirty people to a favorite camping place that had a pond of water lying in a deep box canyon. With two or three men in the advance element and others serving as rear guard, the main body entered the defile. Undetected, a group of Mexicans lying in wait sprang their ambush, keeping all three elements separated. By nightfall, the Apaches' ammunition was expended. The Mexicans closed in, and with gunfire and sticks of dynamite they killed all that were in the ambush zone. Only those in the rear security element lived to tell what happened.[47]

The focus of this chapter has been to look at the capability the Apaches brought to the battlefield in the form of fieldcraft knowledge and individual or small-group tactical preparation. Their skills and training made them difficult foes to bring to ground for the United States military. The way to do this effectively was to include Navajo and Apache scouts who had been trained in similar fashion and who understood the thinking of their adversary. Still, it was extremely difficult, as the next chapter will point out. The Apaches being pursued were not infallible; in fact, there are historical incidences that will make them seem at times to be tactically naive and even foolish. Yet for the most part, the training and procedures that they used made them seem almost invincible to those trying to bring them into a reservation. The scouts opposing them provided the most effective answer for how to defeat this skillful foe.

# CHAPTER FIVE

# Scouts Take to the Field

## Tactics and Techniques

The Apache wars provided the most intense experience for Navajo and Apache scouts during those organizations' existence. Indeed, this conflict was the reason the military formed these two units. It was when these forces reached their highest enrollments as the government accomplished its mission of returning Apaches to their reservations, sending them eventually to Florida. The task was anything but easy as the conflict spread over almost fifteen years. To understand the scouting experience and to place it in context, a brief timeline is provided here. Between 1873 and 1886 there were four different campaigns that took place following the end of conflicts with Mangas Coloradas and Cochise. The newly organized Navajo scouts were first employed against groups of western Apaches who resisted coming into one of the reservations; the scouts were also sent onto the plains during a brief stint in the Red River War against the Kiowas and Comanches. By 1876, problems with reservation lands and inept agents flared into a conflict with Victorio and Nana that did not end until 1880. An attempted arrest followed by a skirmish at Cibecue Creek in 1881 sent many Western Apaches fleeing from their reservation to wage a brushfire war in both Mexico and the United States. This culminated in a large military campaign conducted by General George Crook, who successfully pioneered an approach that championed the use of Apache and Navajo scouts, extensive mule packtrains, cross-border forays, and fair treatment of his foes. His accomplishment of returning his adversary to the San Carlos reservation in 1884 was, without a doubt, a result of these techniques. A year later, Geronimo, with a relatively small group of Apaches, jumped the reservation and did not surrender until October 1886.

In all of these campaigns, Navajo scouts with their Apache scout cousins shared the drudgery of locating and fighting the enemy. Although the Apache scouts hold the limelight in the recorded word, their Navajo allies played an important role in subduing those fleeing and fighting the military. Both earned their laurels in these conflicts. Indeed, Britton Davis, a West Point graduate and officer in charge of an Indian scout company, offered, "The question has often been asked me why we used cumbersome and useless cavalry in these expeditions when the cavalry only retarded the movements of the scouts and hardly ever got into action against the hostiles. The answer is that the cavalry was supposed to serve as a rallying point for the scouts, increasing their morale and protecting the packtrains."[1] The primary focus of this chapter is the examination of this scouting experience, using examples common to both groups while also noting a few instances unique to either the Navajos or Apaches.

## Scout Selection and Organization

Recruiting for Indian scouts centered around specific locations tied to military posts either on or near reservations. While Fort Wingate in New Mexico was the center for Navajo recruitment and control, Fort Apache and the San Carlos reservation were the epicenter for Apache activity, although both Navajo and Apache enlistment also drew upon populations far distant from these locations. Criteria for selection included good health, stamina, reliability, capacity to withstand hardship, and skill in tracking. John Rope mentioned both the diversity of the people applying to be scouts as well as his own personal experience.

> At San Carlos there were lots of Indians gathered to enlist: Yavapais, Tonto Apaches, San Carlos Apaches, and White Mountain people were all there. We lined up to be chosen. My brother was the first one picked. My brother said if he was to be a scout, then he wanted me to go as a scout with him too. He told this to the officers. They asked which one I was and he took them to where I was standing. These officers looked me over to see if I was all right. They felt my arms and legs and pounded my chest to see if I would cough. That's the way they did with all scouts they picked and if you coughed, they would not take you. I was alright, so they took me. After they had picked forty men, they said that was enough. I was twenty or twenty-five years old at that time.[2]

While the Navajos did not culturally have the different band organization that the Apaches did, there is good indication that clan identity
was a factor. Fifty or more different Navajo clans existed at this time and
were spread throughout the reservation. Often there were strong nodules
of clan membership that clustered together as nonbiological relatives who
shared important supportive relationships. Hence, many of those selected
for service, because they had these bonds and lived in the Fort Wingate
area, served together.

The number of scouts enlisted at any given time fluctuated with operational needs, but each enlistment was for a six-month period with an
opportunity to reenlist if their performance was commendable and military activity required it. The largest-sized unit was the company normally
composed of a white officer—usually a lieutenant, an Indian first sergeant,
a second sergeant, two corporals, and twenty-six privates. When there was
a greater demand for leadership, additional sergeants and corporals were
added; at times there might be as many as two hundred scouts operating
in the field. The army, recognizing cultural differences, attempted to keep
different bands and groups together for internal cohesion. Given the fragmented needs of chasing down scattered elements of Apaches, the scouts
were often detailed in small numbers of a dozen or more assigned to one
of the many posts spread over a vast geographical area. On the other hand,
large-scale military operations might have employed over one hundred
scouts dispersed throughout different units. Thus at times, these companies did not function as a cohesive element, but more as a series of special
task forces whose members were assigned to white or black cavalry or infantry forces.[3] They were officially enlisted in the army, received the same
pay of thirteen dollars per month as a white private, and would later be
recognized by the government as official participants in the Indian Wars
and so would be eligible for a pension.

The military took precautions, especially with the Apache scouts who
were working against their own people, to monitor the feelings and attitudes of these men, questioning at times their allegiance. Davis, having
served as the leader of a scout company and also as a temporary agent to
some of the Apaches, emphasized the importance of knowing what was
going on with those he led. Due to language barriers, cultural differences,
social interaction, and daily events, Anglos often missed the nuances of
Indian life. To correct this, the military implemented a spy system to monitor the undercurrent of feelings. It is one of those little-discussed facts of
the scouting experience.

*Apache scouts presenting arms at Fort Wingate, New Mexico. Their uniformity of dress and unnatural pose suggests this staged photo may have been more for propaganda than an accurate portrayal, but once in the field, they were, at times, referred to by white officers as "tigers." (Courtesy of Center for Southwest Research, University of New Mexico, Neg. #000–742–0384)*

In addition to the regular scout enlistments, seven secret scouts were enlisted from the most trustworthy Indians we could find to take the dangerous job. Two of these were for [Lieutenant Charles] Gatewood at Fort Apache. Of those at San Carlos, two were women. One woman and one man went with me later to Turkey Creek [reservation].

The duty of these scouts was to report to us every indication of discontent or hostility that might arise among the Indians on the Reservation. They took no part in the campaigns, but were employed solely to keep us posted on symptoms of unrest or agitation that might lead to serious difficulties in or between the various tribes or even outbreaks; a duty they performed thoroughly and faithfully, enabling us to nip in the bud many situations that might have led to serious trouble.

Their method of communicating with us was, of course, secret. A tap on a window pane shortly after our lights were out would bring the occupant of the room to the door. . . . If any of the Indians suspected the activities of these secret scouts, they gave no intimation of it. Nor was any secret service scout advised that there were others. If they suspected each other, they kept their suspicions to themselves. Following the organization of the scout companies, all the Indians at or near San Carlos were ordered to the military headquarters there, where they were counted. To the males capable of bearing arms, which included all boys from about the age of fourteen up, brass identification tags were issued, which were ordered always to keep on their person. On these tags were letters and numbers indicating the band to which the Indian belonged and his number in the band.[4]

## Terrain Analysis—OCOKA

When tracking the Apaches, there were two major considerations—the terrain and the enemy's tactical capability—which were usually inseparable. Finding the enemy in such diverse territory often challenged the best of scouts, while fighting them was just as difficult because of their use of it. Today's military employs the acronym OCOKA when evaluating land features that can influence how an attacking force approaches, how that terrain can be defended, and how opposing forces can gain battlefield supremacy. The term represents the following characteristics of topography as they relate to tactical concerns. *Observation* allows a defending force to see its enemy, *cover* (protection from direct fire) and *concealment* (seclusion from view) prevents the defending force from taking casualties, and an *obstacle* hinders or stops the enemy from maneuvering and flanking the friendly force. *Key terrain* or a critical part of the land that controls the outcome of the battle may be connected to an *avenue of approach* or route for attacking an objective. Using the acronym OCOKA provides a handy way to recall and evaluate terrain-dictated action on the ground.

Observation could take a number of forms that extended from long-range sight to examination of a moccasin print in the soil. Apaches fleeing their enemy consistently sought high terrain for a number of reasons: there was far less chance of being surprised with lookouts placed strategically to provide early warning, attacking uphill was difficult for the enemy, flight could take place in a number of directions, water sources like springs and rock basins (tinajas) captured rain or snowmelt, and it was easier to signal with mirrors. General Crook noted that when bringing Geronimo to bay, "We found him in a camp on a rocky hill . . . in such a position that a thousand men could not have surrounded them with any possibility of capturing them. They were able upon the approach of an enemy being signaled to scatter and escape through dozens of ravines and canyons, which would later shelter them from pursuit until they reached the higher ranges in the vicinity."[5]

Gravity also assisted defenders. Those fighting in rugged canyon country often piled rocks and boulders on the slope facing expected enemy activity so that they could be released to roll down upon attackers. Jason Betzinez told of a Mexican patrol pursuing some Apaches down a narrow canyon trail. The Indian leaders posted the best fighting men in key positions next to the lower side of the defile while other warriors prepared a rock slide along the draw.

> Finally the head of the military column appeared. Our men let it pass our lower line of warriors who were concealed waiting for them. When the leading enemy soldiers arrived at the top of the canyon our men sprang out and opened fire. The Mexicans turned and ran back. Our men were close on their heels. Then we heard the rocks commencing to roll down into the canyon. . . . The din in the canyon was tremendous, what with the shooting, the yelling, and the crashing of huge boulders. The sound reverberated through the canyon and its side gorges. Although the soldiers outnumbered our side they lost heavily in their initial headlong retreat. After several hours the shooting stopped.[6]

In a similar entrapment of Mexicans pursuing some of Juh's Apaches on a narrow trail up a mountain, those fleeing piled rocks above the path and waited. When the Mexicans entered the ambush site, they were taken under fire, so they decided to retreat. Juh ordered the boulders to be released. "Some of these rocks were so big that they knocked down pine trees. Many soldiers were crushed by the tumbling boulders and falling trees. Not many escaped."[7] The effectiveness of this technique was not lost on Geronimo, who said to Davis, "I don't fight Mexicans with cartridges. I fight them with rocks and keep my cartridges to fight the white soldiers." The lieutenant mused, "At the time I thought he was having fun with me or trying to dodge my request; but now on these steep mountain slopes I could see what he meant and appreciated the effectiveness of his rock ammunition."[8] In a reverse of this practice, when being shot at while moving uphill, some attackers pushed large rocks in front of them as they lay on the ground to avoid enemy fire. As the defenders expended their ammunition, the rocks moved ever closer to the enemy's position until a short rush from behind these shields placed the attackers within easy striking distance at the top of the hill.[9]

Apache invisibility through cover and concealment was an effective tool that lulled the unsuspecting into a trap. Major John C. Cremony, who pursued Apaches through the Southwest for eight years, warned that "when they mean mischief no marks are to be seen—no traces, no tracks, no 'signs' discovered. The unsuspecting traveler, lulled into a fatal belief that none of them are near, relaxes his caution, and is caught as surely as the spider meshes the confiding fly."[10]

Since the pursuer and pursued could be equally involved in offensive and defensive tactics, site selection was important to both. James Kaywaykla recalled that when soldiers were pursuing his people, the Apache leader Kaytennae chose a route that forced the cavalry to go through Dog Canyon. With a restricted avenue of approach, cliff walls providing cover and concealment, good observation, and a spring serving as key terrain for thirsty soldiers, this trail was ideal for an ambush. Kaywaykla remembered the discussion in which Suldeen, one of the warriors, explained the intricate thinking as to why it served as a good site.

> It is a good place for those who wish to ambush the Bluecoats. . . . I know that place well. There is a narrow, winding trail leading into it. The entrance is not very wide, and between it and the narrow gap a short distance back is a spring. Beyond it the walls are so close together that only one horse at a time can pass, and to do so he must scramble up a waist-high ledge. For an enemy coming in from the basin it is a death trap. The Mescaleros and Nana, too, have sent two or three out on the floor to lure cavalry into the ambush. Once through the narrow opening with its perpendicular walls, they can be killed with rocks from above. But to those leaving the canyon there is no protection. They must spend the night in it, for the descent cannot be made in the dark. The women and children must walk down, and the horses must be led by the men. We dare not risk going through the gap till morning. We should start as early as possible, for it is a hard trip across the basin, with little water.[11]

In another incident, David Longstreet and eleven other scouts were driving cattle to the San Carlos reservation when confronted by a group of renegades. He was in front with three other men as they reached the top of a mesa where they were taken under fire. Because of the restricted terrain and the cattle herd, all four were exposed to the enemy, with one man getting shot in the chest, another in the shoulder, and a third having his horse shot out from beneath him. All struggled to make their way through the herd to find some cover. Peering through the dust to spot the enemy, the men fought against an unseen foe. Eventually one of the scouts began talking to the Apaches, who questioned what these scouts were doing. Dissatisfied with what they considered traitorous action, the enemy escaped but eventually turned themselves in. During the fight, the land they selected provided good cover and concealment, a restricted avenue of approach, and the advantage of an escape route that prevented the scouts from following their trail. The attackers made a clean getaway with no scouts able to track them.[12]

## Following the Foe

Generally, Navajo and Apache scouts were invaluable in tracking, pursuing the enemy, and detecting their positions. General Crook provides an excellent contextual summary of a generic scouting experience. He specialized in using Apache scouts, but the same pattern for employment of Navajo scouts was equally true.

> To operate against the Apache we must use Apache methods and Apache soldiers—under, of course, the leadership of the white soldier. The first great difficulty is to discover the whereabouts of the hostiles, and this can be done well only with Indian scouts. Their stronghold once located, the next is to reach it secretly. The marches must be made with the utmost stealth and by night. Fires and noise are absolutely prohibited. The Indian scouts must be kept far enough in front and on the flanks to discover the enemy without being seen themselves, leaving no trail whatever, but slinking along from cover to cover. As soon as they locate the hostile camp, they noiselessly surround it, if possible, meantime sending runners back to us. We make forced marches by night, come up and attack the hostiles, if they have not already flown. It is impossible to pursue them, for every rock may hide an Apache at bay, and with his breechloader he can kill as many pursuers as he pleases, himself secure. Then there is nothing for us to do but to return to our base of supplies, wait until the hostiles begin to feel secure again, then repeat the same tedious operation. A single element of precaution neglected, and failure is certain.[13]

A great deal of information could be obtained about an enemy by the tracks that they leave. For instance, from a person's foot impression and stride, a tracker could determine when the track was made, whether a load was being carried, and how tired they were, as well as the sex and relative age of an individual, direction of travel, number of people in the party, and speed of travel. He could also find the person's rest stops and camps to obtain even more information. To an experienced tracker under favorable conditions, a fairly complete story materialized from the impressions of man and animal. This is why those being pursued went to great lengths to hide or destroy their tracks, including traveling over rocky terrain or certain forest floors, walking in water, or crossing areas where strong winds or rain wiped out the impression. Palmer Valor told of being in a raiding party when the members encountered an open plain that they needed to cross. Everyone walked on their toes and brushed out any trace of their passing.[14] On a different occasion Lieutenant Davis recorded the following:

> Our progress was necessarily slow. The hostiles frequently changed direction to confuse anyone who might be following them. The trail would at times lead due north, switch to the east, bend back toward the west, or turn south. Frequently it would change direction on rocky ground where even the tracks of the mule did not show. In such cases a halt, often for an hour or more, would be necessary to enable the scouts to again find the trail. These tactics, coupled with detours to avoid natural barriers in this mountainous country, forced us to travel a hundred and forty or fifty miles to cover a hundred as the crow flies.[15]

Cremony provides a superlative account of tracking Apaches. The detail he offers and the context in which it is given helps one to understand the skill and attention to minute detail required to be successful. Few other white observers recorded this fine art.

> A knowledge of signals or fires, or bent twigs and pressed grass, or of turned stones, to passes through the sierras, the nature and quantity of the fodder to be had in certain districts, the capacity to distinguish tracks and state with certainty by whom made, and how long before, are absolutely indispensable to a successful campaign among those savages. To the acquirement of all these points I devoted much attention. . . .
>
> Smokes are of various kinds, each one significant of a particular object. A sudden puff, rising into a graceful column from the mountain heights, and almost as suddenly losing its identity by dissolving into the rarified atmosphere of those heights, simply indicates the presence of a strange party upon the plains below; but if those columns are rapidly multiplied and repeated, they serve as a warning to show that the travelers are armed and numerous. If a steady smoke is maintained for some time, the object is to collect the scattered bands of savages at some

designated point, with hostile intention, should it be practicable. These signals are made at night, in the same order, by the use of fires, which being kindled, are either alternately exposed and shrouded from view, or suffered to burn steadily, as occasion may require.

All travelers in Arizona and New Mexico are acquainted with the fact that if the grass be pressed down in a certain direction during the dry season, it will retain the impress and grow daily more and more yellow until the rainy season imparts new life and restores it to pristine vigor and greenness. The Apaches are so well versed in this style of signalizing that they can tell you, by the appearance of the grass, how many days have elapsed since it was trodden upon, whether the party consisted of Indians or whites, about how many there were, and, if Indians, to what particular tribe they belonged. In order to define these points, they select some well-marked footstep, for which they hunt with avidity, and gently pressing down the trodden grass so as not to disturb surrounding herbage, they very carefully examine the print. The difference between the crushing heel of a white man's boot or shoe, and the light imprint left by an Indian's moccasin, is too striking to admit doubt, while the different styles of moccasin used by several divisions of the Apache tribes are well known among them. The time which has elapsed since the passage of the party is determined by discoloration of the herbage and breaking off a few spires to ascertain the approximate amount of natural juice still left in the crushed grass. Numbers are arrived at by the multiplicity of tracks. Signalizing by bent twigs, broken branches and blazed trees, is too well known to deserve special mention here. In these respects, the Apache do not differ from other Indian tribes of this continent.

If a mounted party has been on the road, their numbers, quality and time of passage are determined with exactitude, as well as the precise sex and species of the animals ridden. The moment such a trail is fallen in with, they follow it eagerly, having nothing else to do, until they find some dung, which is immediately broken open, and from its moisture and other properties, the date of travel is arrived at nearly to a certainty, while the constituents almost invariably declare the region from which the party came. This last point depends upon whether the dung is composed of gamma grass, barley and grass, corn, bunch grass, buffalo grass, sacaton, or any of the well-known grasses of the country, for as they are chiefly produced in different districts, the fact of their presence in the dung shows precisely from what district the animal last came. When barley is discovered, the Apaches have reason to believe that Americans have been over the route, and when maize is found they feel confident that the travelers were either Mexicans or people from that country. These remarks apply only to unshod horses, for iron prints speak for themselves. The difference in sexes is easily told by the attitude each assumes while urinating—the male stretching himself and ejecting urine forward of his hind feet, while the female ejects to the rear of the hind prints.

Signalizing by stones is much more difficult to comprehend, and very few have ever arrived at even a distant knowledge of this art. . . . I must confess my inability to do this part of the subject full justice, but will give the result of my observations. The traveler is often surprised to notice a number of stones on one side of the road, lying apparently without set arrangement, when he can observe no others within reach of his eye. A careful observation will convince him that they never grew in that region, but were brought from some other considerable distance. This translation was certainly neither the work of Americans nor Mexicans, but of Indians, and evidently for some fixed purpose. A closer examination will show that these stones are regularly arranged, and that the majority point to some special direction of the compass, while the number of those who planted them is designated by some concerted placement of each stone. For instance, no one need be told that in wild countries like Arizona, where deluges of rain pour down during the rainy season, the heaviest side of a stone will, in course of time, find itself underneath, and when this order is reversed, especially under the circumstances above cited, there is good reason to believe that it has been purposely done. This belief becomes certainty on seeing that each one of the groups, or parcel, is precisely the same way. Besides, a stone which has been long lying on one particular side, soon contracts a quantity of clay or soil on its nether surface, while its upper one has been washed clean. If it be turned over, or partly over, the difference becomes easily discoverable. If one stone be placed on end so as to rest against another, it means that the party so placing it requires aid and assistance. If turned completely over, it indicates disaster during some raid; and if only partly turned, that the expedition has been a failure. Success is noted by the stones being left in a natural position, heavy side down, but so arranged as to be nearly in line. I am not sufficiently expert in this style of signalizing to give any further explanations, and I doubt if anyone but Kit Carson was capable of fully deciphering this kind of Apache warning.[16]

Cremony's tracking tutorial gives a glimpse of the finesse and training it took to be a tracker.

## Pursuit—An Example

Many of the individual skills and observations shared thus far illustrate in a small way the required knowledge of scouting in the larger context of extended field operations. Charles F. Lummis, who in the spring of 1886 worked for the *Los Angeles Times*, reported his three-month experience with the military campaigning against Geronimo. During that period, he observed operations and paid particular attention to past and present activities involving Indian scouts, making frequent mention of their employment. Here, a synopsis is provided to illustrate their multiple duties amid frustration and success. Many place names, personalities, and operational details are not included for the sake of brevity. Elements of the 4th and 9th Cavalry, two pack trains, and 102 Apache scouts left Fort Bowie on July 17, 1885, and headed for Mexico in search of a band of approximately one hundred Apaches who had been raiding along the border. Fresh intelligence from Mexican citizens gave the command the Indians' location as the highest peak in the La Joya Mountains. Six scouts set out to pinpoint the exact location. Twenty-four hours later, two of these men returned, having observed the camp and its activities. Captain Wirt Davis, the leader of this operation, set out at midnight with his force, leaving his mule trains behind while his men rode through the night until sunrise. Ensuring that soldiers and animals were concealed by brush and trees, he waited until dark to move his force up the mountain, leaving the horses behind. All of the scouts had been released previously to join the four that had remained to watch enemy activity. By dawn, the camp was surrounded. The soldiers moved forward but found that its occupants had escaped during the night. The scouts and Davis were chagrined but recognized discarded women's clothing, identifying their intended prey as part of Geronimo's band.

Picking up the trail, they believed the enemy was headed toward a spring and favorite camping place where they traditionally roasted mescal. One scout returned to retrieve the pack train while eighty-six others went in pursuit to gain more information. They rendezvoused with Davis a few days later and reported that they had killed four of the hostiles and had been able to follow the remainder. Seventy-eight scouts and their chief of scouts pursued, agreeing to meet at a certain place after the trains had been replenished and the cavalry moved forward. Those remaining scouts that did not go with this group scoured the countryside in another direction, thinking that another band of Apaches under Chihuahua were in the vicinity. On August 7, the scouts with soldiers attacked Geronimo's camp, killing seven and capturing fifteen women and children. The next three weeks entailed chasing Chihuahua's group, linking up with supply trains, contacting a Mexican cavalry unit that had been in a recent skirmish, and continuing the pursuit, which put the American forces near their quarry. Realizing that they were about to be overtaken, the Apaches killed all their horses and set off on foot, dispersing in small groups to different directions. A rainstorm wiped out all of their tracks, a search around a suspected mountain base turned up no trail, and only hunches provided possibilities. Days stretched into weeks with no results.

On September 14, the raiders stole fourteen horses and mules from a ranch, giving Davis a firm knowledge of where their tracks could be found. Dividing his command and his scouts, he left the cavalry unit, part of his trains, and eighteen scouts with Lieutenant Erwin, and with his own pack train of mules loaded with twenty days of rations and eighty-four scouts, set off on a chase that lasted day and night until the twenty-second. Near the summit of Teres Mountain were deep, narrow canyons through which the fleeing Apache trail led. Davis picked nineteen of his best scouts, gave them several binoculars, and sent them forward to slowly track the enemy without being observed, with the understanding that he would move forward in a few hours with the rest of the command. At 3 p.m. he started up the trail but had not gone far before he heard rifle shots encouraging him to race up the canyon with the main element.

> He hurried his scouts ahead to the firing, and just before sunset they overtook and speedily routed the Indians, who fled into the mountains. It seems that Cooley [Apache scout sergeant in charge of the reconnaissance element] had struck the rear guard of the hostiles and captured their horses, after which he imprudently pushed two other sergeants ahead on their trail. On a ridge covered with dense chapparal, about a mile from where they had captured the horses, the two sergeants literally walked into an ambush which the fleeing hostiles had set. One sergeant, Cooley's brother, was killed *within ten feet* [italics in original] of the man who shot him. That will give you an idea of the skill of the Apache ambush. The other sergeant escaped. In the ensuing fight, Davis' scouts, stripping for the fray according to their custom, showed great spirit. One of them was slightly wounded in the thigh. One hostile was killed, and one or two others must have been wounded, for stained bandages and considerable blood were found on the trail the next day.[17]

The operation continued with additional units, each with a contingent of Apache scouts, adding their expertise to the chase. This particular group of enemy passed out of the mountains, reached a wide open plain where they scattered and disappeared. Davis continued to pursue until September 28, when he turned the chase over to Captain Crawford, whose scouts were relatively fresh compared to those of Davis, who had traveled over nine hundred miles through harsh terrain over ninety days before returning to Fort Bowie to recuperate. Lummis closed his evaluation of this leader and his scouts by writing, "The hardships were cheerfully borne by all. The scouts behaved zealously and did effective service through the whole campaign."[18]

Before leaving this narrative, a few points should be highlighted. Foremost is the role that the scouts played in all aspects of finding, fixing, and fighting the enemy. Indeed, the white units proved to be there more for logistical support and coordination than actually engaging the foe. Davis and other leaders of the scout companies made most of the decisions but were heavily dependent on the scouts to formulate the itinerary as to how to approach the task at hand. Second, the well-known issue of finding the enemy did not end with initial sighting or contact. Even after the Apaches became physically engaged in a raid or ambush, their skills at evasion were sufficient to stymie the scouts to the point of not being able to pick up further signs, and so scouts had to rely on more generalized knowledge of where the enemy may have fled. Britton Davis encountered similar problems of hit-or-miss.

In three days we marched 125 miles, the last day in a hard rainstorm with the mules sinking fetlock deep into the soft ground. The scouts, their moccasins useless in the wet, were all barefoot, and several of them footsore. We had been forced to camp the day before at a water hole that contained alkali in the water. This weakened both men and mules. We were without food and several of the scouts were sick. . . . We cut across the angle and took the trail again, although the chase was now practically hopeless. Our only hope was to continue to push them on the possibility of giving them so little rest they might run into another command.[19]

A final point is how the enemy utilized the principles of OCOKA in every aspect of their flight. Observation (mountain heights, rear guard trail watchers), cover and concealment (ambush, hidden encampments), obstacles (rugged mountains, wide open plains for dispersal), key terrain (mountain defile, water hole), and avenue of approach (restricted movement for the military) all came into play to assist the Apaches when evading or engaging. Knowledge of the land—whether fleeing, finding

*Telltale signs left behind by those fleeing from Navajo scouts and soldiers might be as simple as an impression in the earth, a scrape on a rock, bent vegetation, or refuse. Some indicators may intentionally lead to the pursuers falling into a well-laid ambush; when not intentional, an enemy encampment could potentially be surprised and attacked. (Illustration by Charles Yanito)*

resources, fighting, or planning future movement on it—was critical in this war of resistance.

## Combat—Employing the Principles of War

The remainder of this chapter looks at type and conduct of engagements by the Apaches as well as their effectiveness. For ease of evaluation, we again turn to a contemporary military yardstick to define important qualities in both successful and unsuccessful fights. Whether on a large or limited scale, military leaders, intellectuals, and other interested parties in the past have attempted to codify basic principles leading to success and defeat in combat. In 1921 the United States adopted nine Principles of War that outlined what were believed to be these fundamentals. They were based on years of study and analyses of both success and failure broad enough to encompass a conflict as large as the Civil War or World War I and as small as some of the more minor Indian Wars.[20]

These principles provide the means and measurement for understanding the Apache wars. Each of them is briefly defined here: (1) *Mass*—concentrating combat power at the decisive time and place. (2) *Maneuver*—putting the enemy at a disadvantage through movement and application of combat power. (3) *Objective*—clearly defining a decisive, attainable goal. (4) *Offense*—seizing, retaining, and exploiting the initiative. (5) *Unity of Command*—unifying effort under one responsible leader. (6) *Security*—preventing the enemy from acquiring unexpected advantage. (7) *Surprise*—striking the enemy at a time, place, or manner that is unexpected. (8) *Simplicity*—providing clear, uncomplicated plans and orders for thorough understanding. (9) *Economy of force*—applying minimal essential combat power to secondary efforts. There has been discussion of adding a tenth one to the list—*leadership*—in which personality, knowledge, and skill of those directing forces during a conflict have resulted in a decisive victory. While not all principles apply in every engagement, there will always be some that do. These Principles of War are based in offensive action, which the military believes is the only sure road to eventual victory.

The three main types of offensive operations used by the Apaches were the raid, attack, and ambush. The raid was most often an economic endeavor to obtain wealth or material support for Apache activities and trade. A raiding party was usually small in number, often less than a dozen warriors, who studied their target (objective) to ascertain what was valuable—livestock, ammunition, food, and so forth—then proceeded to seize what they wanted. In applying the Principles of War, these raiding parties were under the command of one leader (unity of command) whose decisions and plans were followed through to the end of the expedition, after which his special status as leader might end. Of primary concern was the approach to the target without being detected (security and maneuver) and the evasion plan after the goods were obtained. Surprise was paramount.

Palmer Valor recalled many of the characteristics of a successful raid he had in Mexico. His party of eleven men traveled seven days and seven nights on foot until they came to a wide open plain and then a mountain. "We had to walk on our toes to be sure that we left no tracks and we hid all our tracks." Seeking mountain terrain during the movement as well as the reconnaissance phase of the journey, the men spent two days searching for horses until they found a stonewall corral that was at first empty, then later filled with horses. To Valor: "There were some men in our party who understood about horse medicine, and it must have been these who made the horses go in the corral like that all by themselves."[21] The leader sent a man to the corral to close the gate while the others waited until dark and then went to the enclosure, where dozens of animals had become entrapped.

> Now the man in charge of us said, "I don't think that the horses will get out of the corral and so you can all go ahead and rope the ones that you want. You have your ropes, so go and do it." The man in charge of a raiding party like this was just like an officer, and when he said something he meant it. . . . Our chief picked out his men just as if they were out on a cattle roundup and set them at different jobs. We got on our horses in the corral and then he told us to open the gate. Two of us he set to lead, and two he told to go on each side of the herd, and the other five of us rode behind and drove.[22]

They traveled for three nights and days before stopping to rest, remaining close to any mountain they could pass, even driving the herd over the top of one mountain. Finally, the leader determined the group was safe, so he had one horse killed for food since the men had not eaten anything substantial for four days, and then they rested. The travel continued—seven days to and seven days from their raid site until they reached home. Success had been built upon surprise, security, simplicity, stealth, and decisive leadership.

The attack and the raid employed these same principles, but their purpose was getting revenge, taking advantage of a target of opportunity, and producing enemy casualties. All of the Principles of War might be employed. A good example in which Navajo and Apache scouts participated took place in Hembrillo Canyon and Basin during April 5–7, 1880, as members of the 9th Cavalry (buffalo soldiers) pursued Victorio and Nana. Captain Henry Carroll commanded a battalion of four companies attempting to locate Victorio's camp and entrap the people. The land, creased with canyons, offered numerous opportunities to be ambushed, and so Carroll divided his forces and chose parallel routes with the opportunity for his elements to support each other if attacked. An advanced company of twenty-nine men and two scouts under Lieutenant John Conline forged ahead down Hembrillo Canyon. As the defile narrowed, the possibility of an ambush became increasingly likely. The scouts warned about going farther when suddenly approximately fifty Apaches moved down the canyon and began their attack. Warriors fanned out on both sides of the soldiers' horseshoe defense, fighting on both flanks and the right rear of the formation. Fortunately, this happened in the later part of the afternoon, so that when dark arrived, the cavalry was able to withdraw and join Carroll's battalion.

The next day, Carroll sent two companies along the same general path that Conline had taken the previous day while taking the rest of his battalion over a less obvious route that brought them into Hembrillo Basin and close to Victorio's camp. The Apaches spotted the advancing cavalry and formed a hasty ambush that took these troops under fire. This action proved so successful that the soldiers had to form a defensive position for protection from the Apaches holding the higher ground. The cavalry maintained their position under harassing fire for the rest of the day and night until the remainder of his other companies under Lieutenant Patrick Cusack, a company from the 6th Cavalry, and two companies of scouts caught up to the main body to relieve the pressure. In the meantime, Victorio sent Nana with the women, children, and elderly to a spot out of danger below the Mexican border while Victorio fought a rearguard action combined with escape and evasion. Carroll sustained four wounded, three killed, and twenty-eight horses killed or captured.[23]

The Apache view of the incident adds detail with a refining perspective. The soldiers were in need of water and so one of their goals was to refill their canteens, water the horses, and secure the area from Apache use. One of Victorio's warriors, Kaytennae, said:

That place had many times afforded refuge to us and our people. . . . On a ledge above it [the spring] Victorio had stationed warriors to command the approach. The cavalry had drunk the water Nana had forbidden us to touch, and so had their horses. Both had become ill from a laxative effect and were weakened until they could hardly travel. We had not poisoned that spring; the illness was caused by a natural mineral [gypsum] that this one time operated in our favor. . . . The troops were easily beaten back until more cavalry came in from the Tularosa Basin. Nana took the women and children up the arroyo and around a point to the Jornada. The trail was very rocky and there was little dust to warn us of the coming of an enemy until they were almost upon us. As the cavalry rounded a point of rocks pretty well lined with mesquite, Grandfather sent the people east, following a rocky ledge, to the shelter of an arroyo. While they were concealing themselves and their horses, the boys hastily did what they could to cover our trail. Fortunately, unshod hoofs make little noise and leave few traces of their passing. Taking advantage of every clump of vegetation, every rock, our people stood with hands ready to press the nostrils of our horses so that they would not betray our position. Mother took off Chenleh's cradle and handed it to Grandmother, freeing her to use her rifle. If the baby had opened her mouth to make a sound it would have been necessary to smother her cries, for the ears of scouts are good. There we waited anxiously until the scouts had passed. I think we could not have been more than a quarter of a mile off the trail, and it seems impossible that our presence was not detected. Not one even glanced in our direction.[24]

The Apache ambush was the most commonly used type of offensive operation and something that Navajo and Apache scouts were constantly watching for. Robert N. Watt in *Apache Tactics, 1830–86* identifies a number of different types whose titles are descriptive of the action. There was the planned ambush; the killing or double ambush (attack of a rescue party for first ambushed group); decoy ambush to draw in victims using tracks, gunfire, and trails; simulated ignorance or simulated panic; and ad hoc or spontaneous ambush such as with a meeting engagement or target of opportunity.[25] All of these shared common elements that made them effective.

Using the fight in Hembrillo Canyon and Basin as an example of Apache ambushes, one can see a solid application of OCOKA and the Principles of War. Holding the high ground surrounding the basin as key terrain, the Indians had excellent observation along with cover and concealment from the rocks and junipers spread all over the slopes. Their rifle fire was directed downward on their pursuers and there was sufficient cover to also let some of the men crawl down near the spring to prevent the soldiers from using their confined avenue of approach to obtain water. In terms of the Principles of War, the Apaches' plan was simple—ambush the soldiers, prevent them from getting water, protect their noncombatants, and kill as many of the cavalry's horses as possible. Both sides wished to out-maneuver the other, but Victorio's people held all of the cards, being able to surround the entrapped white men and fire down from all sides with a sufficient force (mass) to prevent the enemy from moving. At the same time, a group of warriors provided front, rear, and flank security for the women and children fleeing to a predesignated rendezvous spot, illustrating economy of force to accomplish a secondary objective. Victorio as the leader coupled with the sage advice of elderly Nana as an assistant provided unity of command. The soldiers, on the other hand, were not able to obtain their objective of surprising the Indian village nor able to obtain water, were strictly limited in maneuvering, were forced to go on the defense, and struggled to maintain security as the Indians infiltrated close to the white positions to deny them access to water. Until additional troops arrived, Carroll was in a difficult spot to do anything but survive.

A secondary goal of Apache and military offensive action was to kill or capture as many horses and mules and remove as many officers as possible. The high number of animals lost by the whites during the Hembrillo Canyon fight indicate how important this was. The initiation of any ambush focused as much on destroying the animals as it did the men. The same was true in the first major engagement during the Victorio campaign in which elements of Lieutenant Colonel Nathan Dudley's 9th Cavalry became decisively engaged on the Animas River. Navajo scouts advancing up a canyon came under fire, killing one and trapping the remaining scouts and two cavalry troops for a day. Two other troops went to their aid, only to be pinned down. Eventually all elements withdrew and counted their losses—eight men killed, a few wounded—but in terms of horses, there were thirty-two killed, six wounded, and fifty-three horses and mules abandoned. Only two or three Apaches were estimated killed. There is no missing the point that the livestock was as much of a target as the combatants.[26]

Scout Vincintie Begay told of when he and three other Navajos spotted a man on horseback ascending a side draw. "We went to the top of the hill and the Apaches opened fire on us and Mariana Begay got off his horse and the Apaches shot and killed it, and they wounded my horse in the shoulder. We captured some horses belonging to the Apaches and took them into camp."[27] Both sides sought to remove the mobility of the other, not just by killing or wounding the horses, but also by forcing pursuers to go over rough terrain in harsh conditions. Navajo scout Jake Segundo recalled, "The Navajos had their own horses; they went over rocky country and were without water for days. Their horses had no shoes and got sore-footed. They asked for shoes for their horses, and wanted to stay over to rest them. The officers would not let them and some lost their horses on the way back to Fort Wingate."[28] Apache effectiveness in accomplishing this is recorded for the year 1879–80, when the 9th Cavalry reported that it had lost one-third of its mules and that it had more unserviceable horses than serviceable.[29] Not all of the ten cavalry regiments fielded by the army at this time were involved in the Apache wars, but there was enough strain on the system for the military to claim there was no more money left for the purchase of new mounts for that fiscal year.

As for removing officers from the battlefield, Captain Carroll was among those wounded in the fray. Geronimo recounts in another battle that he ordered his warriors to aim for the officers and kill all that they could. To set the example, he crawled through a ditch to approach a force of Mexicans he was about to do battle with. His position allowed him to hear their leader directing the other officers to exterminate every Apache encountered during the battle, including women and children. Just before the meeting ended, Geronimo shot the commander, then returned to his line under a hail of bullets, but he remained unscathed. His bravery enthusiastically encouraged his warriors.[30]

A final example of a soldiers' attack on an Apache camp provides a summary that illustrates OCOKA, the Principles of War, and other tactical measures already discussed. Early in the morning, Jason Betzinez went to his group's horse herd to find his mule when a gunshot rang out. He looked up and saw two troops of 6th Cavalry driving off the animals before anyone could mount, with another detachment of soldiers heading for the Indians' campground.

> All our people took cover in the broken ground at the butte, in some cases several trying to squeeze into the same crevice in the rocks. Our warriors were on the butte firing back at the troops while the rest of us were between the two firing lines. The soldiers were about a half mile away, so our men didn't waste ammunition trying to hit them at that far range. . . . About noon we heard our leaders calling to the men to get ready to attack the soldiers, who now were in the plain southwest of the butte, near the marsh. The warriors stripped off their shirts ready for action. Then under shouted directions from the leaders, the Apaches began sneaking down through the rocks toward the soldiers. . . . The

*Three veterans of the Apache campaign of 1886—Pedro, Gayetenito, and Biziz—pose in the studio of photographer Ben Wittick (1845–1903) at Fort Wingate. It is not surprising that he took the largest number of Navajo scout pictures before the 1920s when the old scouts were seeking pensions. To his credit, the clothing, foliage, and ubiquitous pistol show his flair for accuracy. (Courtesy of Palace of the Governors Photo Archive, New Mexico History Museum, Neg. #015715)*

soldiers kept firing into the rocks in spite of the fact that no Indians were in sight. . . . Several hours passed, with occasional shots being fired from both sides. About noon an old Apache woman climbed up to the highest butte where she stood in plain sight calling out to her son, Toclanny, who was an Indian scout. She thought mistakenly that he was with these particular troops. In vain, she called to him, telling him that we had been run off against our will by hostiles from Mexico. But her son wasn't there; and she was shot and killed.

Early in the afternoon four young warriors slipped through to the southeast and circled around behind the Indian scouts. They attacked the scouts from the rear, driving them out into the plains where they joined the troops. The four warriors ducked behind some rocks and kept on firing. This diversion gave those of us who were between the lines a chance to escape. So while the soldiers and scouts were occupied with this party in their rear, we who were watching from the rocks on the butte ran for the foothills to the east, leaving all of our belongings behind. . . . We were now on foot again, the soldiers having captured all our horses and mules. No doubt they were rejoicing over this and laughing at us in our sorry condition.[31]

Yet Betzinez and others escaped to fight another day. Some would continue to resist for years before there was the final surrender by Geronimo to General Nelson A. Miles in 1886.

Apache warfare took its toll on both man and beast during those thirteen years when Navajo and Apache scouts worked to bring in the enemies of the United States government. The scouts' motivation, how their enemy thought about them, and their ultimate success will be covered next. But from a strictly military point of view, the employment of sound infantry tactics; familiarity with the terrain and its use; tactical knowledge concerning the raid, attack, and ambush; and the physical fitness of the enemy were some of the major challenges the scouts faced in depriving their Apache quarry of what they had traditionally known and used for centuries. Perhaps Captain Dorst, a company commander who served under General Crook in 1885–86, said it best to Lummis:

It was simple idiocy to try to do anything down there [Mexico] without Indian scouts. No one else knows anything about that untraveled country. No one else can follow a trail as they can, and no one else can stand so much fatigue. My scouts will start at the bottom of a steep mountain, fifteen hundred feet high, and go on a trot clear to the top without stopping. There isn't a white man alive who could run fifty yards up the same pitch without stopping to catch his wind. I have been climbing the mountains of Colorado, New Mexico, and Arizona for the last seven years, but I can't keep in sight of these fellows when they start.[32]

# CHAPTER SIX

# Finding, Fixing, and Fighting the Enemy

## Three Personal Accounts

D uring the Apache wars over five hundred Navajos are estimated to have served as scouts. Approximately half that number were recorded with sufficient documentation and a long enough lifespan to be officially registered to receive a government pension during the 1920s for their service in the Indian Wars. Others are lost to history. Poor record-keeping, multiple six-month enlistments (often under different names), individual and unit dispersal over a broad geographical area, combat injury or fatality, and a general lack of interest in tracking Indian activities were some of the reasons that so little is known about the Navajo scouts. Indeed, not until S. F. Stacher, agent for the Eastern Navajo Agency, made a major effort to obtain pensions for these scouts was much of anything recorded about them other than brief glimpses found in military reports. What now remains are a few short paragraphs of testimony and the bare-bones information gleaned from correspondence during the bureaucratic process of certifying who was a scout.

### Wars About with Anger—A Navajo Narrative

Fortunately, linguist Robert W. Young and Navajo linguist William Morgan interviewed and translated information from a number of Navajos during the late 1930s and 1940s, when the two men worked for the Bureau of Indian Affairs (BIA). Both labored tirelessly to record not only Navajo history and culture, but also the Navajo language. Eventually, they produced three pathbreaking works called *The Navajo Language* (1943), *The Navajo Language: A Grammar and Colloquial Dictionary* (1980, 1987), and *Analytical Lexicon of Navajo* (1992). Working in the realm of history as a part of understanding the language, Morgan and Young interviewed elders, one of whom was John Malone, who was intimately familiar with a Navajo scout named Wars About with Anger.[1] His life history is the only lengthy account of the Navajo scout experience that is extant. Perhaps nothing reveals the real essence of the scouting experience like a personal narrative.

John Malone, who was the one actually interviewed by Young and Morgan, tells what Wars About with Anger related to him as a young boy. The elderly scout provided an unvarnished account accurately translated but that lacks some of the polish associated with the written word. Young and Morgan, no doubt, were interested in producing a manuscript that employed a language gloss that maintained the speaker's voice along with the cultural nuance of the narrator. Wars About with Anger offers to the reader a rare glimpse into the daily life of a Navajo scout and the people he worked with. The challenging struggles, interaction with personalities, role of the scout, leadership characteristics of white officers, techniques of scouting, and limited combat provide a view that does not center on the dramatic but that realistically portrays the day-to-day grind of his profession. Comparing and contrasting this account with that of another Navajo scout named Big Hat Charley and with excerpts from Apache John Rope's narrative offers the reader a chance to view shared experiences of three men. Wars About with Anger's report is as follows:

Down in the Apache country there is a place called A Flat Runs into the Rock. It was there that the Apaches received their rations. Beef cattle were distributed among them, which they themselves butchered and ate. Then, on account of their brewing "gray-water" [tizwin], they spoiled things for themselves.[2] They were well taken care of, but would get into brawls with one another. Once twelve of them jumped Gets the Horse and Holds It Back (Geronimo). One was called He Who Whirls His Horse. Another was The Son of Former Water Woman. Those are the only names that I remember. It is said that there were twelve of them. They were probably leaders. They were put into jail on account of that fight. They were put in a tent, but on the morning of the twelfth day they were freed and rode away to another encampment of soldiers elsewhere. It is said that there were seven Navajos in the army at that time. "I feel like shooting Blue Eyes (white men) right in the face," said one of the

Apaches. "We feel like shooting Soft Hat [unidentified] right in the face," they said. They were told not to do it, but they paid no attention.

"No, my friend. What for? You were put in jail for fighting with one another. So don't do it," they were told. But they paid no attention.

"I'm going to die fighting (lit. I'll lie huddled in death holding up my gun)," they all said.

"I'll die holding my bow and arrows (lit. I'll be huddled in death holding up my 'stretchers')" they all said. By "stretchers" they meant their bows and arrows. They were begged not to do it, so fortunately, they left and started back.

On the next day some white soldiers went on horseback to the Apache camp to give out more rations. When they arrived, they found no one there. It turned out that the Apaches had moved away, probably having agreed on a meeting place. The soldiers were ordered to pick up their trail, but they tried in vain to do so. They merely let the Apaches go and staged a horse race. The officer in charge (lit. War Chief) had a very tiny horse. It was said to have been a black one. He got beat as they raced around the track. A white man and a Mexican, who had joined them from somewhere, won the race. They just let the Apaches go, saying that they would find out about them some time or another. After a few more days, they held another horse race. After they did that, they started out in search of the Apaches. They went up to the top of a certain mountain. Some stockmen brought word to them, telling them where the Apaches were, so they went toward where they were. It is said that all of the soldiers went, and the officer with them. Then some remained behind with the officer while several went to some Apache camps on the mountainside. They had recently killed some cattle, and a great quantity of meat was lying around the fire at their camp. So again, the soldiers failed to make peace with the Apaches. They told them in vain not to make war, but they refused saying they were going to keep right on fighting one another. Upon their return, the soldiers reported back to the officer about it. The officer wanted to return to the Apache camp, but the soldiers refused, it is said. They told him no, that the Apaches would kill him. So they didn't take him there. They just went back home.

Sometime later, these Apaches killed some white stockmen. These white stockmen had their homes built out of reeds. The roofs of their houses were sloped, and were made by laying reeds side by side. The Apaches completely burned those houses. That is the news that was brought by a stockman. The soldiers set out for there. Six of the Navajo soldiers stayed in camp, and only one of them set off with this party.

The only one with them was the one called Wars About with Anger. When they arrived on the scene, they found that it was a fact that these white stockmen had been killed. After having burned the dwellings, the Apaches had moved southward. The party of soldiers followed them. After a long time, they came to a hill where there were lots of century plants growing. There they found a white stockman's wife, whom the Apaches had killed, and whose body they had propped up against a century plant in a sitting position. Still further on they came upon the remains of a white baby the Apaches had killed. They just left it lying there, it is said. They followed the trail continuously until the close of the day. At the day's end, they unsaddled the horses and camped for the night. The next day they again started to follow the trail, but they lost it. There was a lot of lava rock and grass there, and because of that nothing could be seen.

Finally, they started following some horse tracks that led off in another direction. This had, perhaps, been made by white stockmen driving horses through. "This is an Apache horse trail. It isn't who we are looking for. Let's go back," said the one referred to as Wars About with Anger. But the officer paid no attention to him and kept riding ahead until the end of another day. At sundown they came to where a little spire of lava stuck up into the air. They found a little spring flowing out from beneath this lava, but there wasn't enough water for the horses. The soldiers got down and dug a pretty good-sized hole in the mud with their hands. Quite a bit of water collected there. They prepared their meal and watered their horses.

On the next morning, just at the break of dawn, the Navajo soldier led his horse to water. He filled his canteen, as well as a flat whiskey bottle that he was carrying. They all ate. After breakfast, the soldiers led their horses to water. Inasmuch as there wasn't a very large supply of water, some of the horses got none. They then set off again, following this horse trail. The one who was a Navajo didn't approve of it, but he trotted along with them anyway. At noon, he again approached the officer in regard to it. "You're leading us down this horse trail for no reason at all. It's not the one. Let's go back there where we lost the trail in the lava rock. They must have gone in some direction from there," he said to him, but he was disregarded, so they merely continued onward.

By mid-afternoon, the horses that had not gotten any water previously began to suffer from thirst. One of the soldiers who was just a boy had the first horse that began to suffer from thirst. This man began trailing far behind on his horse as did a number of his companions. They

soon looked like black dots, one behind the other as their horses became
unable to move fast on account of thirst. Some of the soldiers were thirsty,
too. They set off northward toward some mountains that could be seen
jutting out of a blue haze. The officer said that there was no doubt there
was water over there, but that they were far from it. "It would be better
this way, toward the west," he was told. Pretty soon another soldier got
thirsty. We Navajos at that time used to call him Three (Stripes) Lie on
Him. His horse died under him from thirst. One Navajo was leading
a pack mule loaded with pots and pans and food piled upon it. They
had traveled all of that night and most of the following day. It was then
that Three (Stripes) Lie on Him's horse died. That was when one of the
Navajos said, "Why are we hauling all of these things? Let's throw them
away and let that soldier who lost his horse get on the mule." He said
this to the officer, but he refused. "Well, why not? We've lost many of our
young men for no reason at all. They've died of thirst. Those we were after
have gone off somewhere, and here you are leading us aimlessly about.
You are, indeed, stupid, so let him get on the mule," he said to him. The
officer gave in. They threw away the pack and helped pull the soldier up
onto the mule's back.

At first, one could see our companions trailing far behind, looking
like black specks, but finally they disappeared from view. While the rest
of the party was moving along in a low place, Wars About with Anger
led his horse along onto the edge of the hollow. He came upon many
of these plants called century plants. You've seen yucca with the white
flowers that form on them—these century plants have blossoms like that
on their tips. He took out his knife and cut one of them off, peeled off
the outer layer, then chewed the inner part. He found it juicy, so called to
the soldiers with him who came to him. He told them how to do it and
peeled another one in their presence. They did likewise and really chewed
hard. He cut off another one, peeled it, and took it to his horse, that ate
it. They did this and then started off again with their thirst somewhat
relieved.

The men came to a hill covered with volcanic rocks. There they
found a wide streambed with no water flowing, just pools that stood
where it had collected in little hollows that filled when the stream over-
flowed. There were many cottonwoods there, too. When the soldiers saw
the water, they started rushing toward it. "No! No! Wait! You shouldn't
do that," the Navajo told them. "This is the way it's done," he said. He
led his horse to water, and after it had taken perhaps one swallow, he led
it away and tied it up to one side. Next, he took off his clothing and had

the soldiers follow his example. They took their horses to water then tied them up to one side before they undressed. When the Navajo crawled into the water, they crawled in after him. He took one swallow of water, got back out, and vomited. The soldiers did likewise, standing to one side vomiting, their eyes shining blue. They took their horses to water again, let them have a few more swallows, then led them aside. The horses went over to a grassy spot where they began to graze. After some time, the men again took them to water where they drank their fill. The men, too, drank.

The Navajos had trousers made of white cotton cloth, with a split running alongside the leg as well as a cotton shirt. The army was quite generous with its clothing, but the Navajos didn't want it. It was too tight, and for that reason, a person couldn't run fast enough. That is why they said they didn't want it. At that time, they used to wear about the waist, a broad band of buckskin in which the cartridges were rolled. They drank then the Navajos went up on top of the hill. Just as they reached the summit, two Mexicans riding horses passed by on a wagon trail. Wars About with Anger called to them, but they merely raced their horses toward the hills. He called to them to wait, and fortunately, they reined in their horses and sat there while he called to them to come over, but they wouldn't do so. "No," they said. "You must be an Apache. You're just saying that so you can kill us." "No, you probably have a knife," they said to him. "No, I haven't so much as a knife," he said as he took his knife sheath and bent it double before their eyes. However, they didn't believe him. "The soldiers are nearby. I'm with them," he told them, but in vain. Even with the soldiers it was hard to get them to come over. When they finally came, they all went over to where the soldiers sat waiting for the Navajo. Then they all set out for the place nearby where the Mexicans had their home. As soon as they arrived, they ate, hitched horses to a wagon, filled water barrels in the wagon, and put in some food. Then the Mexicans started off to where the stragglers had been left, while the soldiers remained at the Mexicans' place. When the Mexicans got there, the soldiers let the horses that had been dying of thirst over drink, not knowing about how to handle such things. Many more of the horses were lost. The Mexicans brought back the soldiers that were still alive, who spent the night with them at the Mexicans' place.

The soldiers all set out anew then came to a place where many more Mexicans lived. I don't know what the name of the place (town) was. Some of them were afoot when they got there because they had lost their horses. From that place the officer sent a written request for more horses which were brought there to them. On the day the horses arrived, word was passed that they would start back home on the next day. But one of the Navajos became drunk, drinking with the Mexicans. When he was discovered missing, the soldiers went in search of him. They found him and brought him back. He had bought some whiskey, which he was carrying, so they brought it back for him. When they got him to the camp, they put him in a tent, but he was drunk that night, the next day, and still another day. Then just about sunrise, he leaped up. "Oh yeah, we were supposed to be going home today (he had lost two days)." He wondered where his horse was and started after it, but it was right there in the corral. The officer sent word for him to report, so he did. "Yesterday we were going to start back home, but you disappeared on us. So for that reason, we didn't start back. You spent two days drunk. This is your whiskey. Here, take it and don't you dare drink any more of it. Now we'll start home," the officer said to him. "Very well, that's the way it will be," the Navajo said, and then they set out.

On their way back, they saw a big cloud of dust approaching to their front. The soldiers went on top of a hill and tried to make out what it was, but they couldn't determine what it was because the dust cloud was so large. They said it might be Apaches or soldiers, but they did not find out until it was very near. It turned out to be some soldiers. The other Navajos who were in the army, and who had stayed behind, were in this party. Hoolyo was among them as well as the man called The Nephew of the One Who Keeps Adding Peaches to It. He was the son of Lisolini. Another was called Little Boy since he was still young. There were seven Navajos in the army. I don't remember the names of some of them, but they were with the soldiers.

The one I mentioned as Hoolyo asked Wars About with Anger to go again with them. "My older brother, come with us. We'll be together with this party of soldiers. Let those you are with now go home," he said, begging him. The one who told this story said he tried to turn them down, but they would not take no for an answer so he joined them. "My former companions started back alone," he said. We again started off toward a mountain, the base of which was thickly grown with brush— century plants, scrub oak, mesquite and a plant called tsildili. A wagon trail had been cut through there.

The sun went down before they got to the mountain. While it was still daylight, the one called Hoolyo said, "Let's kill a deer. We'll use it for food," they told the officer, and he at once gave his approval. "Two shots are all you're allowed. When you have shot one deer that will be all. If you miss with the first shot, you can shoot again, but you can only shoot twice," he told them. While the soldiers were unsaddling the horses off to one side, two of the Navajos went down along the rim of a canyon. Before they had gone far, a fawn suddenly came running out of the brush. They knew that it must be with a fully grown deer so they just stood there. Sure enough, after a while a deer came running out into the open on the opposite side. It was a fine, big deer. With one shot the deer fell over and was butchered there on the spot. They left it where it had fallen and went back to where the soldiers were. Some of them went after the meat and packed it back. They ate it and spent the night there.

The following day, they again set out. The Navajos were told to scout ahead, so they went far in advance, reconnoitering. The soldiers followed at some distance. Presently, they came upon some yucca stretching across the trail in front of them. There were pieces of dried meat through which the yucca was passed, the pieces being threaded on it and strung across the trail. The soldiers caught up with the Navajos as they sat on their horses at the barrier. They told the officer about it and he immediately jumped his horse at it. Cursing, he broke the thing that stretched across the trail and the group went on through.

They went over another hill where on the other side they found a beautiful meadow with springs in it and the place where the Apaches had camped. Perhaps they had seen the soldiers the day before, so had moved on. The soldiers started after them, following their trail that led into a blind canyon in the mountain. Water flowed out of this canyon. The pursuers went up onto the rim then descended into the canyon.

No doubt back at the place I first told about, where I said the soldiers went to the Apache camp on the mountain top and tried unsuccessfully to make peace, one of the Navajos had made an agreement with the Apaches. This came to light later. The Apaches had said, "Wherever we may be lying in ambush, we'll place two rocks, one upon the other." Sure enough, there were two rocks, one on top of the other. The only one who knew about it was the one named Hoolyo. Long after this event, he told about it. The Apaches had told him, "Wherever we may fight with the soldiers, you Navajos will ride through our ranks and then join us in the shooting." Hoolyo kept this plan a secret.

They crossed the stream and started moving up the canyon. It was there that we noticed that Hoolyo was jittery, because he knew what lay ahead, as the soldiers moved along at a considerable distance behind. Thickets of small oaks grew on both sides of the canyon, and among them lay large boulders of lava rocks. "First, we'll wait here and let the

soldiers catch up with us. Then they can lead our horses for us while we
go on foot," the Navajos said. "The soldiers can go to the canyon's end,
while we will go up onto the rim," they said. When the soldiers arrived,
the Navajos turned over to them the horses they had been riding then
climbed the canyon wall. They were nearly to the top, when an Apache
woman was seen running and shouting loudly, letting out whoops with
her hand held intermittently over her mouth. The Navajos at that point,
boosted one of their number up a ledge of lava rock at the canyon rim. As
he was just getting on top, an Apache shot him from another direction.
He toppled back down, but the Navajo scouts below caught him. The
soldiers had disappeared into the canyon, and at that moment, from the
direction in which they had gone, there came the sound of heavy gunfire.
"I'm mortally wounded (literally—They have done such to me that one
cannot again become a man). Do your utmost. Now, go ahead," he told
them.

Then the Navajos dashed down into the canyon among the oaks,
separating then running in different directions. Wars About with Anger
told how he had run to a place where there was a deep pocket in the
streambed (the farthest point to which the water had thus far cut its
deepening channel in the water course). From up the canyon came the
sound of heavy gunfire and the sound of people cursing one another.
"You Hoolyo from hell; we'll kill you for sure. We'll kill every last one of
you," the Apaches were heard to say, cursing lustily. It was on account
of Hoolyo's broken agreement that they said this to him. Sticking their
heads up from behind rocks and ducking down again, the Apaches and
soldiers fired at one another. It continued in that way until the latter part
of the afternoon. Then the Navajos saw their horses, which had gone up
on the side of the canyon among the oaks. Thinking that the Apaches
were after their horses, they tried unsuccessfully to catch the animals.
Presently the stud that had been carrying Wars About with Anger fled
with his tail sticking up in the air. He ran through the oaks, but when
he was about to disappear running over the crest of the hill, he halted
and looked back before starting to run again and disappearing over the
hill. He kept on running right back to the soldiers' camp, bringing the
news that something had happened. The soldiers probably thought that
everyone had been wiped out when the horse came back riderless, so they
set out at once.

All day long the soldiers and the Apaches continued to stick their
heads up, shoot and duck back down. The other horses milled around in
the canyon, but when they clustered together in a flat spot, the Apaches

*Terrain analyses of a battlefield played an important role on both sides of a conflict. The Apaches were highly skilled in applying the principles of today's acronym OCOKA in order to place their foe in the least advantageous position. (Drawing by Kelly Pugh)*

fired on them, killing every single one. At dusk, the Apaches began to thin out, giving up the fight in preparation for leaving that night. Those soldiers still alive assembled together. One of the white men wounded in the leg was found lying by the water's edge. Wars About with Anger located him. After a while two more of the party appeared, one of whom was the officer accompanied by the bugler. Of the Navajo soldiers, three of them were unscathed but two had been slain. One was merely wounded in the leg when he struck his leg against the lava and nearly broke off his knee cap.

Carrying the wounded on their backs, the soldiers made their way onto the canyon rim. As they were moving homeward, daylight found them a considerable distance toward their destination. They put the wounded down by a little stream so that in the daylight the officer, with a needle, sewed up the knee of the man who was wounded. All the wounded were told to stay there by those who had carried them. They reminded the wounded that when they first came through this spot, there had been a cow wandering about with a broken leg. If the soldiers could find it, they would kill it and feed the injured men the meat. As the soldiers were leaving, the wounded Navajo began to cry. "Each one of you pitch in as many cartridges as you can spare for me," he said, so they did. Everyone contributed. Then he immediately left them as his companions sat there. The party found the cow with the broken leg, killed it, built a fire, and cooked part of the meat since that was all they had to eat. Then Hoolyo and Wars About with Anger packed some of the meat back to the wounded men, but when they arrived, they found only a white man still there. He was lying there chewing acorns which the wounded Navajo had brought to him. That Navajo had gone to get water, sliding himself along on his buttocks. Hoolyo and Wars About with Anger brought him back, put him and the white man together, and went back to where the officer waited with the soldiers. After the party had traveled farther, they suddenly met up with reinforcements and joyfully shook hands. Some of the soldiers brought horses back to the wounded then we all set off for home, returning to the place called A Flat Runs into The Rock. When they arrived there, Wars About with Anger saw his horse standing in the corral. He went up to it, pulled out his pollen, and put some of it on the horse and in its mouth. Then he prayed. That is what they did.[3]

## Big Hat Charley—Navajo Scout Diplomacy

A second Navajo scout, Big Hat Charley, gives an uncharacteristically long statement that has detail and historical color. He began by relating events that occurred in the mid-1870s.

While we were living around Fort Wingate, the word came that they [military] wanted the Navajos to enlist to go against the Apaches. We started off on foot. Only five of the Indians had horses and the others went afoot. We only had one wagon to haul the provisions. There were about 80 cavalry soldiers with us. They were in three bunches and each bunch had two officers. They had yellow stripes on their pants and also yellow soldier straps. The Indians called one of them "Red-headed" because he was baldheaded. One of the men had a star on his shoulder straps. Only one of the officers wore shoulder straps. He carried a sword. The others wore stripes on their sleeves. They wore hats of a gray color which were brought up to a point with four indentations. The soldiers wore light black uniforms. The Indians did not wear any uniforms.

About three days after we enlisted, we left Fort Wingate and were on our way for seven days until we came to where the Apaches live. We came to an Apache village where everything was quiet and peaceful. The Apaches received rations. In about two days after they were given green coffee, flour, and brown sugar they all left in the night. The following day we were told the Apaches had all left and we were told to go after them and find where they had gone. We left as soon as we were notified. We followed their trail and the first evening we came to where there was an old Apache woman with her arm cut off at the shoulder. It had been cut off some time before then. I do not know how it was cut off. She was suffering and had been left behind as they were going so fast. We gave her something to eat and drink, told her to go back to where she had left and that we were going to get the rest of the Apaches and take them back there. We Navajo scouts followed the Apache trail through the night and the soldiers followed us. We could follow the trail by feeling the horses' tracks.

In the morning, we stopped by a stream to prepare our breakfast and while there, the officers through field glasses saw the Apache camp on the top of the mountain. While we were eating breakfast two of the Apaches came to our camp. They did not come to where we had eaten breakfast but after we had breakfast we went on to where the Apaches had encamped and as we approached it, they all scattered in different directions. We told them to go out and tell the rest of them that we were after them to take them back to their homes. We found that one of their horses had been killed going up the mountain and that they had eaten it before we arrived at their camp. Then we sent the two Apaches out to tell the others that we did not want to fight them but wanted to take them back to their homes where they would be taken care of and given something to eat; we gave them some provisions for the others. The same day some of them commenced to come into our camp and the next day others came.

We moved our camp the same day that we sent the two Apaches out after the others and took the Apaches that had come in with us. The second night we were told that the chief had gone on with some of the men. There were five chiefs with the Apaches. The second day, all came in but one chief and his men and the third day they came in but some of the men were still missing. All of the women were in and they said their men would come in as they wanted to take their wives with them. We did not wait for them but started back to their village. After we got them all together, we counted and found that the men, women, and children, there were 140 Apaches. At our night camp, the stragglers came in. When we arrived back at headquarters, we took them to a big log house and as they went into it, we counted them. We arrived back on the fourth day. The Apaches were told in the log house that all that was wanted of them was to be good and live peaceably. The Apaches called that place Tai-ni-di-cai which means a weed that grows tall in a lake. The white people called it Bel-le-los.

The next day we started farther south. We left our wagon there and took three pack mules loaded with provisions. All of the scouts and soldiers went. We left the Apaches there. We were on our way four days before we got over the mountain; I do not know its name. The fourth day we killed a big brown bear. It was not fat enough to eat, so we took the feet and left the rest. The next day, one of the soldiers accidentally killed his horse. He was fooling with a gun and it went off and accidently killed the horse. The horse furnished the first good meat we had to eat. The soldiers did not eat the horse but the Indians did.

The next day we came to a town where white people lived and stayed there a few days. I do not know the name of the town. We went off east to the foot of a mountain, to the south there was no mountain. We got a wagon and a spring wagon (two wagons). We did not have a road over the mountain we had gone over and that was why we used pack mules. After we left the white town, we followed a road along the foot of the mountain. On the second day a horse that one of the officers rode burst his side. We ate him. We came to a river where some Mexicans lived. We got some ripe corn and some ripe melons. I do not know the name of the river but it is below Se-go-ia mountain. We stopped there two days, eating melons and ripe corn. We went on to where there was a deep well. It was the only place near there where we could get water. It was Sunday and we stayed there two days. The second day from there we came to a place where they were getting salt; people were hauling it away by the wagon load. I do not know the name of the place. We went on to a place where there was a lot of pigs and so we killed and ate one of them. It did not taste good and we only ate part of it.

The same day we arrived at Mescalero. The officer we called Redhead, myself, and two other scouts had gone on ahead. The rest of the scouts and the soldiers came in the evening. At Mescalero, we saw some Mescalero Apaches that some of the Navajo scouts knew. The scouts became acquainted with them when they were at Fort Sumner for four years. They were glad to see each other and shook hands. I was at Fort

Sumner but I worked around the camp and did not get acquainted with the Mescalero Indians.

Some Utes were encamped at Mescalero and we went to make them a friendly visit. The Utes had gone down from this part of the country trading. I am not sure if they were Utes. They were not friendly and the Mescaleros warned us to be careful, or the Utes would kill us. We were there three days. The army was going around trying to make friends with the Indians by giving them something to eat. The Mescalero Apaches were also receiving rations at an army camp at Mescalero as were the Utes. The Utes got scared and moved out and we followed them up to around Santa Fe. They got away from us. There was a heavy rain which washed out their trail and we did not get them. We went down to where there was a watermill. Five of the scouts were sent out to find the Utes' trail. When they came back, they said they found it. Five men were called to volunteer to go after the Utes. The five Indians who had horses and the soldiers went after the Utes. The rest of us backed out. Only about half of the soldiers went and the rest stayed with the 20 scouts. We went back to where the Mescalero Apaches lived. We waited there several days and during that time, we did not hear anything from the party that had followed the Utes. We were told it was uncertain as to when they would be heard of and that we might as well go home.

The 20 scouts and one white man who drove the wagon started for home. After we had gone part of the way, the white man said he would take the wagon to the Apache village and the rest of us could go home. We divided into parties and went to our different homes. . . . Later we heard that the five Indians got back. We went over to Fort Wingate for our pay. Some of the Indians had gotten their pay in money, but I was late in getting there and was told I would have to trade mine out at the store. I do not know how much pay I received, but it was not very much as I only received fifty cents a day and I was out three months.[4]

## John Rope—An Apache Perspective

White Mountain Apache John Rope, as a scout, shared many of the same concerns and struggles as Wars About with Anger, and yet their situations were different. Here, Rope, born about 1855 and whose Apache name was "Black Rope," tells his experiences, which were recorded in 1932 with Grenville Goodwin.[5] He had more than a half dozen six-month enlistments including General Crook's 1883 campaign against the Chiricahua

*This group of Navajo scouts included men of different ages and experience levels, but all lived a rugged life when operating on the trail. Big Hat Charley's account shares part of the humdrum of daily scouting, the constant search for food, and some less-dramatic interaction with those he pursued. (Courtesy of Cline Library, Northern Arizona University, Neg. #7792)*

Apaches. Since his narrative is close to one hundred pages long, only excerpts that emphasize his scouting activities are shared here. Note, in particular, the interaction between the scouts and the military as well as the ongoing dynamics between various Apache groups as friend and foe. This autobiographical account illustrates the very human side of scouting—aspects of interpersonal relationships that seldom make their way into the written reports and tactical analyses of the Apache wars. At this point in Rope's narrative, he was well into his scouting experience and searching for the Chiricahua Apaches near Hachita Mountain in southern New Mexico. A friendly group of Chiricahuas under the leadership of Chihuahua entered the soldiers' camp and offered their services as scouts. Game was plentiful, and so many of the scouts and newcomers went hunting together.

> We waited up on the mountain till all of the unpacking was done, and
> then we went down to them, carrying our game. The scouts with the

soldiers had killed lots of deer also. Two canvases were spread, one for the friendly Chiricahuas, the other for us White Mountain scouts. All the game was put on each canvas. Our sergeant saw us and told us to come over and put our meat on the White Mountain canvas, which we did. Then the white soldiers and officers came over to the meat and started taking all of it from us and the friendly Chiricahuas as well. Chihuahua got mad and called over He Is Building Something, our sergeant. He said, "They are doing the same with your meat as well as ours. This is not fair. The soldiers did not shoot this meat. They ride horses and we go on foot, and now they want all the meat. These white soldiers are like nothing to us. If they keep this up, we will kill them and take all of their horses."

The lieutenant came to the sergeant and said, "Don't hold back this meat now from the soldiers or you will get discharged." I guess the head officer did not know what was going on. Now the top sergeant (He Is Wide) of my company, to whom the lieutenant was talking, got mad and said, "All right, I'll quit now." He threw his gun and cartridge belt down on the ground.

About this time the white interpreter whom we had with us went to the head officer and told him what was going on. The head officer came back down to where the meat was. He brought the other officers with him. He asked He Is Wide what was going on. "I don't know about this taking away of the meat," he said, "it was not my orders." He asked if this had been going on before in the other camps. The sergeant said no, that they had only made a present of the hind quarters of the deer and antelope to the soldiers and kept the front part for themselves. The captain told him to pick up his gun and belt, saying that he was a scout and he had not ordered him to quit that way, that the lieutenant had no right to fire him by himself. The captain said, "You scouts travel only on foot and have a hard time of it, work hard to kill meat. From this time on, the meat that you kill is entirely for you." Then we cooked up our meat and ate it.[6]

There were different types of motivation that encouraged a warrior to become a scout. Whether on a band, family, or individual level, the scouts' reasons to enlist included individual revenge, opportunity to prove oneself, escape from the stifling life of the reservation, the need for employment and booty, encouragement by others, or fulfillment of a debt. Rope shared some of the reasons he and other White Mountain Apaches served. During one of his earlier enlistments, he listened to the urging of some elders.

> When the morning came, we scouts were called together and talked to. The first speaker was an old woman, one who knew about war medicine. She said, "You boys are like close relatives to me. I want you to look out for yourselves and do things the right way. If you see the Warm Springs people, follow them and don't let them get away." Then a chief talked to us and said, "The Warm Springs people are born from women only. You are born from women also. If you see the Warm Springs people, go right after them. Don't run away, but go to them and stay fighting them." They talked with us that way because of the White Mountain chief who had been killed by the Warm Springs people.[7]

During a later enlistment, there was further urging.

> We heard that some Chiricahuas had killed some of our people at Fort Apache. It was at that time that they issued a gun and belt to me and put me on special duty. I no longer was a policeman. I was just carrying arms to shoot the Chiricahuas if they should come. Al Sieber [Albert Sieber—chief of scouts] said that the Chiricahuas had killed some of my relatives and so he was giving me this rifle to guard myself with. Later on, he said he was going to make me a scout.
>
> When they began enlisting scouts again, I joined. They kept us at San Carlos for one month while they were getting together one hundred Indians for scouts. There were two sergeants for us White Mountain scouts and two for the San Carlos scouts and Tontos. The officer made some of the scouts practice shooting at this time. Before we left, we put up a big dance. First, we had the war dance and then the social dance. There were lots of White Mountain and San Carlos people there and lots of girls and women. We danced all night.[8]

The line between trust and mistrust was often a fine distinction on either side of the scout-soldier fence. The important role of the scouts could not be missed, and so they wielded power in their own way. Given the skills and knowledge of the Apache scouts, the military clearly recognized its dependence on these men. A white leader would have to think twice and even backpedal to ensure that he did not lose the most important, but also temperamental, arm of his operational command. Rope illustrated this point.

We scouts had for an interpreter a man who had been captured by the white people from the Navajo country. He was a Navajo Indian. After supper, the officer called us scouts over to his camp. The soldiers were all lined up, three companies of them. There were four officers and one army doctor. The head officer spoke. He said, "These two scouts killed an elk two days ago, but then I did not say anything about it and gave them another chance. Today, the same two shot a burro. It seems to me as if they were trying to help the Warm Springs people and warn them by shooting this way. Tomorrow I am going to discharge these two, send them back home, and take their rifles, canteens, and cartridge belts from them."

One of these men was related to our sergeant, so he said that he did not want these scouts sent back. The officer would not listen to him. All of us scouts felt the same way, that we did not want these two men sent home, as they were far from home and might get killed by wild animals on the way back. The sergeant said that if these two men were discharged, we all might as well turn in our outfit and start back tomorrow. The officers talked among themselves, and I guess they changed their minds, because the head officer said, "All right, we will keep these two men, but from now on they will have to take the place right at the head of the column." Next morning, we started out.[9]

At the next point in his story, John had been working with a large contingent of scouts to locate a band of Chiricahua Apaches that had raided extensively in both Arizona and New Mexico as well as dipping down into Mexico. One day, a scout spotted a flash on the slope of a nearby mountain while others discovered tracks and the remnants of a recent Apache campsite. Other scouts with binoculars picked up the enemy's shelters on top of a ridge on an opposing mountain. John and the other scouts prepared for action.

Sieber said that fifty scouts were to be ahead and that the pack mules and the rest would follow some distance behind. I was one of these fifty. At that time, I had never fought with the Chiricahua and did not know how mean they were, so I was always in the front. We crossed over a canyon, going in single file. First there would be ten scouts, then a mule, then ten scouts, then a mule, that way. We scouts in front heard someone whistle in the brush. We stopped and listened and heard the whistle again. We all thought it was the Chiricahuas and started to run back. One man tripped and fell in a waterhole. Afterwards the whistle turned out to be only the wind blowing on an acorn with a hole in it, which was on a blue oak tree. . . .

On a level place near the camp all the horses of the Chiricahuas were grazing. There were lots of them. We all hurried back and there we could see the camp alright. There were quite a few Chiricahuas in it. Sieber sent two scouts back to tell the other soldiers and scouts who were way behind to hurry up here and to come that same night. Some of the scouts were afraid. It was only a mile across the valley from where we were to the Chiricahua camp. That night we could not sleep but sat and talked in whispers. Later on, we slept a little. Early in the morning, the troop and other scouts got in there. They told us all to eat and tie the horses up, as it would be daylight soon.

Now we looked at the Chiricahua camp again. There was lots of smoke coming up from there. We started out, down across, and up towards the camp. Part of the soldiers and scouts went on the left side and part on the right. In the middle went Alchise and his scouts. This way we were going to surround the Chiricahua camp before they found out we were there. One of the scouts on our side of the line went off to one side to urinate. Right then he saw two Chiricahua men riding towards the scouts. He told the others and they waited to surround the two Chiricahuas. One sergeant on the other side of us down the canyon had his gun all cocked, ready to fire. The gun went off by accident, but even so, the Chiricahuas did not seem to hear and kept right on coming. Then we scouts started shooting at them but missed. The two men jumped off their mules and beat it off in the rocks and brush, but they did not go back to their camp.

Now we scouts all ran down into the canyon and drank there, dipping the water up with our hands. Some of the scouts started to say their knees hurt them as an excuse to keep in the rear. Some of them were always doing this because they were afraid. We all started on for the Chiricahua camp, going up over some rocks where there was lots of water. Right above there some of us could see three Chiricahuas herding some horses to a grassy place. They were coming our way, so we waited. Right behind these three a boy and a girl were riding, each leading a horse behind them. We waited, hiding in the brush till the boy and girl were right opposite us.

Then Much Water called to them. "Shew," he said, "come here." He was a Warm Springs man so, of course, he talked like them. The two stopped, but did not come. Much Water called again. "Come here. Hurry up," he said. They dropped the ropes of the lead horses and came over, but

*John Rope (center), with two more contemporary Apache servicemen, portray the warrior spirit passed through generations. Rope's account is one of the most detailed of all those collected about the Apache scouts, thus preserving the "face" of scouting. (Courtesy of Wikimedia Commons)*

they could not yet see us. When they were close to us, we made for them. I grabbed the girl and Much Water got the boy. The girl had lots of beads made from the roots of a kind of brush that grows down there. She had four strings of them and I started to take those off of her. Then Much Water said, "No, that girl belongs to a friend of mine and I want to trade you this boy for her." I said all right, and he took the girl and I the boy. Now all the rest of us started to shoot at the three Chiricahua men who were driving the horses. The scouts had told the three to stand still, but they started to run off in the pine woods. Only one of them was shot. The boy I had captured saw all of the scouts in a line shooting with their red headbands. "What kind of people are these?" he asked. "These are scouts," I told him, "and they are all after your people." Then he started to cry. The girl did not cry at all. She just stood there quietly. I told the boy, "If you try to run away, I am going to shoot you, so you had better stay with me." The girl spoke to me. "My friend, don't shoot him," she said. I was wearing two belts of fifty cartridges each, but I did not shoot more than three times because I was satisfied with having helped to catch these two Chiricahuas. My brother was there and I told him to go on to the

Chiricahua camp, but he did not want to, so I told him to keep my boy for me and I went towards the camp myself.

Near the place where the one Chiricahua had been killed, I saw someone's heels sticking out of a clump of bushes. I grabbed this person by the heels and pulled him out. It was one of the other two Chiricahuas who had been with the one who was killed. This was only a boy and there was no blood on him, so I thought he was all right. Just then some of the other scouts came along and said they wanted me to give them the boy, but I said no, that I had found him and was going to keep him. I told the boy to run ahead of me to the camp. He was only a little boy, but he ran fast and we got there quickly. I found where the Chiricahuas had been butchering a horse and the front quarters were cut off already. One man had got to the camp before me and had captured a white mule with a saddle on it. I found an old worn-out Navajo blanket for the boy and put him up with the scout on the white mule to ride double.

This camp was Chihuahua's and he and his brother had just come from the warpath with lots of cattle. The Chiricahuas had been butchering there and there was meat lying around on the bushes to dry. I found a good thick cowhide and doubled it over, putting a lot of dry meat and grease inside. This I also gave to the scout on the white mule, allowing him half of it for himself. There was some mescal spread around to dry on the bushes and some just boiled. We took this also. I found an old Mexican saddle, bridle, and rope and put these all at the side of the camp together, so that the others would know that they were mine.

They yelled for all of the San Carlos scouts to surround the Chiricahua horses, which they did. Two Chiricahua men got up on a high rocky shoulder above us. They shot down at us a couple of times, then they yelled, "All right, you're doing this way with us now, but some time we will do the same to you," and then went off. One of the sergeants called to us to come up where he was and help him surround a bunch of mules. Seven of us went up to him but there were no mules. There were, however, some pine trees and a woman had left her little girl at the foot of one. The girl was hiding behind the trunk, so I went and reached around the tree and grabbed her. She was wearing a string of beads around her neck from which hung a Mexican silver cross. I took the silver cross for myself.

I started back and the first man I met was one of the scouts. "Here," I said, "I'm giving this little girl to you." He laughed, took her, then gave her to He Knows a Lot, who was riding a horse and was also a scout. He Knows a Lot held her and started riding down the hill, singing the victory dance song as he went. All the other scouts laughed when they heard him singing this song. This is the song of thanks that they used to sing long ago when a successful war party came back and they gave a victory dance in which men and women danced together.

After we got back to the Chiricahua camp, we burned all the mescal that was left and also a lot of a kind of big juniper berries that grow down in Mexico and which the Chiricahuas had gathered for food. One of the scouts caught five horses and drove them to camp. There was one fat sorrel mare, which I took for myself and put the saddle and bridle I had captured on her. One scout came to me and said one of the boys I had caught was the son of the daughter of Nachise, who was a good friend of his. For this reason, he wanted to trade me eighty dollars, a horse, and saddle for the boy, but I would not do it. One scout called Big Coyote had also caught a sixteen-year-old girl when she had come down for water. This girl was taken back to Fort Apache and is still living on North Fork.

Only four of the Chiricahuas had been killed. One of these was an old woman shot by some San Carlos scouts. She had stood up when they came to her and asked them not to kill her but just to take her captive. The San Carlos scouts shot her anyway. We White Mountain men talked to the San Carlos scouts and said, "Why did you kill that old woman? You ought not to have killed her." The San Carlos men said they had come after these Chiricahuas and they were going to kill them.

We started out from the Chiricahua camp, General Crook riding in front. I shot my gun off some because I was feeling happy about what I had done in the fight. The others were shooting too, just for fun. Some of the other scouts were joking with me about firing only three shots in the fight. I said, "I have done better than you. I caught three Chiricahuas." Pretty soon my horse gave out, so I killed her and gave my saddle to the man who had given me the horse. I also gave him the boy to carry.

After we had gone a way, we stopped and made camp. I took out my dried meat and fat from the hide and divided it up among the others. We cooked and ate. Then the man who had wanted my boy came again to me. "My cousin," he said, "give me that boy like I asked you. I want him and will buy him from you." But I told him no, that I did not want him to be that way. He kept right on asking me. Then Mickey Free came over and spoke to him. "Don't ask for that boy like that. We are on the warpath now and don't know for sure if this boy belongs to the daughter of your friend or not."

That night they put fifteen scouts out to guard on all four sides of the camp we were in. General Crook said to make all our Chiricahua prisoners lie down together and sleep and for us to watch and see that they did not get away. That night the oldest Chiricahua girl we had caught said that almost all of the Chiricahua men had gone out on a raid that very day. The next morning General Crook said to bring all the captives to his place. There he asked the oldest girl which was the best one of the horses we had captured. She answered that a certain grey one was. General Crook sent for this horse, but a scout had already taken it for his own and would not give it up. General Crook sent again for it and said, "Bring that grey horse to me here right now." The horse was brought and although the scout who had claimed it was there, he said nothing. They saddled this horse for the two oldest Chiricahua girls and gave them food, also tobacco for Chihuahua.

Now General Crook said, "Go to Chihuahua and tell him that we have only come to take his people back to San Carlos and not make war." They took the girls back to the Chiricahua camp we had attacked and from there the two followed the Chiricahua tracks. The girls had been told to tell the Chiricahua that the raiding of their camp yesterday was an accident and that it had not meant war. Also, that our camp would be at the right end of the mountain and that we wanted the Chiricahuas to come in to that place to talk. Much Water had told the girl to tell his brother and sister to come in to our camp right away. Twelve scouts and Much Water took the girls back to the Chiricahua camp. Some of the Chiricahua had been to their camp again, but had gone back up on top of the mountain.[10]

The attack had been devastating for Chihuahua and his people. Crook sent out scouts to inform the Apache leader that he had come only to bring his people into San Carlos and not start a war, but Chihuahua, in a face-to-face confrontation with Crook, asked why he had killed the old lady, who was his aunt, and others. Still, there had been enough pressure exerted and enough property lost to convince Chihuahua that it was time to surrender—there was also time for revenge, especially with the scouts. Appearances were meant to be deceiving.

Now we all mixed with the Chiricahuas like friends. About noon the Chiricahuas went apart and started to make a victory dance. Sieber told all of us scouts to stay away from the dance and so only the Chiricahuas themselves were there. But all the same, one scout went over to the dance that night and danced. A Chiricahua woman made him pay her twenty cartridges. Some White Mountain scouts reported on this man and the officer made him go back and get the cartridges from that woman. The Chiricahuas had driven in the cattle they had captured. They gave three head to us White Mountain men. . . .

The Chiricahuas were camped apart from us and Cartridges All Gone went back there to a council they were holding. The Chiricahua chiefs were talking. They said that this night they were going to put on a social dance for the White Mountain scouts and let the Chiricahua girls dance with them. Then all the Chiricahua men would get behind, and while the scouts were dancing, they would kill them all. It did not matter if they themselves, the Chiricahuas, got killed, but they would get us scouts anyway. They sent word to Pine Pitch House to come to the council. When he got there, they told him what they planned to do and asked him to join in. Pine Pitch House said, "I won't join in this because the White Mountain people are like relatives of mine," and then he went back to his camp. . . . That night they started to hold the dance, but one of the scouts, Long Ears, had died that day and Sieber sent word for them to stop the dance on account of this, so they did.[11]

Nothing else came from this incident.

Rope remained on duty even after the Apaches returned to San Carlos. Much of his time was taken in apprehending Apaches who had killed other Apaches and had then fled the reservation. He found this police work tiring and so was not bothered when it came to a close.

We were lined up for inspection, all with clean clothes on and our rifles shined up. This way we knew that our time was pretty near up and we soon would get paid off. In a couple of days, we were discharged. Sieber, who knew me well and whom I liked a lot, asked me three times to rejoin the scouts, but I would not do it. Those long scouts we used to make at first, down to the southeast and around Fort Bowie, were good and we could save some money. But this being stationed at San Carlos all the time was no good, as there was always somebody killing someone else, and we were having to go out after them. Then, too, we could never save our pay because we had our families to care for. . . . You see me here still alive and well. That is because I have been good and minded my own business. Lots of the other scouts did not, and they are dead.[12]

In summarizing what can be gained from these three scout memoirs, at the top of the list has to be the inside Navajo and Apache perspective. Personal accounts share that insight in a way that nothing else can. Daily life—beyond the dramatic large events—puts grist in the mill of understanding relationships and operations. Many things are shared that would never make their way into more formal reports, for whatever reason. Wars About with Anger, Big Hat Charley, and John Rope become representatives, in a small way, of what so many other Navajos and Apaches encountered but never had an opportunity to share. With the passing of their generation, these men became the voice of many silent participants who worked so hard during the Apache wars in the last quarter of the nineteenth century.

CHAPTER SEVEN

# The End and a Beginning

Closing Perspectives on the Apache Wars

F ollowing the removal to Florida of Geronimo and his Chiricahua band, including the Apache scouts that had served so faithfully, the military breathed a sigh of relief, turning its attention to maintaining peace in other aspects of the diminishing frontier. There was also time for all involved in the Apache wars to reflect upon the role the scouts had played in ending this conflict. There were as many opinions on their effectiveness as participants, but for those who had worked extensively with or against the scouts the feelings ran fairly consistent. All sides recognized that without the Navajo and Apache scouts the entire conflict could have dragged on for years. Even those who were not in favor of using these Indians and who feared that those working for the military actually served as a fifth column had to begrudgingly admit at the end that the scouts were indispensable in terminating the war.

## Friend or Foe—Who Is Asking?

Beginning with the United States military—"the employer"—many of its leaders charged with rounding up recalcitrant Apaches recognized the impossibility of bringing to bay groups, large or small, who knew the land and how to use it to their advantage for lightning-fast raids, well-disguised ambushes, and eking food and water from a stingy environment. General George Crook, the strongest advocate for using Indian scouts, employed hundreds in his operations and was unflinching in his praise of their work.

> Without Apache scouts we could have made no progress. I first began using them in 1872, and have used them ever since. Nothing has ever

143

been accomplished without their help. Have they acted in good faith? We have every assurance that they have. They followed the hostiles' trails almost as well as bloodhounds. It is nonsense to think that white trailers could have done the work. These white mountaineers howl against the Apache scouts—but how does it happen that they and the cowboys together never killed a hostile? The scouts have put in on the chase the most tremendous work men ever did; and when they succeeded in catching up with the hostiles, they have invariably fought well. But there is a great uproar because the Chiricahuas have been employed as scouts. A good many people think that any Indian scout will do, but this is not so. The average Indian scout is almost invariably better in his peculiar line than a white man, but the ordinary Indian, and even the ordinary Apache, is totally unable to cope with the Chiricahua. . . . [They] are the supreme scouts, and all the other tribes acknowledge it.[1]

Crook realized there was also a secondary value that accompanied his use of Apache scouts, one that worked at the roots of tribal dynamics. The general understood that beyond the purely functional aspect of having men trained and knowledgeable about the foe being pursued, there were social and family dynamics that became fractured as one group worked against another. Splintering into factions fostered the breakdown of family, community, and band ties, encouraging cultural rifts.

To polish a diamond there is nothing like its own dust. It is the same with these fellows. Nothing breaks them up like turning their own people against them. They don't fear the white soldiers, whom they easily surpass in the peculiar style of warfare which they force upon us, but put upon their trail an enemy of their own blood, an enemy as tireless, as foxy, and as stealthy and familiar with the country as themselves, and it breaks them all up. It is not merely a question of catching them better with Indians, but a broader and more enduring aim—their disintegration.[2]

James Kaywaykla, one of those Apaches pursued by Indian scouts, testified that these men were the real problem. "General Crook put eighty companies of cavalry and infantry in the field. But it was the scouts whom the Apaches dreaded, for only they knew the trails and the hiding places. And only they could traverse the country rapidly enough to be a menace. They got close enough to capture many horses and nearly all of the supplies."[3] Nana, an old warrior who used supernatural abilities in outwitting his pursuers and in obtaining supplies, especially ammunition, recalled his hatred for what he considered turncoats against his people. Yet he also recognized their effectiveness.

> At the fire that night, Nana talked of Juh's stronghold in the Sierra Madre, picturing the peace and security there. He spoke of how we might live indefinitely even if the trail were destroyed and we were cut off from all the rest of the world. We would be as those who are gone to the Happy Place of the Dead—provided with all necessities, protected from all enemies. "Could no one find us there?" "Only the scouts, the accursed scouts." When they first began working with the cavalry it was to run down our enemies. Now they are used against their own people, and for what? Only the silver—the eight pieces of silver they get every moon. They might guide the cavalry to the foot of that trail, but they could never climb it. They would be buried under a landslide if they attempted it.[4]

More than money induced the scouts to work against their people. Already mentioned were the interband rivalries, where individuals or families killed those from another camp, initiating a series of vengeful attacks. At other times there were thefts, interfamily or intergroup conflict, or territorial disputes that raised friction. However, there were also cultural inducements that encouraged a warrior to take up arms. Apache society honored its warriors. Fighting offered an opportunity to prove one's bravery, protect loved ones, and follow the patterns established by Killer of Enemies and Child of the Water, the ideals of manhood. Once Apaches and Navajos were forced into a more peaceful existence, access to weapons—the tools of a warrior—were sometimes restricted. For the Apaches, especially those who embraced conflict after the Fort Sumner period, owning weapons on the reservation was curtailed. By enlisting as a scout, the military provided rifles and ammunition, something that encouraged many to enlist. Kaywaykla understood this reasoning. "Ours was a race of fighting men—war was our occupation. Our rifle was our most cherished possession. And though the scouts were permitted to have only five bullets at a time, and had to account for each one fired, a weapon is a weapon. And, believe me, there was not a man who did not envy the scout his rifle."[5] In other instances, the scouts received a fifty-cartridge ammunition belt, not just the five rounds mentioned here.

In addition to the obvious symbol of manhood made evident by having a rifle, it was also a ticket to get off of the reservation and go on the warrior's path. Kaywaykla further explained as he discussed the feelings of those Apaches watching their own people work against them.

When General Crook first employed scouts to guide the cavalry, it was against their enemies. Being chosen as scouts was a recognition of a warrior's ability to fight, and it was a relief from the dreary, monotonous existence on the reservation. To Apaches, a reservation is a prison. Scouts were admired and envied by other men—not for the meager pay, for at that time money meant nothing to them. What they valued was the possession of a rifle and ammunition, for they had been deprived of arms when they went on the reservation. In addition, Crook used the scouts against their enemies the Pimas. The Chiricahua and Warm Springs had fought occasionally also with the Tontos, though they were Apaches. The name Tonto, meaning fool, was given them because they were considered inferior in intelligence. So scouts who fought against the Tontos were not despised by their own people. [Kaywaykla then shifts to the scouts pursuing his people.]

Chihuahua, Tissnothos, and Speckle Face were riding close, Chihuahua's warriors wearing the red head-cord that was their badge of servitude. Good and true warriors inveigled into military service and now used against their own people! Those who attempted to leave the service were grimly informed of the punishment meted out to deserters. These three had gone to San Carlos with Cochise's band and found existence unendurable. Kaytennae's heart burned within him as he thought of how these men who should have been fighting with him were the allies of his enemies.

They were cutting for sign before coming into the water. Not once did they look toward the ledge. He waited while they drank, one at a time, with the others keeping watch. When they had finished, he was so enraged that he leaped to his feet and yelled, "Come up here!" He had them covered. "We'll give you metal, more than you want. I have sharp metal for your treacherous hearts. Brave warriors who fight their people deserve a reward. We'll give it. Come!"

The scouts fled. Suldeen reproved him. The cavalry would be warned and would prevent our crossing the basin to the Organs on its western edge. Kaytennae admitted he had been hasty, but reasoned that without water the cavalry would turn south to Hueco Tanks or the Rio Grande.[6]

Charles Gatewood observed a similar attitude of scorn when chasing Victorio, who had become disgruntled with the government system and fled the reservation at Tularosa with sixty men. Major Albert P. Morrow sent cavalry elements with Navajo scouts in pursuit, while Gatewood and twenty Apache scouts joined later in the chase. Victorio ambushed the first element in a canyon, killing ten men and thirty-two horses, along with capturing another twenty-one mounts and most of the military's supplies. Lieutenant Gatewood and his scouts with additional cavalry units soon caught up to the beleaguered element and followed the fleeing Apaches. His scouts, well in advance of the main party, surprised Victorio's warriors, which had by now doubled in number. Caught in a small canyon in the middle of preparing their evening meal, these Apaches jokingly asked their pursuers to join them for supper. After exchanging insults, the two groups opened fire, each holding their own until the larger force of cavalry arrived and pushed the enemy up into the canyon walls. When night settled in, the fighting stopped, only to resume in the morning. The echoing booms of rifle fire made it difficult to tell who was shooting and where they were located as the two sides skirmished for an upper hand. Gatewood noted the confusion. "When the scouts began to appear, it was impossible for us to tell whether they were hostiles, [until we] heard the fog-horn voice of Sergeant Jack Long bellowing 'Mucho bueno! God damn, come on!' I didn't think there was a sane man in the country, except the corporal, who coolly informed me after a while that I was sitting on the wrong side of a boulder and pointed out to me the folly of protecting a rock."[7] When the Apaches felt they had enough, they broke contact and escaped with their captured supplies and livestock.

There were other times when goodwill existed between the pursuers and the pursued. At one point, Chihuahua was chasing Kaytennae and got dangerously close. The fleeing Apache, in his haste, needed a fresh horse and so abandoned his tired mount and cut the harness of a fresh one from a team of horses attached to a nearby buckboard. The horse became skittish, refusing to obey his rider. Kaytennae, realizing this was fruitless, dismounted and headed for an arroyo in which to hide until the approaching night could provide additional cover to escape. Providence smiled upon the fleeing warrior, since "the scouts knew all the time where he was, but they pretended they couldn't find him. They let him get away and catch up with Nana."[8] No explanation was given by Eugene Chihuahua, the raconteur, as to what encouraged the scouts to allow for the escape, but there was doubtless some kind of bond between the two opposing sides.

Perhaps one reason for this type of behavior was that there were no clear long-lasting divisions between who was friend at one time and foe at another. Sympathies could shift between the two. One of the major criticisms that Crook faced for using Apaches to hunt down Apaches was the possibility of changing sides. Could one be trusted to faithfully conduct field operations against a group that may comprise family and friends?

Add to this the fact that the government was arming and equipping these scouts as well as making them aware of plans to entrap those fleeing, which gave rise to speculation that the reason those Apaches being chased were so successful in evading was due to leaked prior knowledge. Crook adamantly refuted this idea vouching for his scouts' loyalty. Gatewood, on the other hand, understood the shifting dynamics in Apache culture and was not quite as convinced that all were ever faithful. He wrote:

> They seemed to take turn-about in annual eruptions, it seldom happening that more than one tribe raided the white settlements at one time. And if they did, each went out independent of the other. It therefore happened that the scouts of one year would be turning the territory topsy-turvy the next, and the officer commanding a company would be pursuing a party of ex-scouts with an assortment of ex-hostiles. They could be relied on provided due care was taken to make enlistments from those who had old scores to settle with the renegades. These could generally be found by anyone who had some idea of the many feuds that exist among them. These feuds, by the way, extend to bands of the same tribe and even exist among families of the same band.[9]

An example of a shift in allegiance between sides is provided by Jason Betzinez. As a young man and relative of Geronimo and one who often lived in his camp, he told of a Navajo who had joined forces with the Apache leader. But friction arose, ending in his death. "The only unusual happening was when one of our Apaches, a man named She-neah, suddenly decided to shoot the lone Navajo who had been with Geronimo all this time. The Navajo, while previously serving as a U. S. scout, had killed one of She-neah's relatives. As usual the Apache never forgot or forgave, so without warning She-neah killed the Navajo. We were all sorry this happened but no one did anything about it."[10]

The Navajo experience of scouting against Apaches is far more straightforward. In general, most Navajos viewed these cousins as competitors and enemies, and so recruiting trackers was not a problem. Navajo warriors appreciated the opportunity to hone their warrior skills in the tradition of Monster Slayer and Born for Water, to enjoy the break from reservation boredom, to obtain pay, and to readily accept whatever booty they gathered. The Navajos were also a more settled people, isolated on an ever-expanding reservation, whereas the Apaches were generally on an ever-decreasing land base that, for the most part, was far less desirable. To the Navajos, the Apaches were fierce fighters but lacked the cultural sophistication of their own tribe. They also worked closely with the military, who, for the most part, did not question their loyalty or their desire to aid and abet the enemy. Field commanders appreciated their skills, and although there were times of disagreement and refusal, the Navajo scouts earned a good reputation. Major William Price summarized his experience following his campaign against the Mescaleros in 1873. "The Navajos were splendid as trailers and allies and seemed to terrify the whole of them. They never deceived me in any instance and were prompt to obey all of my wishes." In the same breath, he revealed the Navajo attitude toward the Apaches when he quoted their leader as saying, "Manuelito, the war chief of the Navajos, when selecting the Indians that were to come with me on this scout said, 'You take the Apaches, bridle them, saddle them, put a load on them and then get on and ride them as you did us and they will behave themselves ever afterwards.'"[11]

In summarizing this period of warfare that brought Navajo and Apache enlistments to their height and saw the most intense conflicts, one can observe two very different cultural approaches to war. Given the terrain, training, logistical requirements, and religious and cultural beliefs, the Native American system was fully adapted for the fighting encountered. The U.S. military, whose heritage hearkened back to European-style conflict and which had most recently found its largest expression in the Civil War, had to forgo many of its accepted practices and operate more on its enemies' terms and turf. Logistically and numerically, the Americans were superior, but when it came to tactics and physical conditioning, it took an Indian to defeat an Indian. Maneuver, surprise, security, and simplicity were Principles of War that the Apaches capitalized on, given his hit-and-run brand of warfare, while the cavalry emphasized mass, unity of command, and offensive operations when applicable. Both practiced economy of force and had their own objectives; both drew upon all of the Principles of War in different instances.

Britton Davis, who scouted with and fought against the Apaches and was a keen observer, explained their psyche and what motivated them.

> The Apache was unlike any other Indian tribe the whites have ever fought since civilization began to creep over the North American continent. His mode of warfare was peculiarly his own. He saw no reason for fighting unless there was something tangible and immediate to be gained. To satisfy his pressing needs for arms, ammunition, food, or clothing he would raid isolated ranches, the suburbs of small Mexican towns, or ambush travelers. But he had no such sense of bravado as animated other Indian

tribes, who resisting encroachment by the whites on the Indian's domain, fought us man to man in the open. His creed was "fight and run away, live to fight another day." Corner him, however, and you would find him as desperate and dangerous as a wounded wolf. Only when cornered, or to delay pursuit of his women and children, would he engage a force anywhere near the strength of his own. To fight soldiers merely in defense of his country, he considered the height of folly; and he never committed that folly if he could avoid it.[12]

John Cremony, another military man who studied the Apaches, also listened to their opinion of what motivated their adversary. Not surprising, it is contrary to what Britton Davis viewed as Apache beliefs.

The Apache regards our reckless onsets as vain and foolish. He is in the habit of saying, "The Americans are brave, but they lack astuteness. They build a great fire which throws out so much heat that they cannot approach it to warm themselves, and when they hear a gun fired, they are absurd enough to rush to the spot. But it is not so with us; we build small fires in secluded nooks which cannot be seen by persons unless close by, and we gather near to them so as to obtain the warmth, and when we hear a gun fired, we get away as soon as possible to some place from which we can ascertain the cause." They regard our daring as folly, and think "discretion is the better part of valor." I am not so sure but that they are incorrect in this idea, as well as in several others.[13]

In conclusion, there is no doubt who won the war, but it was fought on the terms of those who lost.

## Navajo Scouts—A Potpourri of Service

The Apache wars dominated the military's efforts in the Southwest, consumed large chunks of the army's budget, and commanded readers' attention in newspaper headlines. The controversy over using Apache scouts and discussion of their effectiveness dimmed the contribution of Navajo scouts, who soldiered admirably but often remained out of the limelight. In reality, they performed a wide variety of jobs associated with both the ongoing war and many necessary day-to-day tasks that contributed to keeping the frontier army operating. There was usually nothing dramatic about their service, just routine and tedious, but most records indicate it was necessary and well done. To get an idea of the variety of service and the commitment of those performing it, we turn to the abbreviated muster rolls of the 9th Cavalry and view selected entries, covering the period from May 19, 1876, to October 31, 1911, when the final Navajo scouts' enlistment ended.

May 19, 1876—"Marched from Ft. Wingate July 12, 1876, for Camp Vincent, N.M. Arrived August 6—187 miles. 70 scouts left Camp Vincent for scouting duties in Mogollon Mountains, distant marched 104 miles. As good as Indian scouts are usually found."

October 31, 1876—Discipline: "Good for Indian." 25 scouts enrolled.

February 28, 1877—"Jose, Pedro, and Charley Chavis were engaged in Lt. Wright's fight with Apache Indians in the Florida Mountains on January 24, 1877 and behaved gallantly."

August 31, 1877—Sergeant Kite and detachment of nine scouts left Fort Bayard for Ft. Wingate, NM July 12 1877 to bring stolen horses and Apache captives to the former post, returning August 8, 1877. LT. Wright with detachment of 10 scouts left Fort Bayard on July 26, 1877 in pursuit of deserters, returned August 8.

October 31, 1877—2nd Lt. H. H. Wright, 9th Cavalry and 20 scouts on detached service from August 29 to September 22. Scouting in Mogollon, Mimbres, Hatchet, Las Animas, Pyramid, and Burro mountains. Distance marched 532 miles. The detached (23) Navajo scouts left Fort Bayard, September 30 with Battalion 9th Cavalry for field service. They engaged in tracking and scouting until October 20. Distance marched, 334 miles. Total distance September and October, 866 miles. Corporals Pedro and Jack in an engagement with Apaches, each killed an Indian, capturing their horses, arms, and equipment.

February 28, 1878—The scouts absent in detached service have been guarding and escorting mail in Arizona since January 17. Those at the Post have been employed as sentries over the quartermaster haystack and performing escort duty.

December 31, 1878—Escorted Apache captives to Camp Apache via Ft. Wingate, 308 miles.

April 30, 1879—5 scouts—good—have been doing courier duty up to the time they were discharged.

October 31, 1879—the scouts have been employed operating against the Warm Springs Apaches. In the action with Victorio—two were killed—Sam and Baraja.

August 31, 1893—Scout John Vandiver court martialed. Awaiting to be tried in Albuquerque, NM, for killing San Juan, a Navajo.

August 31, 1894—Quite a few scouts on furlough. Officer and 19 scouts left on August 15 to pursue Navajo prisoners who escaped. 2 prisoners captured and returned August 17.

October 1894—Eleven scouts on detachment courier duty to as far as Old Ft. Tularosa.

June 30, 1896—Only 4 scouts

April 30, 1902—Scouts Jeff King, Joe Murphy, Henry Rosenow, Julian Smith, and John Tom sent to Red Rock, NM, to fight forest fires.

October 31, 1911—The six Navajo scouts authorized to be discharged. During this period, the scouts performed duties necessary in connection with the work of abandoning Fort Wingate. [All six scouts received the following final rating: "discipline—very good; instruction—very good for scouts; military appearance—good; arms—good; accouterments—good; clothing—good."][14]

Navajo scouts also served in other activities that might be considered tangential to their military mission of chasing the enemy. With the end of the Apache wars the necessity of maintaining a large number of scouts diminished, but the many skills they had were still needed on a lesser scale. They were in demand as interpreters, translators during disputes, supporters of reservation police, trackers for law enforcement, assistants for placing children in school at a time when it was unpopular, guides, laborers on roads and in gardens, and hunters and fishermen.[15] At certain points in the historical record, there is confusion about who performed a certain task—reservation police or scouts. This will be discussed in the next chapter, but suffice it to say that each agency had a police force that ensured law and order on a small scale. However, if there was a controversy large enough to demand that the military be called in, which was often at the discretion of the agent, then the scouts became involved. Still, their main function was as a cultural go-between who understood the Navajo people, who could defuse heated situations, and who could see beneath the subterfuge that lay within an incident. Four examples follow, each illustrating a different aspect of the scouts' role from 1879 to 1908.

The Monument Valley–Navajo Mountain region had a bad reputation in the 1870s and 1880s. According to army doctor Bernard J. Byrne, stationed at Fort Lewis, Colorado, during the 1880s, local folks called the Four Corners area the "Dark Corner" because "a man makes his own laws there. There ain't no pertection 'cept what a man makes himself. . . . Down in the Dark Corner, if a man kills another man he just steps over to Utah. If he steals a horse in Arizona he slides across to New Mexico."[16] With the

*Large contingents of Navajo scouts, as shown in this Ben Wittick photo, were needed during the Apache campaigns but dramatically decreased after the surrender of Geronimo. The military still required the skills and language capability of the scouts to prevent conflict, identify those who broke the law, and confront aggressors. (Courtesy of Palace of the Governors Photo Archive, New Mexico History Museum, Neg. #016338)*

Navajo Agency hundreds of miles away, the Southern Ute Agency focused on the main body of Utes in Colorado, and the number of settlements throughout this region being so scant, many peacekeepers turned to the military to investigate murders and hostile incidents. Mining activities and cattle grazing drew people to this forbidding area, a trend that many of the native inhabitants resented. It was also an invitation for conflict. The Monument Valley–Navajo Mountain area saw different parties crisscross over the land with hopes of discovering rich veins of silver, something that had been rumored for years, but the Navajos, Utes, and Paiutes in the area wanted nothing to do with them. The best known of the hopefuls were two men—Charles S. Myrick (sometimes incorrectly spelled Merrick or Merritt) and Hernan D. Mitchell, for which two large buttes in Monument Valley are named. Only part of that story is told here about how a handful of Paiutes managed to immortalize these two men.

A band of Paiutes had planned a surprise attack at daybreak, but when they came to the men's camping place, they found them already mounted. The Paiutes told them that they had been using Paiute water to which they had no right.

"We were sent to that water," replied the white men calmly.

The efforts of the Paiutes to make them angry and pick a quarrel were fruitless.

"Give me a chew of tobacco," demanded one Paiute [later identified as Big Mouth Mike].

Mitchell reached into his pocket for a plug of tobacco. At the same time the Paiute grabbed for the gun on his [the white man's] hip. A moment later Mitchell lay dead on the ground, with a bullet from his gun through his head. Merrick whirled at the shot, and seeing his partner past help, put spurs to his own horse and fled, shooting as he rode.

For three miles he rode, to the foot of the great rock formation which later was to be named for him, Merrick Butte. There, knowing that he had been wounded, and fearing that he might have cartridges left, his pursuers turned back. Alone among the rocks he died.[17]

Because this occurred in Navajo country, they were automatically implicated, although the Utes and Paiutes had strong relational ties, and according to Henry Mitchell, Hernan's father, they were acting "sausy."[18] In February the two miners' bodies were found, Mitchell went to retrieve them, and he was led to the site by a Navajo guide. No single Indian group claimed responsibility, the Navajos blaming the Utes and the Utes blaming the Navajos, with the Paiutes serving as another culprit.[19] The first indication of who might be guilty was when a Navajo, Boy with Many Horses, visited a Paiute camp sixty miles above Lee's Ferry. There he saw four mules taken by the Paiutes after they had killed their owners. Since the Navajos were often blamed for deeds they did not commit, they were anxious to have it investigated.[20] The agent sent out Navajo scouts to determine who committed the murders. They returned with word that the guilty party was composed of renegades who were not attached to any agency.[21] A second inquiry by a Navajo scout and a Mexican named Jesus Alviso confirmed that three of the four Indians of Ute-Paiute ancestry, living north of San Juan, had killed the two miners.[22] Thus the true accounting for events was discovered by the scouts, who knew all three groups involved and had the cultural understanding, linguistic ability, and stature to get to the bottom of the crime. This was very much in keeping with similar events.

Take for instance what has been called the Walcott-McNally incident, which occurred two years later in the Navajo Mountain area. This offers a particularly good example since two agents—Galen Eastman and John Bowman, his replacement—recorded much of their effort, the military became involved, the Navajos provided excellent oral accounts, and most important, the role the scouts played is obvious and instructive.[23] In early April 1884, word filtered south to Fort Defiance that Navajos had killed two prospectors—Samuel T. Walcott and James McNally—in the vicinity of Navajo Mountain, sitting astride the Utah-Arizona border. Agent Riordan did what he could as he packed his bags, but he left the main share of the chore to the incoming Bowman, who was of a more aggressive nature and interested in determining what had happened to the two miners. Having previously been a sheriff in Gunnison, Colorado, he started the wheels of justice rolling toward Navajo Mountain as soon as he took office. This area was the preferred hiding spot for Navajos, Utes, and Paiutes fleeing retribution. Thus, when word first reached Riordan and later Bowman that Navajos who killed two prospectors near the mountain were defiant, it was one more example in a long string of incidents that played off of the isolation and lack of information concerning this territory.

First news of the Walcott-McNally incident filtered into the agency via word-of-mouth. Riordan sent a Navajo scout named Pete to investigate. Since February 8, 1884, when Walcott and McNally split from a group of prospectors and set out to find rumored rich deposits of copper, they had lost touch and were not following a planned schedule of contact. Concern grew for the lost miners. Riordan wrote to the commissioner of Indian affairs that he had already had a run-in with the rumored Navajo perpetrators who had one time cornered him and another white man. The Indians debated the two men's fate for several hours before letting them go. As far as the agent was concerned, "this band of cut throats in that region" needed to be punished, "and if the party sent out is not strong enough to bring them in, I propose to send the entire force at my command and if that will not do, I shall ask for troops. If my resignation was not pending, I would go myself and get those men or they'd get me."[24]

Several accounts of the murders emerged, but for brevity, the one provided by scout Pete when he returned to Fort Defiance on April 19, is one of the clearest detailed reports provided by eyewitnesses. Near the southeast corner of Navajo Mountain lived the powerful headman Hashkéneinii with his son, Hashkéneinii Biye'. These men had held residence there for more than two decades, ever since the Long Walk period began. They were well known and respected for both the physical and supernatural power they commanded. When the two prospectors showed up in their territory, Hashkéneinii Biye' saw it as an opportunity to take revenge for past wrongs, although those misdeeds had nothing to do with these two white men. There had been no satisfaction, no payback, on the perpetrators. Now, the time seemed right to exact revenge on the two peacefully camped miners with the help of some other local Navajos. A young boy and three men along with Hashkéneinii Biye' drifted into the camp. "Let's kill these Americans. They are always mean and have no accommodation about them." The boy readily agreed, but Slim Man cautioned both that their relatives would not like them to do it; the other two did not seem to care. Hashkéneinii Biye' told the boy to pick up one of the miner's rifles leaning against a log while he grabbed for an ax. Walcott went to the adult first, trying to wrest the tool out of his hands until the Indian told him he was just checking the blade for sharpness. He then went to the boy to get his rifle as the youth began to remove it from its scabbard. Walcott bent over to secure it, allowing Hashkéneinii Biye' to strike him in the back of the head with the ax, killing him instantly. Slim Man arose from his seat as two older Navajos joined the group asking, "What have you boys been doing fighting?" Slim Man explained what happened, which raised the question of what course to follow with McNally. The answer from one of the old men, Little Mustache (Dághaa' Yázhí), who had just joined the group, was, "As long as one is killed, it is better to kill the other one too, for if they are murdered, no one will ever know anything about it."[25]

The Navajos withdrew a short distance from the camp but as McNally approached, Hashkéneinii Biye' began shooting at him with the newly acquired Winchester rifle. The prospector immediately tied all three horses he had together to form a standing breastwork until all of the animals fell mortally wounded. McNally lay behind his dead mounts and returned fire. Soon Hashkéneinii Biye' had used all eight cartridges in the rifle and decided that he and his companions needed to crawl as close as they could toward their victim, then engage him with their pistols. Little Mustache got the closest, twenty-five feet to the barricade, before they all began firing. When he raised himself up to see above a tuft of grass, the miner spotted him, shot, and hit him in the head, the bullet entering near his right eye and exiting behind his ear. The wounded Indian jumped up and stumbled away, occasionally falling. The others broke contact, secured their wounded friend, and brought him to a nearby hogan where he could be warmed and cared for. They also sent word to Hashkéneinii's camp to make the headman aware of the incident. Shortly after dark the leader arrived with a group of followers. He sent an observer to see if McNally

*Hashkéneinii Biye' played a central role in the Walcott–McNally incident, which became apparent when details of the murders unfolded thanks to the Navajo scouts. He is pictured here over fifty years after the incident, still a prominent medicine man and leader in the Monument Valley area. (Courtesy of Utah State Historical Society)*

had moved and if so, where. The scout eventually returned saying that the white man had left; he did not know when or in which direction, but he was definitely gone. Father and son along with a number of others in this group took up the trail, lighting matches to follow the tracks. The next day it was over; they killed McNally.

Pete's report offers fine-grained detail from a man who interviewed effectively and understood the language as well as the cultural motivation. As a Navajo scout, he provided that detail in a way that made sense to both parties involved. He added that Slim Man buried Walcott; collected and burned the men's blankets, saddles, and equipment, which were all covered with blood; and captured their two remaining horses as well as two others coming from a recent fracas at Henry Mitchell's trading post on the San Juan River. He accompanied the scout as far as Pete's home in Chinle Valley and planned to come to the agency with animals and equipment once the horses were able to travel again, indicating that he trusted the scout. Slim Man would also make a statement of the events he witnessed. Riordan appreciated this testimony, which corroborated that these murders added to "scores of white men during the past ten years [who] have paid the penalty of daring to examine the country outside of this reservation with their lives."[26]

Additional information trickled in. According to another Navajo scout, Sam-Boo-ko-di, with a less convincing report, Walcott was much more the aggressor: he spoke sharply to the Navajos, was the first to draw his gun, and shot one of the Navajos as he peacefully sat around the campfire. The scout also asserted that McNally was badly wounded before leaving his horse barricade and that other uninvolved Navajos while looking for horses found him dead. As for the badly wounded Little Mustache, he was still alive.[27] Sharply at odds with this report is the eyewitness testimony of Slim Man, who came into the agency on May 5. According to his account, when Man with White Horses first approached the camp the night before, he and the two miners shook hands with the Indians and "hugged each other all around," followed by a gift exchange of tobacco. The next morning after breakfast the white men gave all three of the new visitors tobacco, but Hashkéneinii Biye' "was moving around all the time while the other two sat by the fire."[28] After the Navajo killed Walcott, he removed a pistol and holster that he had tried to trade for earlier but had been refused.

Once Bowman took charge of the Navajo Agency on June 30, he assumed responsibility for appropriate action on the ground. He sent word to the miscreants that they had ten days to travel the 175 miles to the agency and give themselves up or he would assign Navajo scouts, or if necessary the military, to apprehend them.[29] Things started to happen. Colonel L. P. Bradley ordered one of the officers of the 6th Cavalry operating along the San Juan to find the graves of the two men in preparation for moving them to Fort Lewis once the weather was cold enough. Transporting them in the summer was too difficult. He also directed that a detachment of soldiers be available to Bowman on request, should it be necessary to ferret out the murderers.[30]

At first this did not seem necessary. On July 10, within the ten-day ultimatum, Hashkéneinii Biye's father turned himself in, then traveled to Fort Wingate under guard. A day later Little Mustache, described as a very old man still suffering from his head wound, came in with some Navajo scouts.[31] Before leaving for his incarceration, he provided a statement, insisting that Hashkéneinii Biye' and Slim Man were the two trying to kill McNally and that he had been wounded by chance as he innocently walked near the battlefield.[32] A week later, Navajo scouts brought in Slim Man, who with Little Mustache joined Hashkéneinii in jail at Fort Wingate.[33] The effectiveness of the scouts was apparent since, according to Bowman, the "troops move so slowly that it is much easier to accomplish arrests with the scouts when the opposition is not too strong."[34]

It became too strong when the Ute and Paiute faction, prominent in southeastern Utah conflicts, entered the ring. Fresh from giving the cavalry from Fort Lewis a drubbing in July at the Soldier Crossing fight, these warriors with their families fell into their normal pattern of fight-and-flight-then-disperse, some making their way to Navajo Mountain. The Utes "took charge" of Hashkéneinii Biye', promising to protect him. Bowman headed north with ten scouts, where he rendezvoused with forty soldiers of Troop K, 6th Cavalry under First Lieutenant H. P. Kingsbury from Fort Wingate. On August 14 the agent met with five hundred Navajos at Thomas V. Keam's trading post in Keams Canyon, Arizona, then moved toward Navajo Mountain.[35]

Kingsbury provides a detailed report of his involvement.[36] Having traveled 122 miles from Fort Wingate to Keams Canyon in three days, the officer learned that Hashkéneinii Biye' was camped with a band of Utes that had twelve men, while two other groups nearby composed a total complement of thirty-two warriors. The next day, August 19, in company with Bowman and his scouts, the lieutenant traveled thirty-eight miles over a very rough and indistinct trail; another day of travel covered thirty-five miles with little water available; after a few hours rest, the command mounted at midnight and rode until daybreak. Kingsbury struck the reported camp only to find that the Utes had fled a few hours previous, scattering into the desolate canyon country.

Kingsbury backtracked twelve miles to meet with his pack train, then established camp near the foot of Navajo Mountain for the next three days while Bowman secured Walcott's remains, later to be buried at Fort Wingate. He also tried unsuccessfully to acquire any stock belonging to the murderers, only to find the animals had been "run out of the country and up into the mountains." Efforts to find McNally's body proved fruitless, since only the guilty knew where it was. According to one Navajo account, McNally made it "close to Kayenta," where he was caught and killed.[37] As Bowman continued with his duties, the lieutenant had time to ponder his failure. In his mind it was easily explained: "The reason I did not surprise the Utes is plain: the Navajos were cowards and politicians; being afraid of the Utes they did not want them killed for protecting the murderer; they were afraid the Utes would retaliate on them; they therefore kept the Utes posted every night as to my whereabouts; they persistently lied about distance; they were spies the entire route."[38]

After the soldiers spent three days in this encampment, they took five more returning to Fort Defiance, then two more on the way to Fort Wingate, arriving on September 1. This completed a round-trip excursion of 359 miles.[39] In Kingsbury's concluding remarks of his report, he commented that he would need one hundred mounted men and thirty days to "run the Utes, who are protecting the murderer, to ground . . . [and that] the Navajos should be given to understand that condign punishment would follow treachery and tale bearing, and it should be meted out to the first caught going ahead of the marching column."[40] This was not to be. Hashkéneinii Biye' remained at large, the government released his father and the other prisoners after about a year, McNally's body remained where it fell, and the military moved on to other pressing problems. One of the bright spots in the entire affair was the role played by the Navajo scouts. Many of the eyewitness accounts stress the difficulty of the sinuous canyon country terrain, the lack of water, and the necessity of trying to get ahead of a well-informed enemy. As in the Apache wars, the logistical trains, the slow-moving cavalry, and the ability to get misrouted were problems all too apparent for the military. Navajo scouts kept the operation on a solid path.

Fast-forward thirteen years to a time when the army would soon end using Navajo scouts. Significant changes had already occurred as the military mission of fighting and controlling Indians in the Southwest had all but ended. Indeed, this last example is often touted as the final conflict between white men and Indians in which a cavalry charge as part of a battle occurred in the United States. Control in Indian relations had now shifted more to the agents who had a significant police force to keep the peace on their respective reservation. In this case, Agent William T. Shelton established the Shiprock Agency for the northern part of the reservation in 1903. Known for being a strict disciplinarian, staunch Christian, and a progressive reformer, he turned the Northern Navajo Agency into a model of his contemporary values by controlling gambling, forbidding consumption of alcohol, establishing an exemplary school, teaching economic independence and scientific improvement, and propagating other progressive values of this era. To enforce these ideas, there were the agency police.[41]

Many Navajo people appreciated the opportunities he offered, but there were also those who did not. One of these was a powerful medicine man named Ba'álílee, who fought against every change Shelton implemented, reveled in conflict, and had amassed a following of disciples who remained close to his camp on the San Juan River near Aneth, Utah. Ba'álílee had been a thorn in Shelton's side from the beginning and sought every opportunity to resist on any level. The agent, on the other hand, was no admirer of the old medicine man and saw him as a relic of the past that needed to be controlled. Confrontation followed confrontation until finally Shelton removed his velvet gloves. Realizing that his Navajo police force was woefully outnumbered and unprepared for a real fight, the agent fired off a letter to the commissioner of Indian affairs requesting two troops of cavalry to either arrest Ba'álílee or remain in the vicinity of his camp to suppress his activities. He even suggested the soldiers come from Fort Wingate, New Mexico, 150 miles away, because the roads were excellent, hay could be delivered to Aneth at fifteen dollars a ton, and more importantly, no advance warning of troop movements would be communicated. That was Shelton's recommendation in a letter dated September 18; by October 15, the commissioner of Indian affairs, the secretary of war, the regional commanding general, and the commander of Fort Wingate had signed off on the plan. At 8 a.m., October 22, 1907, Captain Harry O. Williard with Troops I and K of the 5th Cavalry began their ride to southern Utah.[42]

Williard's force, comprising four officers, seventy-four enlisted men, a surgeon with two medics, and three Indian scouts, arrived at Shiprock four days later. What would have been a larger number of scouts had diminished because they were being phased out with the hope that the Navajo police could fill the void. The next morning, October 27, the soldiers moved again, fearing that word would spread among the Navajos that a military force was present. Shelton and Williard devised a plan that capitalized on speed of movement, secrecy, and a night march to decrease the probability of detection. Shelton let slip a rumor for the Navajos that the troops were in the area to control the unruly Utes and Paiutes in Bluff, masking the real intent.[43] Whether it was the Navajo scouts or police who spread the word is not indicated in the official report, but whoever it was could not raise suspicion. All excess baggage remained at the agency. The quartermaster issued each man one hundred rounds of rifle ammunition and twenty rounds for his revolver. Wagons loaded with six days of rations and additional equipment rumbled toward their first stop at the Four Corners Trading Post, estimated by Williard as thirty-two miles distant.[44] The cavalry accompanied them on the first leg of the journey.

Ba'álílee's camp was large, with relatives living in or near his home. He enjoyed a log and a stone house as well as a number of hogans and a "medicine lodge" next to his fields that were serviced by an irrigation ditch. Around his camp, and sectioning off parts within, was a heavy log fence that kept his livestock out of the gardens, confining them to the corrals where they belonged.

Shelton, all his police, and a contingent of Navajo leaders reached the Four Corners Trading Post an hour before the military force arrived. In the interim, Shelton secured any local Navajos who came to the store, preventing them from leaving before 11 a.m. the next day. Security and surprise were paramount. Among those detained was Sis-co, one of Ba'álílee's followers and a persistent troublemaker.[45] He remained in custody and eventually joined the group sent to jail. Shelton ate lunch, then moved on to Aneth to determine the exact location of Ba'álílee. He would inform Williard of the medicine man's presence, but if he did not, the soldiers were to proceed on their own. The captain arrived at the post in the afternoon, shortly after Shelton departed. Williard, learning about the situation, felt that a night march offered the greatest chance of surprise, and that a direct assault rather than a diversion through Aneth would net the best results.

At 1:30 a.m. on October 28, the command awakened its soldiers, who ate a hurried breakfast, quietly saddled their horses, and started down the road an hour later under the light of a half moon. Navajo police, scouts, and headmen took the lead. The logistical trains remained behind with orders to break camp in the light of day and move to Aneth. The cavalry horses trotted rapidly over the fourteen miles to a spot where the San Juan River was fordable.[46] Known as "Soldier/Police Move Across" (Siláo Ha'naa Nínínú), this place was still some distance from Ba'álílee's camp, but was inhabited by a number of Navajo families. The horses' pace quickened once

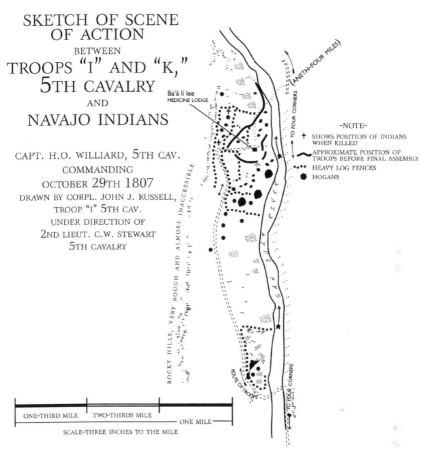

SKETCH OF SCENE
OF ACTION
BETWEEN
TROOPS "I" AND "K,"
5TH CAVALRY
AND
NAVAJO INDIANS

CAPT. H.O. WILLIARD, 5TH CAV.
COMMANDING
OCTOBER 29TH 1807
DRAWN BY CORPL. JOHN J. RUSSELL,
TROOP "I" 5TH CAV.
UNDER DIRECTION OF
2ND LIEUT. C.W. STEWART
5TH CAVALRY

Ba'á lí lee
MEDICINE LODGE

-NOTE-
+  SHOWS POSITION OF INDIANS
   WHEN KILLED
   APPROXIMATE POSITION OF
   TROOPS BEFORE FINAL ASSEMBLY
   HEAVY LOG FENCES
●  HOGANS

ONE-THIRD MILE    TWO-THIRDS MILE
                        — ONE MILE —
SCALE-THREE INCHES TO THE MILE

*This sketch map was drawn the day after the battle. (Courtesy of Utah State Historical Society)*

across, the troopers pressed forward, and a half mile from the objective, the formation fanned out to surround Ba'álílee's hogan.

Dawn was breaking when Williard, Navajo interpreter Robert Martin, and some of the soldiers rushed inside the hogan. Ba'álílee and two other men stumbled to their feet. A scuffle ensued with increasing numbers of soldiers piling into the fray. Several women, a child, and a sick man avoided involvement, but in Williard's words, "The Indians strenuously resisted arrest and capture to such a degree that it was necessary to use considerable force before they were overcome, secured, and handcuffed."[47] By now people in the community were gathering. Surrounded by relatives'

*Ba'álílee, living near Aneth, Utah, was a powerful medicine man who confronted the U.S. military and a few Navajo scouts before being arrested and imprisoned. At this point, the scouting program was phasing out with agency police from Shiprock, New Mexico, assuming many of the duties. (Courtesy of Utah State Historical Society)*

camps, Ba'álílee was sure to draw assistance. Some came with weapons, others armed only with curiosity, but Williard took no chances; he arrested everyone and "all resisted." Finding eight hogans in Ba'álílee's camp alone, with other Navajo homes spread over a larger area than he had planned, the captain directed Martin, the Indian police, and Troop I to secure the more distant parts of the objective. Within minutes gunfire erupted in their direction. Little Warrior (Naabaahii Yázhí), also known as "Smarty," Ba'álílee's son-in-law, opened fire and received a shot through the torso. Although the soldiers dressed his wounds, by noon the next day, he was dead.[48] A detachment from Troop K spurred their horses toward the sound of firing, followed in a short while by Williard, who had remained behind to ensure all the prisoners were secured. The shooting lasted for only a few more minutes, then silence. On his way to Troop I, the captain heard a cry for help and dispatched soldiers to investigate. They found the first sergeant afoot without his rifle, which had disappeared beneath his wounded horse shot out from under him. The Indian assailant, Little Wet One (Ditłéé'ii Yázhí), Ba'álílee's son-in-law, was out of range of the first sergeant's revolver. Another sergeant drew his rifle and shot the man in the head, killing him instantly.

Williard returned to ten prisoners he had secured, moved his force a half mile to a ford on the river, and sounded assembly. Following roll call, the officers reported that they had met resistance from some of Ba'álílee's followers, who had opened fire on the police, not noticing the approach of the soldiers. The fifteen-to-twenty-minute battle resulted in the death of Little Warrior, Ba'álílee's son-in-law, and the cessation of all opposition. The command crossed the river with its walking prisoners and by 7:30 a.m. arrived in Aneth. The soldiers established camp near the trading post, jailed the prisoners in a log house, purchased three sheep for lunch, and waited for the supply trains to arrive in the late afternoon. Two days later, Shelton and Williard, with prisoners in tow, started the march back to the Shiprock Agency, and by November 12, Williard received orders to return to Fort Wingate with his prisoners. In December the prisoners continued on to Fort Huachuca, Arizona, to serve their imposed sentences.

The role of the scouts in this incident is instructive. Their small number and diminished presence in the record was in part due to the role that the Navajo police under Shelton's direction assumed. Little mention is made of their part in the fight, only that they were present, while the cavalry served as the hammer, a reversal of much of the fighting witnessed in the Apache wars. With interpreters, uniformed police, men familiar with the country, graveled roads to the objective, a trading post, and Navajo settlements along the way, as well as tailored logistical support, the old days of scouting had been squeezed to a close. In less than four years, the government disbanded the Navajo scouts.

A final footnote to this era and the type of service rendered by these scouts came a year later, when Lieutenant Colonel George H. Hunter, 5th Cavalry, took command of an expedition to the Four Corners area. Specifically, in addition to the Ba'álílee incident there had been Navajo unrest in the Black Mountains farther to the south; he was to conduct a military tour de force with four cavalry troops, a machine-gun platoon, and "detachments of Apache and Navajo Indian scouts."[49] How many were included in these detachments was not specified; however, they must have played a significant role due to the results. The expedition departed Fort Defiance on August 19, 1908, and made its way to Chinle, Arizona, where two more cavalry troops joined Hunter's command before moving on to Oljato. Drought conditions affecting accessibility of water and grass as well as poor road maintenance proved discouraging. By August 9, most of the leaders representing various Navajo communities within ninety miles of the John Wetherill trading post at Oljato had assembled and were prepared for a three-day conference. Two hundred attended. Topics such as establishment of a school and subagency, relations with white neighbors, subsistence methods, receipt of government agricultural equipment, livestock improvement, and range conditions were discussed. Later, four of the troops visited different areas—Navajo Mountain, Carrizo Mountains, Black Mountain, and Bluff along the San Juan River. All returned with area reports identifying population numbers, leaders and relationships, subsistence, location of water sources, trafficability of the area, and neighbor relations. By August 25, the members of the expedition had returned to Fort Wingate or were en route to their various duty stations. Much of their detailed information could not have been obtained without people who understood the language and culture of those interviewed. Most likely, Navajo scouts played a significant role in collecting what is now a snapshot of these northern communities at the turn of the century.

CHAPTER EIGHT

# "The Times, They Are A-Changin'"

Troop L and the Navajo Police

B y 1890 the Indian Wars were over. The final gasp—the massacre at Wounded Knee, South Dakota, in December of that year, provided one last graphic example of how different the Indian world was from that of the white man. The event was also a wake-up call for those who wished to help Native Americans get their feet solidly on the ground for the approaching twentieth century. Much of the Anglo population in the Trans-Mississippi West still had too many raw nerves and remembrances that conjured up past conflicts, but those in the East assumed a more sympathetic stance. As for the native peoples, many had reached the nadir of their existence—and from the white perspective—would soon be disappearing as a race. Stuck on reservations, many of them desolate, at the mercy of government handouts and crippling policies, suffering from cultural loss, and no clear plan for the future, many collapsed under the weight of their burdens.

The situation was ripe for change—an experiment that could shift the situation for good. The idea for a new approach emerged from the long history of American Indians as opponents who had lost their lands, a significant portion of their cultural heritage, and their ability for self-determination. The one point that most people inside and outside of the culture could agree upon was that Indians had been formidable foes on the battlefield and placed great emphasis on bravery and warrior ethics. Why not take these highly sought-after values and put them to use in the military establishment that wished to inculcate these same beliefs in its soldiers?

167

For three years from 1891 to 1894, the army enlisted men from various tribes to capitalize on these desirable traits. A number of excellent studies have analyzed its success and failures, but all agreed that this valiant experiment in change failed to accomplish its goals because of the large cultural gap between the two different ways of life.[1] A brief discussion of what happened is given here, focusing on "L" Troop, 2nd Cavalry, an all-Navajo unit, the only one of its kind. It also serves as a representative example of many of the other Indian companies stationed elsewhere. While this unit was separate from the Navajo scouts, there were many who joined for a number of reasons, and so it is included here as one of the elements that had an impact and became a change agent for those men.

## Troop L—Transforming Traditional Warriors

Three weeks before Wounded Knee, General Nelson A. Miles wrote to the secretary of war suggesting that the Indian nations had been mistreated and robbed of their inheritance and that the government should make amends in some way for the wrongs. From a less philanthropic vantage point, Miles suggested that the warrior ethics with which an Indian was raised could be made more productive by enlisting young men in the military as soldiers, alleviating the problem of having to quell their martial spirit while putting those values to work for the government.

> The savage cannot be converted into a civilized man in one generation. At least one entire generation must pass away before, under the process of education of youth, the Indian nature can be materially changed. . . . They are natural soldiers. There is in their mind no employment worthy of an Indian brave but that of a soldier. They eagerly enlist in the service of the United States as scouts under Army officers, and their efficiency as such has been proved on multiple occasions. Indeed, their fidelity in the service with troops has been so marked that they are relied upon almost implicitly. It is therefore proposed to enlist quite a large number of young Indian braves and educate them for service with regular troops. Indeed, treat them in all respects as soldiers.[2]

The idea soon caught on so that in the Trans-Mississippi West, the government recruited Native American men into all-Indian infantry companies ("I") or cavalry troops ("L") to work side by side with white sister units stationed at the same post. Each element would have a fifty-five-man limit and develop its own NCO leadership corps of four sergeants and four corporals. But until an Indian could be found with the English and math skills to handle the necessary paperwork demanded on a battalion and post-level, the first sergeant could be an Anglo. At least one white officer, usually a lieutenant, was in command. For instance, as Troop L at Fort Wingate began to build, Sergeant F. S. Hay transferred from a neighboring unit to serve as the ranking NCO with a higher pay grade since "it will take several years before a Navajo soldier of the troop will be found capable of undertaking the duties and responsibilities of this position."[3] The expanding force structure across the West added eight cavalry troops and nineteen infantry companies to the army. In Arizona, what this meant is two "I" companies composed of Apaches and Mojaves were assigned to the 9th and 10th Infantry, while an "L" Troop of Navajo soldiers became part of the 2nd Cavalry stationed at Fort Wingate. Those joining would initially receive thirteen dollars a month, as did their white counterparts, a clothing allowance, food and shelter, and canteen privileges—an opportunity that later created some issues.

At the same time, the number of scouts working with white units was drastically reduced from 1,000 to 150 authorized slots; in Arizona there were to be a total of 50 scouts to serve with military units at Fort Wingate and near San Carlos. This action had the express purpose of denying those who wanted to be scouts by pushing them into the full-time active-duty elements with men who had enlisted for five years through a regular army contract as opposed to the scouts' six-month contract. As Major General John M. Schofield, commanding general of the army, directed:

> One of the first steps to be taken should, doubtless be, to discharge all of the scouts who are not actually required for present service. Indeed, the law authorizing the employment of scouts contemplates their discharge when their services are no longer necessary as scouts, and it is only in an emergency requiring their services as scouts that the extraordinary pay allowed to them, including that for their horses, could be justifiable. When the Indians find that only a very small number of them can be employed as scouts, the others will be more inclined to accept what ought to be to them very satisfactory compensation—that of a cavalry soldier.[4]

The two types of service were to be reported separately.[5] According to historian Michael Tate, who has studied the Apache experience:

> Although a majority probably preferred duty as scouts, because it entailed less discipline and regimentation, they recognized that the regular army

offered a better future than they would find among the jobless on the reservation. The first Apache unit—Company I, Ninth Infantry—was organized on the San Carlos Reservation in Arizona. A second company would later be assigned to Fort Apache. It was mustered during mid-May [1891]. . . . After an initial practice march of over fifty miles with the Indian troops, Lt. Charles Dodge wrote to Secretary of War Redfield Proctor, that his Apache company was "as fine a set of young men as were ever recruited for the Army."[6]

The army outlined its expectations, most of which are not surprising given the normal procedures of an Anglo military unit. The officers in the Indian troop were to be energetic, patient, and sympathetic to their charges. They should also be free from extra post duties so that they could devote full attention to building their companies. Indian recruits should generally range in age from 18 to 25, but if exceptional, those up to 35 years of age who had served "honestly and faithfully as a scout could be enlisted. In general, full-blood Indians, being more faithful and obedient, will make the best soldiers, and not more than 10 or 15 percent of a company should be mixed bloods."[7] Not surprisingly, gambling and uncontrolled drinking was forbidden, only a limited number of dependents for married men were allowed to live on post, and strict adherence to cleanliness, dress uniformity, and maintenance of equipment followed army guidelines. For those in cavalry units, the larger "American" horse was to be issued in place of the Indian pony with no daily reimbursement as the scouts received for using their own horses. For many Indians, because of their slighter stature, this created some problems in controlling the larger mounts.

Each candidate received a strict, standard medical examination to eliminate those with health issues. There were exceptions. A Navajo named Chiquito, who had served three years as a scout, attempted to enlist in L Troop 2nd Cavalry but was declined because of a heart problem. His past record portrayed him as an active scout and an excellent soldier with no sickness. Even with his previous commander strongly recommending him, his application went through seven levels of endorsement, each one denying his enlistment, until it reached Washington and General Schofield, who gave his approval, overriding the previous subordinates.[8] Other Indians had no such problems and filled the open ranks quickly so that by May 26, 1891, Troop L, 2nd Cavalry at Wingate and I Company, 9th Infantry stationed at Whipple Barracks were filled with Navajo and Apache soldiers respectively, meeting the Arizona quota.

*The U.S. military recruited heavily from the Navajo scout program. Navajos joining an L Troop received a standard physical exam before enlisting, as did this Anglo soldier from K Troop, 4th Cavalry, Fort Wingate. Intercultural communication, however, proved more challenging than the physical requirements. (Courtesy of Palace of the Governors Photo Archive, New Mexico History Museum, #086944)*

What were these new enlistees like? From the start, a few significant problems emerged, one of the main ones being language. Lieutenant C. B. Hoppin, commander of the newly formed L Troop at Fort Wingate noted, "When enlisted, but very few of these Indians could talk any English. A few could understand the general meaning of some sentences if short, but none were proficient in understanding or speaking the language. They could not count in English nor did they know the meaning of left and right. In fact, they were unable to understand anything that was told them collectively, but if taken separately and great care was used in explaining graphically, there were several who could understand fairly well."[9] The manual of arms, marching and facing movements, and other activities taken from the *School of the Soldier* were drilled for two months. Learning how to keep in step was particularly challenging, but they were "quick to imitate and anxious to learn." Most soldiers were involved in fatigue (post maintenance) duty, while others worked at becoming blacksmiths, cooks, and saddlers. The number of married men with dependents on post increased to 37 out of 55, but only ten families received quarters from the military. The army did not pay for feeding and caring for these dependents while enlisted pay did not meet the needs of family expenses. Consequently, prostitution became an increasing problem. Along with this vice came alcohol, accompanied with permission from the military that all soldiers could drink at the post canteen. Many commanders on the ground wished to see this privilege curtailed with no access to alcohol, but the regulations were clear that all soldiers could drink. Eventually, local commanders received authority to close the spigot, but there were those as well as enlisted men who continued to supply some Indians with beverage.

Troop L's muster roll paints a brief picture of the men's activities at Fort Wingate. Continuous fatigue duty and various types of drill, both mounted and dismounted, gave way to entries like this: "2nd Lt. B. B. Wallace and 24 men Troop L, 2nd Cavalry fully armed and equipped with 27 horses and pack mules, left Ft. W. on the 12th day of May 1892 with the Navajo Commission under command of Brigadier General Cook, commanding the Department of Arizona for the Carrizo Mts., establishing a courier line between Ft. W. and the camp of the Navajo Commission near the Carrizo Mountains." Another example: "The troop consisted of 39 enlisted men (Navajo Indians) with 4 men attached and 50 horses properly armed and equipped, commanded by 1st Lt. L. H. Brett left Ft. W. Sept. 6, 1892 for camp of instruction, Camp Duane, N.M. Instruction was imparted in internal post duty, advance and rearguard reconnoitering, and screening—70 miles."[10]

On December 31, 1891, L Troop received its first official evaluation from Major Theodore Schwan, assistant adjutant general from Fort Meade, South Dakota. He observed that the fifty-four full-blooded Navajos in the unit were

> very fair in their appearance and would have been good but for the fact that a part of them wore their hair quite long. Having refused to enlist if not allowed to retain their long hair, Lieutenant Hoppin, rather than see the scheme of raising a Navajo troop defeated, agreed that they should not be compelled to part with it; but yielding to inducements, such as full dress, that were offered to those who should voluntarily do so, quite a number have had their hair cut short, and it is believed that the others will soon follow the example thus set them.[11]

Otherwise, the men looked as good as those found in any other Indian unit. Not so, however, with the equipment they had been issued, when compared with that of the other elements stationed at Wingate. Schwan felt that equality should be enforced.

Further inspection netted additional irregularities. The issue of Indian ponies versus the larger "American" horse was addressed through attrition—as the smaller animals became no longer serviceable; they were to be replaced with the larger size. By December the Navajos moved out of their canvas tents and into wooden barracks, while ten homes for dependent family members had also been constructed. These became magnets for Navajo visitors coming from the reservation, with large numbers descending for social and family activity. To the white community that did not understand the importance of Navajo relationships or cultural practices like maintaining long hair for religious purposes, these types of issues were noteworthy. The mess hall served good and adequate food, but there was a separate dining facility for a half dozen white soldiers who had been attached to assist L Troop. They were now directed to either eat at the company mess or go back to their parent unit.

On a more positive note, four Navajo corporals and two sergeants performed their duties well, while the two assigned officers received accolades for their dedication.

> No two officers could have been selected for service with this body of young Indians, who are better calculated than Lieutenants Hoppin and [R. B.] Wallace to make a fine cavalry troop of it. They are not only willing to put forth every effort to accomplish this end, but they are confident that their efforts will be attended with complete success. They are proud of their men and believe that they possess high soldierly qualities. They have also an implicit faith in the effectiveness of the Army as a civilizing instrumentality, and believe that when relegated to their tribe, their men will be far better fitted than heretofore to grapple with the problems that confront the Indian.[12]

There was no issue with serving alcohol to Indians at the canteen, very little gambling, and a lower number of those attending sick call than those found in white and black companies serving at the same post. Both troop officers testified to the "obedience and loyalty of their men, who are very particular in the observance of military courtesies."[13]

The biggest issue, bar none, was that of communication. Indeed, this was one of the major factors for the eventual abandoning of the all-Indian-unit-experiment throughout the West. Schwan, who had worked with the Sioux and the Crows, felt that they were far more proficient in education and the English language than the Navajos. This was not a comment on their intelligence, which this officer felt was comparable to that of the white man, but rather the depth to which Navajo culture was still rooted. "When the organization of the Navajo troop had been completed, it was found that none spoke English fluently or sufficiently to act as interpreter, although one man could make himself understood without difficulty and three or four others knew a few words and phrases. Since their enlistment some 30 members of the troop have been daily instructed in the English names of things and subjects pertaining to their duties, but no systematic effort to give them the rudiments of an English education has been made." Schwan went to the post commander, Colonel G. G. Huntt, 2nd Cavalry, and obtained permission for an hour-and-a-half class to be taught each weekday as part of all of the men's mandatory training. Both lieutenants were highly supportive, an enlisted man from another unit serving as the teacher and submitting special requisitions for school materials. By doing this, Schwan felt that the troop would be prepared for more advanced military training in the spring and that eventually "they will become leaders of their people in their march toward civilization."[14] This goal did not quite pan out as envisioned, but it did remain at the center of the conduct of this three-year experiment.

By the end of 1892, L Troop had filled its quota of four sergeants and four corporals, none of whom could read and write enough to work as first sergeant. There were two enlisted men—Sergeant William Fleming and Private Henry Blank on temporary duty—assigned to work with L Troop. Blank served as a teacher and knew the names and disposition of all of his students. He received a field promotion to sergeant, then was given the responsibility not only of teaching but also of being the first sergeant of the troop with all of its administrative duties. Eighteen months later, Blank was still hard at work and obtaining success. According to his commander, Colonel Huntt, "It is doubtful whether a private could be found in this command who would take much interest in the instruction of these Indians and it is therefore thought best to ask for the detail of Sergeant Blank, who has always manifested a great deal of interest in these Indians and met with considerable success in their instruction."[15]

There was every indication that the enlistment of Navajos in L Troop, 2nd Cavalry was an ongoing success. Two years after the unit had achieved 100 percent strength, it still maintained 46 committed soldiers with losses over this period coming from discharge (9), death (1), and desertion (2).[16] The report that accompanied these statistics stated that "the enlisted Indians of the Navajo Tribe offer every encouragement to the continuance of this policy. . . . The conditions of the military service are now well understood by them and the benefits to be derived from service are sufficiently recognized by them as furnished all recruits which may be needed." The younger enlistees between eighteen and twenty-one were particularly desirable because they were more "conservative, free from any rooted evil practices and more receptive." At no time was there any problem with disobedience or insubordination but only "faithful service in a very commendable manner." For some there was the issue of off-duty drinking, but fines that withdrew money from the monthly paycheck seemed to have a positive impact on curtailing this activity. L Troop had worked with all of the other elements stationed at Fort Wingate and "have received and absorbed intelligently the same instruction in minor tactics as the white troops. . . . In their military instruction, they compare favorably with any organization at this post and perform all manual labor required of them cheerfully. They are by no means free from those traits of character which are kept alive by the presence of the worthless Indians who hang around the military post. . . . The reservation influences are demoralizing; they should be where there are no other Indians about them."[17] Still, the final report concluded that all that had been accomplished should be hailed as a success and that the program, with a few slight modifications, should continue.

There was, however, another side to this coin. Major General Schofield, in his annual report on the army, had a different perspective as he viewed what had been eight cavalry troops and nineteen Indian infantry companies. In terms of recruitment, the first year of 1891 had brought in a total of 417, the next year had reached a peak of 780, and the current year had only 547.[18] At the time of his report, October 1, 1894, there were only six Indian troops and four infantry companies still in existence. While trying to keep a stiff upper lip by declaring that the program of recruitment had met its larger objective to "demonstrate the present and prospective value for military purposes of several Indian tribes," once he got down to the details, he did not run short of reasons for its failure. "Lack of knowledge of the English language, restlessness and discontent under absolutely new conditions of life and habits, marriage, demoralization when stationed near Indian reservations, are among the causes which have interfered to prevent the Indian from becoming a valuable American soldier. As the object for which these enlistments were authorized has been fully accomplished, I am of the opinion that further attempts to incorporate Indians as a part of the Army will neither benefit them nor the service."[19] An accompanying report rendered by Brigadier General A. M'D. M'Cook, who commanded the Department of the Colorado, which encompassed the State of Colorado and territories of Utah, Arizona, and New Mexico, noted that all of the L troops and I Companies within his jurisdiction were gone, with the exception of the one serving with the 2nd Cavalry at Wingate.[20]

While this unit maintained a suitable number of enlistees, there were those Navajos who either saw other units failing or for some personal reason decided to get out. Many asked for their discharge in accordance with General Orders Number 80, Series 1890, which allowed those who had enlisted for five years to be released without completing that commitment. For Huntt at Fort Wingate, the question remained: Should recruitment of new soldiers take place or would the program die a natural death through attrition? He needed direction if he were to save the floundering effort at his post, assuming the army wanted to continue the experiment. In a month and a half, the answer arrived. There was to be no more recruiting until the dust had settled, and those seeking discharge should be allowed to do so, and in the meantime, they would wait and see what developed.[21]

Criticism arose. Colonel Huntt felt that the service of the Navajo troops did not have much value at Fort Wingate because if they were called out to quell local problems, they would have trouble operating against their people. Navajo police on the reservation could handle any of those issues, and so the better thing to do with L Troop was to reassign it to Fort Huachuca, where it could solve problems with different Indian people. Another officer felt that a lot of the issues on post could be handled if the soldiers moved to a place where friends and relatives were not around to bother or influence them. Language was another concern. "The chief objection to the deployment of Indians as soldiers is their dislike to speak the English language. Indians never like to be laughed at and as they are very liable to make ridiculous blunders in any effort to speak English, they persist in using their native tongue, so that they may shift blunders to other shoulders than their own."[22] Interpreters, on the other hand, increased the soldiers' proficiency, but also became a crutch in learning English. So much of the official business between the first sergeant and the other enlisted men required an interpreter that a lot of time was wasted.[23] Language continued to be a huge barrier. Seven months later, enlisted strength was down to twenty-nine people, as well as three American mounts and fifty-four Navajo ponies. Even the horses raised controversy.

The final word came to First Lieutenant Hoppin when he requested assistance in identifying horses for his L Troop command. Although he was down to twenty-eight men, he reported that there were "ten now and a considerable number of desirable men ready and waiting to enlist." Should he proceed in enlisting men and obtaining more horses or were discharges and transfers in the wind? The answer was short but not sweet. "This troop has not been of much, if any, value to the government, and therefore its continuance in the service and further recruitment is not approved by the Major General Commanding who desires the papers to be placed before the Secretary of War with the recommendation that the twenty-eight men remaining in the troop be discharged from the service."[24] On November 13, 1894, it became official through Special Order No. 267. All remaining soldiers were discharged and sent home.

The official enlistment of five years was shortened to three so that each soldier could complete a full term of service. The last L Troop to be decommissioned was in the 7th Cavalry at Fort Sill, Oklahoma, in May 1897.[25]

The experiment had ended. A lot had been learned by both cultures, but the barriers between the two appeared insurmountable—at least from the official point of view. On the Lieutenant Hoppin level, there was great hope and satisfaction in the success he had achieved. The respect and loyalty he earned over the years came from the patience he fostered and the cultural understanding he obtained. Although he did not leave much of a paper trail, the correspondence that we do have seems to paint a picture of a commander devoted to his troops with his men responding. The real issue for most of the army was its lack of understanding and acceptance of Indian ways. In the case of the Navajos, there was some leeway—not having to cut their hair, which was tied into deep religious beliefs connected with spiritual identity. The constant flow of family and friends on post to visit was another cultural trait that went deep into Navajo relationships, which from their perspective was all-encompassing. They were at the core of understanding how life interacts with both animate and inanimate beings. Language was a central value, something the Navajos obtained from the holy people. While learning an additional language was seen as beneficial—in fact often considered a strength—entirely giving up the daily use of their mother tongue went against Navajo beliefs, and it required a thoroughly different way of viewing and acting in the physical world. Little wonder that for those who had not made this leap but were fortunate enough to have remained as scouts, there was a far more comfortable cultural fit.

## Scouts as Policemen—The Early Years

A second institution where Navajo scouts released from duty could find employment was the Navajo police force, whose origin in the early 1870s has already been discussed. This organization's growth and development has its own story, separate from that of the scouts. As the influence of the military lessened on the reservation, the role of the police increased and took over some of the tasks that scouts had performed when a heavier hand backed by government troops was necessary. The early police force originated in the Fort Defiance area, where the first Navajo Agency began. Law enforcement emanated from this corner of the reservation; however, as reservation lands expanded through presidential executive orders and congressional legislation, the necessity of having a larger mobile force grew. As time progressed, the reservation became so large in size, with an ever-expanding population, that a series of subagencies arose, each with its own police force. Subject to the rise and fall of congressional appropriations, the number of law enforcement officers ranged from two or three individuals to a force of twenty, depending on the need of the specific agency.

The selection of who could serve as a policeman in the early days was left to the whim of the agent. He looked for men who were respected in their community, accepted the government programs meant to further the welfare of the Navajos as they transitioned into the dominant culture, obeyed orders that often brought them into confrontation with their own people, and fostered the ability to interface with white men surrounding the edges of the reservation. Some of the tasks that fell in the domain of the scouts and many others that were new to an evolving situation became part of their job description. This included returning pilfered livestock; bringing in thieves and murderers; quelling confrontations with people who opposed government programs like sheep dipping and later livestock reduction; interdicting bootlegging operations; enforcing mandatory school attendance for children with resisting parents; supporting the agent's rules concerning cultural issues such as witchcraft, polygamy, and child marriages; and siding with the government when controversy arose. This was a tall order for most Navajo men who were invested in their culture and community, had little or no training in law enforcement, and received paltry pay for their efforts.

As time progressed, conditions changed, but the early years were rough. A few agents' evaluations paint a bleak picture. Agent D. M. Riordan in 1883 bemoaned:

> I have had no police. Navajos cannot be had for any such sum as $5 a month. The right to fix the pay of police should be vested in the Secretary of the Interior, and not be arbitrarily named by men who have no conception of the duties required. I have had to go after red horse thieves and white; to remove unlawful traders from the reserve; to recover stolen

stock; to chase criminals; and to do it all myself—be agent, clerk, chief of police, an entire force, hostler, courier, everything, to be able to cope with single-handed, and to wisely treat all questions arising between 17,000 Indians and their white neighbors; and to personally watch over and guard every item of government property at the agency.[26]

Eight years later, things had improved. Pay was higher, the Apache wars had ended, and Troop L recruitment accompanied by scout downsizing released partly trained Navajo men into their communities. No doubt some of the Navajos who had found employment as scouts were now joining the police force, bringing their previous experience and orientation to the task. Agent David L. Shipley noted, "The services of the Indian police have, I believe, generally given satisfaction, having proved very valuable in a number of instances. I think the presence of a well-organized police force has a very good effect upon these people, serving to discourage misconduct which, without the lawful force to bear upon it, would finally produce discord."[27] That was in 1891. Not until 1934 did the Navajo Nation totally reorganize its pan-tribal police force, comprising thirty young men who were FBI trained and riding horses provided by the government. Even with this more standardized force, the number of policemen fluctuated with funding cycles, descending to as low as fifteen officers.

How much of this trend toward improvement can be credited to released Navajo scouts or L Troop participants is difficult to determine. Alfred W. Yazzie, himself a twenty-year veteran of the Navajo police force (1953–74), names at least four men he knew that had served as scouts— Captain Belone, Curley Haired Policeman, White Haired Policeman, and John Daw. According to Yazzie:

> These men served as scouts for the United States cavalry as young men and proved themselves as brave, dependable, honest men. None of them had any formal schooling so they could not read, write, speak, or understand the English language except through an interpreter, but with their knowledge and abilities, they had proven themselves as good lawmen who could assume leadership at any time. . . . Several of these men were involved in the campaign against the Apaches while they were still serving as scouts. There were many other Navajo men who served as scouts and as Navajo police officers, but this was mostly on a short time basis.[28]

Charlie Mitchell was another person who served as both scout and policeman, and later, like many other former scouts, he became a community leader. He said about these formative experiences, "This is how I learned about the white man's law."[29]

Identifying those men who served as scouts and then transitioned to the police force is more than difficult. There are hints in some of the records that help make this connection, but it often required someone in the white community intimately familiar with the Navajo man and interested enough in an incident to identify the relationship. Take for instance Nakai John, whom Agent Albert H. Kneale referred to as both a tracker and policeman. Most likely the tracking title came from his work as a scout, although the agent was not specific enough. The incident that Nakai John participated in was of high interest and so made it into the newspapers, reports, and local oral history, thus preserving the actions of the scout. The episode started at a well-known trading post on the reservation.

A seasoned trader named Roswell Nelson began working at the Two Grey Hills store with his wife Mildred in 1927. As with most traders, his involvement in private and public events was expected. Thus it was not surprising that on September 25, he offered to give a tourist having car trouble a ride to Newcomb, about a half hour away. He was joined by the post's owner, Willis Martin, who was visiting their store with his wife on a Sunday afternoon. Around 7 p.m. Mildred Nelson answered a knock on the door from an unfamiliar Navajo man asking to buy hay. She wanted to wait until the men returned, but the Indian persisted, and so she relented, took the keys for the doors of both hay barns, and headed out in the gathering twilight. As she moved toward the most distant barn, the man picked up a single tree sitting on a nearby baler and struck her on the nape of the neck, knocking her unconscious. Next, he pulled her body closer to a pet bear the Nelsons kept, hoping the animal would be drawn to the blood, mutilate the body, and erase any signs of foul play. The Indian next returned to the post hoping to steal from it, but to his surprise found Mrs. Martin, newborn baby in arms, at the door. He asked where the men were and when he learned they would be there any minute, he mounted his horse and hastily fled.

For approximately a half hour, Mildred lay in the barnyard, while Mrs. Martin assumed that she was feeding the chickens. But when Roswell's headlights flashed upon the prostrate form of his wife in the dirt, he and the Martins went into action. They sent for the government doctor, J. D. Kennedy, stationed at Toadlena. The physician rendered what aid he could, then rode with the Nelsons to the hospital in Farmington, arriving at 7 a.m. Diagnosed with a fractured skull, Mildred required three weeks of bed rest before she returned to her duties at Two Grey Hills. In the meantime, the Navajos in the community were incensed at the misdeed of the thief, later identified as Juan Cavallero, who hailed from around Crystal, New Mexico. Agent Kneale dispatched Navajo tracker and policeman Nakai John, who followed the fleeing culprit over the Lukachukai Mountains. The trail was difficult to trace because it ascended rocky and mountainous terrain, crossed extensive beds of pine needles, and had been trampled by the hooves of a herd of horses the assailant drove before him to cover the tracks. Still, not only was John able to pursue him, but he even determined that he had changed horses along the way without dismounting. The policeman's efforts eventually paid off; he captured the criminal in Gallup and brought him back to Shiprock. The court determined that Cavallero was mentally unstable, and so he received a short sentence in a federal penitentiary and was soon released.[30]

When the *Farmington Times Hustler* published the initial story of the attack on Mrs. Nelson, there was a short paragraph at the end of the piece referencing another side of law enforcement that was very much a part of the Navajo experience. In this instance, a medicine man named Hastiin Klah visited the Newcombs, who were traders at the nearby Nava Post (later renamed Newcomb), and ceremonially diagnosed through divination (type unspecified) what had happened in the attack and what the future outcome would be. Klah predicted "that Wednesday night Mrs. Nelson would get much better and that Thursday the criminal's 'hands would be tied' meaning that he would be captured. Mrs. Nelson did get much better on Wednesday night, even though all that day her recovery was much in doubt and at this writing (Thursday evening) we do not know if the would-be-murderer has been captured or not."[31] Later, Agent Kneale filled in the details. Klah went to the agent on Wednesday afternoon, and after telling of Mildred's anticipated recovery said, "My medicine also tells me that your policeman will overtake the would-be murderer tonight and tomorrow morning you will have him safely lodged in jail."[32] The next morning, Nakai John sat in the agent's office with prisoner in hand. The tracking skills, so prevalent during the Apache wars, were still relevant forty years after Geronimo surrendered.

## John Daw—Paramount Tracker

There is no other Navajo who has gained more fame as both a scout and a policeman than John Daw. A number of reasons assured this renown. Often recognized as the "last Navajo scout," dying in 1965 at the age of ninety-seven, he was among the first to enlist in L Troop at Fort Wingate and among the last twenty-six men to be discharged when that experiment ended. In Special Orders No. 267, issued on November 13, 1894, he is listed as one of two trumpeters being released. According to his oral testimony, he had previously served five years as a scout working against the Apaches. It was during this time that he received the name of "Big Policeman" (Silaoo Tsoh—Big Policeman/Soldier). He remembered, "When I was with the scouts, we fought the Apaches with the Army on the other side of Mogollon Baldy. Many scouts lost their lives there. At the time the Navajos were at Fort Wingate, some Apaches came in and said that just a few warriors were doing all of the killing."[33]

In 1905 Daw assumed his duties as a policeman in the Tuba City/ Western Agency area and established his home near the Red Lake Trading Post. His duties took him over a large geographical region that included the Navajo Mountain territory. Traders, entrepreneurs, and brothers Hubert, Cecil, and Gladwell Richardson, with their father S. I., wished to capitalize on guided tours to Rainbow Bridge, a large stone arch that was a Navajo sacred site as well as an awe-inspiring natural wonder near the mountain. To access it, an old Ute war trail threaded its way through the high plateau canyon system, but at this point in 1923, few people remembered it and no one had developed the possibility. Daw, however, who had been throughout the area, offered to guide the Richardsons and assist in building a road suitable for pack animals and automobiles alike. He agreed to lead the road construction crew to the foot of Navajo Mountain, but from there he would let the Richardsons explore a route to a site with enough water to support the operation of a lodge and the tourist business that it would attract. Incidents along the way reveal this Navajo's personality.

Briefly, there were other traders—John Wetherill and Clyde Colville, in particular, from the Kayenta area—who wanted to maintain a monopoly on their trading and touring business, so they hired local Navajos to threaten, cajole, and if necessary, stop by force the construction of this road.[34] The Richardsons hired Daw and a crew of Navajos to help with the building of the dirt pathway, but eventually all but the old scout were scared away, with only S. I. and Cecil remaining with him. A lone messenger from the opposition warned that if the men did not stop their labor, they would be killed. According to Gladwell Richardson, Daw told his two white companions what had been said, then alone went to where forty of these protesters had gathered, only to learn that they were planning to attack the next day, kill the road builders, destroy their equipment, and fulfill their agreement with Wetherill. When they arrived, "John Daw remained alone on a new stretch of road—S. I. and Cecil, by prearrangement,

*John Daw—scout, L Troop soldier, and policeman, epitomized the skills and tenacity of Navajo military and civilian service. Known to many as an expert tracker, he was able to read events left at a scene or follow a trail by studying the slightest variations he discovered. This picture was taken in Tuba City, Arizona, 1919. (Courtesy of Cline Library, Northern Arizona University, NAU. PH 516.116)*

had dropped down behind some cover, wide apart, where rifles and six-guns were hidden for emergency use. The leaders eventually expended their wild talk, whereupon Daw picked up a stout cudgel, informing them, 'If you have come to fight, get down off your horses and let us get to it. If you have not come to fight, then go, for we have this road to build!'"[35] He continued to berate them for foolishly becoming involved in this white man business.

Each succeeding night, enemy Navajos prowled about the camp, their activities recorded in their tracks and signs left behind for the morning light. At one point when S. I. was separated from his party, a number of his opponents descended upon him and began to beat him with fists, rocks, and clubs until Daw and Cecil arrived to break up the melee and send the enemy packing. Exploding sticks of dynamite later served as a suitable chaser. A shortage of supplies created another problem, and although Daw was able to find a local Navajo interested in selling food, the entrepreneur was soon run off. More verbal clashes followed, but additional resources came in while local Navajo leaders heard about the confrontation with these Navajos from the Kayenta area and demanded that they leave and not return. Daw completed his assignment in guiding for this part of the journey and left future development of the road and the lodge to the Richardsons. His fearless determination to see the project through is best summarized when S. I. suggested that he may not want to go against his people in a showdown. His answer: "I finish what I start. Besides, these people are not so tough."[36]

One of the best examples of this man using his scouting abilities of tracking, unearthing evidence, deductive and inductive reasoning, and familiarity with the land and its people began in November 1937, when Tillman Hadley, chief of Navajo police in Tuba City, Arizona, contacted Daw. A lengthy article authored by Hadley gives a detailed accounting of the steps that he and his friend went through to apprehend a murderer.[37] An abbreviated account is given here, emphasizing how this retired Navajo scout used his skills successfully, boosting his already famous reputation as a tracker and policeman.

A number of law enforcement officials and community leaders had, along with Daw, been summoned to a crime scene in the desert outside of Tuba City. An old Anglo itinerant had been shot once in the neck with a .22-caliber rifle, his body dragged across an arroyo, and his few belongings, including his riding shoes, either stolen or left in the fork of a juniper tree. There was no identifying information as to who this individual was or who had committed the crime other than the murderer's footprints left in the sand beside the road and in the arroyo. Daw examined the narrow ribbon of road and determined that there were a half dozen cars and three riders on horseback that had passed over this section of sandy pathway on the afternoon of the shooting. He eliminated three of the cars and two of the horses as possibilities by studying the tracks. A coroner determined the time of death, and the FBI discovered the victim's identity—D. E. Pugh—as well as his earlier travel itinerary, but the real work of catching the murderer remained with the two Navajo policemen. Hadley explained:

> Then it was, that furnished with the approximate time Pugh died, John Daw figured out the deceased had been standing in a certain spot when a sedan coming from Kaibetoh trading post had also passed him; that two or three minutes later a truck going toward Kaibetoh had also passed him; that immediately behind this big truck appeared a man on a horse. Bearing in mind that before and after the appearance of the two machines and the rider, others had also traveled over the road, don't ask me how it was possible for John Daw to narrow the suspected list down to those three. Only John Daw, born and reared on the desert . . . could explain how he accomplished the feat. But he did so by careful deduction and, when eventually we had the slayer, his deductions were proven to be correct.[38]

The police and FBI were able to identify all three drivers of the vehicles and ruled them out as suspects, leaving a rider on horseback as the main target of the investigation. A month passed but no leads, even though the two Navajo policemen interviewed community members extensively. Then one day, as the two officers visited the Tonalea trading post seventeen miles distant from the crime scene, something caught Daw's eye. Near the concrete steps of the building in a section of windblown sand, the scout saw the footprint of the dead man's riding shoes. Realizing that no Navajo would wear a dead man's clothing, the officers entered the building to find many Indians but no suspect. They did, however, question those present and learned of a man riding a buckskin pinto in the vicinity of the murder, but who was too far away to identify. Two witnesses took Daw to the place where they had spotted this individual, allowing Daw to confirm that the horse tracks were identical to the ones found at the murder site. The policemen tried to backtrack, but the trail had been destroyed by a large flock of sheep passing over the prints. At least now he had a description of the guilty party's horse.

Further clues, derived through interviews, confirmed that a man who was half Paiute and half Navajo and had a criminal record was the most likely candidate as the murderer. A search of his hogan did not provide any evidence, he was wearing shoes that did not match either the murderer's or Pugh's footwear, and no one recalled him riding a buckskin pinto. In spite of the apparent dead end, Daw continued to investigate and learned that the man, Howard Balli Begay, once owned a pinto, had been seen with a .22-caliber rifle, and was in the area at the time of the murder. The old scout maintained a network of people who reported Begay's activities. In the spring of 1938, he appeared at sheepshearing time to claim livestock that was not his. A woman tried to stop him, receiving a beating with a rope for her efforts. That became the break in the case. She went to Daw, explained what happened, and added that he was the man the officer was looking for and that his wives knew all about the murder. That was enough for Daw. He confronted the two women about their husband's activities, and although they feared him, they lived with the hope that if he was sent off to jail for a second time, he could not hurt them. This was true for other members of the community who knew a lot more of what had happened than they had let on. A rumor reached Daw about some objects being buried in a sandhill, so he investigated. There he found a .22 rifle and Pugh's boots, whose heels and soles had been altered to throw off the tracker; as for the pinto, it had died a mysterious death. Borrowing a horse from a Navajo family, Daw set out to bring his man in. When night fell, he slept at a friend's hogan until 3 o'clock in the morning, when Begay showed up to turn himself in—for what he thought were the charges of beating the woman at the livestock corral. Instead, Daw informed him of the murder charges, secured him as a prisoner, and made the seventy-mile ride to the Tuba City Agency in record time without stopping for a break.

Once Begay learned that there were a number of witnesses ready to testify against him, he admitted to his crime. With this acknowledgment came a strong confirmation that all that Daw had determined by reading signs was correct. Daw's reputation preceded him so that when Begay learned that this particular law enforcement officer was on his trail, he knew that his time as a fugitive was limited. According to Begay:

Yes, I killed the white man. I saw him the day of November 21st. I rode to him on the road the next day. I followed him all afternoon, until about sundown when he went up the low red hills into the cedars. I heard a car coming, so I rode over behind some trees. Pretty soon that car went by, then a government truck passed. When it was gone, I went on up the road and came to the old white man. He stopped still and turned around to look at me. I made signs that I was going to kill him. He picked up a rock, motioning for me to go away. Then after I made more signs, the white man showed with his hands that, if I killed him, I would be hanged with a rope. He turned to go and when he did, I raised the rifle from the saddle where I had carried it, and shot him once in the back of the neck.[39]

Begay had hoped to get a lot of money, not just the seventeen dollars he was able to pull off the corpse. What he did receive, however, was a life sentence served at McNeil Island, Washington.

John Daw died in 1965 at the age of ninety-seven. With his passing went the memories of his service as a scout, as one of the last members of L Troop at Fort Wingate, and as a distinguished police officer famous for his tracking ability. Unfortunately, he also shared the fate of many Navajo scouts—that of dying in poverty. John, with his wife Jane, lived off a pension of less than $200 derived from his military and civil service. His windowless hogan near Tonalea boasted a metal stove, a small cot, some sheepskins that covered the sleeping area on the hard-packed dirt floor, and some shelves holding family possessions and implements needed for daily life. Still, there were no complaints from this aged, almost deaf veteran as he spoke of his former life. In his words, "My life has been pleasant, and I have settled here. I haven't been to any more places. I am old and can do no more. I just stay home. Even then, I am still useful as a medicine man when people ask for my help."[40] Six months later he died and was buried under a piñon tree near the Tonalea trading post.

# CHAPTER NINE

# Tracking the Trackers, Unearthing the Past

## S. F. Stacher and the Eastern Navajo Agency Experience

As Navajo scouts spent much of their time tracking the enemy, they found every sign an indicator of something that had happened—a shift in direction by the enemy or the condition of their horses, bent grass or a scrape on a bush, the remaining heat from an extinguished campfire, and the remnants of food eaten. All were part of a story that became woven together in an increasingly complete picture. Through inductive and deductive reasoning, eyewitness accounts, telltale remains, pattern analysis, an understanding of the enemy, and a host of other insights, the tracker pieced together what had occurred. These invaluable skills were in demand until 1911, when the scout program ended. For approximately fifteen years, the men and their experiences were forgotten, viewed by many as a relic from the past requiring skills no longer necessary for the increasingly sophisticated, modern army.

Yet there were those who remembered after World War I because of the contributions made by Native Americans who had been integrated into regular units. Some people became more aware of veterans in general and how they could be quickly forgotten with the cessation of hostilities. Still others sought to help an impoverished people, many of whom were living in the twilight of life. Previously, over 150 Navajo scouts alone had served in the Apache campaigns of 1885–86 and deserved recognition and assistance.[1] Whatever the reason, the Indian War Pension Act of March 4, 1917, covering 1859–91 and later expanded to 1896, recognized the Indians' prior service. It proved, however, to be inadequate in meeting their needs. By providing written proof of their military enlistment through War Department or Treasury Department records or muster rolls, the scouts became eligible for a pension, but little of the necessary documentation was readily available. The amount initially offered on a monthly basis was a scant twenty dollars; for those Navajo scout veterans still living, estimated at over ninety in number, they were unaware of how to access this help and improve their situation. The Eastern Agency at Crown Point, New Mexico, became the nexus of meeting their needs, thanks to Agent Samuel F. Stacher (1875–1952), who had worked in the Indian Service since 1903. This seasoned administrator in 1925 assumed the difficult task of helping the Navajo scouts receive a pension that officially increased in value in 1927 with passage of the Leatherwood Bill (H.R. 15532) and Smoot Bill (S. 4501). This legislation allowed a veteran at age 62 to obtain $30 per month, $40 at age 67, and $50 at 72, while those with service-related disabilities received $72 per month. Widows and children of a scout could also apply and receive benefits of $30 per month or $8 per month until the age of sixteen. The government also accepted, beyond written documents, statements from at least two witnesses with personal knowledge of the applicant's service or the scout's widow's circumstance. Stacher, in a sense, became a scout tracker. Working through the maze of government records, conducting numerous interviews, hunting down material witnesses, sifting through the information and misinformation that came across his desk, and piecing together evidence from past events, he devotedly went to work on behalf of these forgotten soldiers, extending a lifeline of hope to help many Navajo scouts and their relatives.[2]

## Tracking Scouts

Grasping this lifeline could be exhausting. A number of avenues were pursued, but the one depending on the white man's paperwork was tenuous at best. The process started with a man walking through the agency's door and declaring himself a scout, say in the 1885–86 Apache campaign. If the Navajo had a certificate of discharge in hand, the process moved forward, his identity or that of the scout's widow was confirmed, and the application for the claim was initiated. This was the ideal but not usual. Given the living circumstances on the reservation at this time with a person residing in a hogan, subject to the whims of nature, being unable to read, and unaccustomed to the Anglo world of paperwork—the chances of this document surviving were slim. Some of the explanations given by scouts as to what had happened to their certificate of discharge provide a sense of why not everyone could produce these important papers. For instance, one scout had his papers cut up and used to wrap tobacco for cigarettes, another had them used to start fires, another had his destroyed by his children, and another had them stolen. Scout Marianito testified, "I had it [the certificate] in the pocket of my pants and they were hanging in my hogan and while I was out with the horses, a big rain came and washed away the hogan and my pants and I never found the certificate."[3] Julio Francisco (Hólaa) kept his certificate of discharge in the pocket of his coat, which hung on his hogan wall. A gust of wind blew the coat into the fire, burning both it and the papers.[4]

Fortunately, by the mid-1920s, Navajo testimony given by confirmed scouts, as long as they were not relatives of the applicant, could be used to establish a candidate's eligibility. These statements were collected by Stacher and a government reviewer, in most instances at Crown Point by C. R. (Charles R.) Franks, and then verified through interviews as well as supporting records in Washington, D.C. Those who testified on behalf of the individual were, with a handful of exceptions, honest and exacting when testifying. If they were not sure or had negative knowledge, they were forthcoming in saying so. The scouts took pride in their accomplishments and were not about to cheapen their experience or word by falsely testifying. They were the best safeguard against those men and women who tried to commit fraud in attempting to obtain an unearned benefit.

Take for instance Tom, who applied for a pension. Three highly reputable scouts, each of whom had served in one of the three separate companies in 1885–86, testified that Tom had not been a scout, was known as Charley Yazza, and that the men he claimed to have served with denied working with him in their company. Franks then commented, "It is my opinion the claimant was afraid to come to Crown Point and face the scouts, as he knew they would denounce him in public, as they have a brutal manner of sticking their finger under a person's nose and declaring him a liar; [there was] no taking one around the corner and asking that the matter be kept confidential."[5]

A translator who was highly conversant in both Navajo and English would conduct a thorough interview, which could also spin off into other areas of interest for the inspector. Good translation of these languages was critical, with John Perry and Tom Torlino often serving as interpreters. Torlino became famous for two photos of him taken before and after he attended Richard H. Pratt's Carlisle Indian Industrial School in Carlisle, Pennsylvania. People often looked at these pictures that seemed to indicate so clearly the future of the American Indian—complete adoption into the

*These two images of Tom Torlino were taken to illustrate the before and after of a "wild" Navajo and a citizen who fit in with the dominant culture. His years of training at the Carlisle Boarding School were modeled after the military, providing him with good linguistic skills in English but not a desire to enter mainstream America. He returned to the reservation and assumed many traditional practices but later used his English to help the old scouts receive a pension. (Courtesy of Wikimedia Commons)*

dominant culture. In reality, when Torlino returned to the reservation, he maintained many of his traditional ways. Still, these two men's facility with both languages provided the accuracy that Franks and Stacher required.

The government, in the form of the pension office, derived a list of questions to be asked those applying for a pension. Instructions insisted "the claimant should state, as nearly as he may be capable of" answers to the following queries:

1. How many times he enlisted?
2. Place of each enlistment? [Note: Fort Wingate for most Navajo scouts]
3. Place of each discharge?
4. Names of first and other sergeants of each company in which he served? [In the 1885–86 campaigns, there were three Navajo scout companies, each with approximately fifty men. The military referred to them as A, B, and C companies, while the Navajo used First, Second, and Third, which made more sense in their language.]
5. Whether he participated in any battles or skirmishes?

6.  If he did, who was the chief or leader of the opposing force?
7.  Whether any were killed, wounded, or injured on either side with names and nature or character of wounds or injuries?
8.  Where fighting occurred, if any?
9.  Was he paid for his service? If so, at what rate?
10. What tribe or band was he a member of? Who was its chief?
11. How many names has he had? Which one did he serve under as a scout?
12. Was there another Indian of the same or similar name?
13. Does he know of any other scout or scouts who served with him in the same company? If he does, is he positive they were in the same company?
14. How would other scouts who served with him be able to recognize or distinguish him from others?
15. Any mark, scar, or peculiarity?
16. What is his exact height?
17. Who was the captain or commanding officer?[6]

This was the bulk of the required information.

The conduct of the interviews was just as important. C. R. Franks gave an excellent description of the process he and Stacher went through to obtain verifiable testimony. One well-known scout, Casa Miri, provided what Franks called a "key case" or stellar example of what the two government men were able to achieve. Franks started his report by saying that none of the Navajos interviewed could read or write, and so Stacher ended up filing claims "for all Indians on the reservation who had title for pension."[7] Navajos came in from as far away as 150 miles to lay their claim, and once collected as a group, remained at the agency for eighteen days. Franks, noting Stacher's hand in facilitating this opportunity for the scouts to gather and confirm their status, wrote:

Had it not been for his help, we could not have reached these men in a year's time and the expense in travel over the desert roads, with little hope of locating them, would have run into hundreds of dollars. In suspicious cases he did everything possible to learn the facts, as results, especially in some of the widow's claims as it will show. There was a time when I was somewhat afraid that Mr. Stacher was a trifle too zealous regarding Indian claims, but that suspicion was uncalled for. His attitude as well as the attitude of the older and more reliable Indians indicated they were trying to be absolutely honest in this matter, and I feel sure they were, as subsequent events proved.[8]

## Testimonial Honesty

To ensure honesty on everyone's part, the agent "pounded into them" that incorrect information or intentional lying could damage that Navajo's claim.

> I can say for the Indians that not once did we find where they told an untruth regarding any applicant, and if one was not sure, he would name someone who did know. We also had two scout cases which they were sure were frauds. There are some claims filed which were not among the claims I had, and inquiry among the Indians indicated they were not straight. . . . It may appear strange to the Bureau that all the Indians appear to know each other. They were born and raised on the reservation. Not a month passes that they do not have a big feast, Yé'ii Bicheii, or some Indian doings and they all gather at one time or another.[9]

Time and age of the person testifying also helped to maintain accuracy. Instead of the months of the year, a more general "fall" or "winter" and an annual reference point of the Fort Sumner period or some other important event was used in place of a specific date. Ages given during the enlisting process varied from accurate to ballpark. Further discussion sometimes narrowed the time gap in age.

As the process of confirmation got underway, Stacher identified a handful of old scouts who had served for much of the time and who recalled details about events and individuals that were found to be highly accurate when checked against the written record. They also knew most of the men who had served as scouts and were honest in their evaluation of individuals. Men like Casa Miri, Largo, Mariana Begay, and Hosteen Nascha (Hastiin Nééshjaa') were valuable assets in confirming information about the scouts' activities. Jake Segundo was particularly effective, with Franks stating, "Jake is a very intelligent Indian and a reliable one. . . . He was one of the Indians relied upon in establishing identity of some of those who claimed service in 1880 or near that time, as this man knew all of them well. . . . Jake was a sort of bureau of information. They recognize Jake as one of the older scouts and know that he had several services and personally knew each and every man who had served in the scouts who enlisted from Wingate."[10] Time after time, when Stacher and Franks reached an impasse in determining the accuracy of a claim, they would turn to these trusted sources of information who could say definitively from the Navajo perspective what the scouts experienced.

Sitting at the agency and waiting for applicants to arrive to start the pension process was only part of the story. Verification also took the government men into the field, illustrating their commitment to see that the job was done right. In 1932 Washington, D.C., sent out a field inspector named S. L. Hoover to find answers in some of the more questionable cases. One involving scout Jose Chavez raised issues concerning benefits for four Navajo wives, two of whom made conflicting claims. Much could be either verified or denied, but in the case of one of the women, Kiddespah, connections between husband and wife grew foggy, since he was dead and she had no clear documentation. Hoover illustrated the conscientious lengths he went to determine her status.

> I was not authorized to investigate Kiddespah, but I felt this was the only logical course to pursue in the interest of economy and efficiency, and as I was already at Crown Point, I proceeded to develop this claim from every angle. I conferred with Superintendent Stacher and urged him to help me get in touch with every available Indian who could assist in the solution of this case. I have explained in reporting other Indian claims during this trip of the terrible weather conditions I encountered while here. I felt that Slim Jim was an important witness in this case. We started out in the snow and mud to find him. He lived twelve miles from Crown Point. After dragging through mud and snow for hours, we finally contacted him, but his testimony on this point or in this claim, was not what I had hoped for. Supt. Stacher then suggested Jeff King and Jake Segundo. Jeff King gave good testimony; Jake Segundo failed us.
>
> I told Supt. Stacher that it was necessary to see Kiddespah and her son Peter Martin. We had exhausted all available witnesses around Crown Point and I felt that if we could see Kiddespah, I could get some information which would enable me to continue the investigation. Supt. Stacher cooperated with me nobly. He agreed to go to see her but said the conditions over the desert were not favorable. She lives at Tohatchi, twenty-five to thirty miles from Gallup. There are no roads. It is just a track across the desert. In wet weather, the mud is a foot deep. Supt. Stacher said he would go with me. It is in order here to say a word about this man Stacher. He is one of the finest men I have ever met and is admirably fitted for the place he holds in the Indian Service. He takes a

*S. F. Stacher poses with his highly esteemed and trusted group of scouts that played a key role in identifying and confirming applicant claims for a pension. These men had served faithfully and remembered clearly those Navajos who had worked as scouts. They could often relate, in detail, what an individual had done. For those making fraudulent claims, this group of men was a source to be reckoned with. (Courtesy of National Anthropological Archives, Smithsonian Institution, NAA INV.02277500)*

> real interest in his Indians. Besides, he is the most persistent man I have ever met. When we went to find Slim Jim or Jim Cuddy, we encountered difficulties which I did not see how we could overcome, but he persisted. We plowed on and were finally successful. When we started out to find Kiddespah, it seemed to me that as soon as we struck the soft ground of the desert, that to make 25 miles of this would be an utterly impossible thing. But he persisted in still going on until the engine became so hot, we had to stop, and finally after we had gone four miles and it was then getting late toward night, he had to give up and gave the order to return. I simply mention the above to show that everything was done within the range of the possible to complete this claim at this time. It could not be done. There is no use to try to buck the impossible.[11]

Further investigation raised other questions, so it appears Kiddespah did not receive the benefits she had applied for.

At times, there were those who fooled the system. Jack, a.k.a. Mamuzzo, a.k.a. Willeto, was such a man. He obtained a certificate of discharge from a woman that presumably belonged to her husband or a relative. Jack promised that he would make the fraudulent claim, then give her half of the initial payment, amounting to a total sum of $1,800. She received only $200, and so she went to the agent to expose the crime. Scouts also testified against Jack, searched old photographs to show that the person he was impersonating was not him, and supported the agent's action. Stacher began disciplinary procedures by targeting Jack's sheep amounting to $600, retrieving $170 from Jack's grandson and $175 from the woman involved, withholding checks at the agency, and putting a hold on $150 credit.[12] The power of the federal government came to bear to correct the situation.

Stacher, however, also did what he could to support those who may not have had a perfect record but were still deserving. One old scout, Juan Martine, was now totally blind but had served for three years in L Troop beginning in 1891. He had never received his honorable discharge papers, perhaps because of three incidents of drunkenness, "but his conduct in the main was good." On the other hand, a scout named Charley Davis had deserted during his years of service but was now receiving a pension. According to the records in Washington, because Juan did not have an honorable discharge, he should not receive a pension. For Stacher, "Anything you can do for him will be appreciated by this old scout as well as myself. . . . Appreciating all that you have done for various scouts and hoping that you will be able to do something for Juan, I am sincerely yours, S. F. Stacher."[13] He felt the same way about Jake, a.k.a. Delgadito, who in the second month of his enlistment had broken his arm when his horse fell on him. He went to a hospital, where a doctor removed part of the shattered bone, but he was unable to reconnect the two pieces of good arm bone so that the appendage could function. Following a period of recuperation, Jake returned to Fort Wingate, where his enlistment ended, but his civilian life of pain and incapacity had just begun. By the time he appeared before Stacher for a pension, he was also totally blind. The agent was able to secure a government award for the scout's disability.[14]

## What Is in a Name?

One of the most basic necessities in the pension process was identifying the scout by name. While this may seem fundamentally obvious, it was a task that took hours of investigation and multiple witnesses to corroborate. Before discussing that experience, it is helpful to put the Navajo naming process in perspective in order to better understand how some scouts ended up with so many titles. Few of these men spoke English, and few of the Anglos working with them spoke the Navajo language. Yet everybody needed to be called by something, and so the bestowal of names became a natural outgrowth of this interaction. Since the spelling of the Navajo language did not start to become standardized until the late 1930s, names were spelled phonetically by the writer. In this study, I have both followed what is in the documents and enlisted the help of Navajo linguists in providing the correct spelling. Some names could be discerned, but others could not, so those have been left as they were originally recorded.

In Navajo culture, soon after a child is born, he or she receives a sacred name that is used only in ceremonies. By this title, the holy people recognize the individual while also establishing the child's social status among the people. Family members will also know what it is, but outsiders, especially those who might ceremonially use it against the person, should never be aware of it. When an individual is going to offer a prayer and talk to the holy people, this name is used by way of introduction. At the same time, a child might receive a family name or a title that denotes a characteristic, and he or she might obtain relational kinship terms such as son or grandson. These names are used in daily life by everyone that the child interacts with and may be changed at various life stages or when the person does something noteworthy. The bearer may or may not know what they are, depending on how they are used and who uses them. For instance, a person may have a social name that carries great prestige because it links him or her to a respected individual, or it may denote a personal peculiarity, physical or temperamental quality, occupation, ability, achievement, occurrence, characteristic of a place he or she lives, clan relationship, or ceremony he performs.[15] Thus, a male or female may be known by a number of names at any given stage of life.

When Big Hat Charley, also known as Black Horse, at the age of eighty-nine gave a statement to Stacher as to his service as a scout, he also revealed the various names by which he was known. This testimony gives a clear explanation of the naming process that so many other scouts went through.

> I was born in Canyon de Chelly. In that canyon there is an Inscription Rock. My uncle did the inscribing on the rock and when I was a boy, I was called the Boy from Inscription Rock. Later on, I was given the name of Dugai. My full name was Dugai Bitsui [Daghaa' Bitsói—Mustache's Grandchild]. I was also called One Who Lives in the Canyon [Tségi'nii]. I lived in the canyon at the foot of Black Mountain from my birth until I enlisted in the United States service. I was going around in search of something to eat and went to Fort Wingate where there were some Army

officers enrolling Indians. There were also some Indians there that had already enlisted. They wanted me to join as I understood a little English and a little Spanish. I did not want to enlist at first and held off two days. A friend of mine called Jack had already enlisted and wanted me to enlist so I finally did so. Jack's Indian name was Na-pa-gi-gin [Blanket with Dirty Edges], named after the old-time Navajo blanket that he wore and means Blanket that Is Black around the Edge. He called me by both my names—Dugai Bitsui and Tsegi ni. I do not know under which name I was enrolled. After I had joined, we started for the Apache country where a mail carrier was missing for three days. We found where he had been killed by some Apache Indians. After that I was called Black Horse, a name I kept for as long as I was in the service as a scout. I was given that name because I rode a black horse. After I came back from being in the war with the Apaches, my people called me Diné en ni which means Navajo Indian Warrior. The Indians have called me by that name ever since. The white people have called me Big Hat Charley because when I was carrying the mail between here and Flagstaff, I wore a big white hat. I have given you all of the names by which I have been known. I served for two years. Both times I enlisted at Fort Wingate and so the first time we went on foot, but the second time, we rode our own horses.[16]

The white officers doing the enlisting, in some cases, tried to get the Navajo pronunciation of names correct, yet much of it turned into a Gordian knot. When Narbon or Barbon Segundo (Big Mustache Second) applied for his pension, another man named Nagarito came in to assist and mentioned two men that Segundo had served with. Enter complexity and uncertainty.

Among these men were two scouts named Hosteen Soize [Hastiin Ts'ósí—Slender Man] and Hosteen Yashie [Hastiin Yázhí—Small Man]. . . . Nagarito names Hosteen Soize as one of them. Could the other claimant be Hosteen Yashie? It will be noted that this man had several enlistments and was along with the men named by Nagarito and claimant, and apparently Nagarito was correct when he states he served as Juan Martin, for that same name is shown on the list of scouts. Neither of the scouts recalled a man named Hosteen Yashie. While the old Indian is not mentally capable of making a full and complete statement regarding his service, he does tell a fairly accurate story about this one service and it would appear he was one of the scouts in that particular organization. But which one is hard to tell as the name was a secondary matter with the Indians, and either the white officer or enlisting interpreter tacked on a name most suitable for the occasion, which should be remembered when the Indian names some of his comrades, as many were known to the Indians by one name and to the whites by another. . . . The older Indians know him as an alleged scout and think, as the writer does, that the old man had service, but under what name, no one knows.[17]

Another example of mistranslation and misunderstanding of names came with Julio Francisco when he was enlisting. He obviously did not know what was being said and so he responded with the word "Hólaa," meaning "I do not understand" or "I do not know." It became one of his scout names. Another man was known to the Navajos as Lost Reader while yet another person was "No Weno" (Bueno) or "No Good" to the officers but to the Indians was "To-Ah-Hal-Ien" (Doo Áhalyání—One Who Is Crazy). Billy Gonna received his name from the Navajo word Bilagáana meaning "Whiteman" because he spoke a little English. Naat'áanii (Leader) morphed from Charley Boy to Charlie Bowie, and since there was more than one Charlie, the second one received the name of Charlie Primero or Charlie One. There was also a Charlie Two, Three, and Four. The name of San Juan changed to Seguine or Say-geen. A Navajo named Mosto had a label close enough to Mose that he assumed that name while he was serving as a scout, and then he received a new title when he enlisted in L Troop, 6th Cavalry, for three years. He became Tom Brown. Nakaii Chehe (Naakai Chįįh Snézi) enlisted under the name that means "Long Nose Mexican." He served for a couple of months as a blacksmith, but was kicked by a horse while shoeing it, remained unconscious for several days, and was eventually discharged. A Navajo named Tłitso (Yellow) took his place and assumed the name of Nakaii Chehe. It did not end there. Nakaii waited a little over a month for his pay after getting out, but never received it. "In the fall of that year after the scouts mustered out, the Indians gave a big dance near Gallup and I went. While I was there, I saw this man Yellow and he told me that he had drawn my money and spent it. He had my discharge certificate."[18] White officers serving with the Navajos received their own names, such as Lieutenant Albert B. Scott, who was called "The Man Who Always Smokes," or Captain Tom, known as "Breadmaker," or General George Crook, who earned the title of "Gray Fox." No one was above getting a label.

While the Navajos had their opportunity for expression of creativity, the soldiers and recruiters also had their day in the sun. There was nothing Navajo about a scout being named Robin Hood, Slim Jim, Grover, Louis,

Dick, Aleck, Mr. Mud Face, or Mark Twain. This last name went to a scout who first enlisted as Nasdui (Náshdóítsoh—Mountain Lion). During his next enlistment he obtained the name of Louis from a Mexican interpreter. Following the Geronimo trouble, he received a final title of "Nig." "I stayed around Fort Wingate after my second service and there was a nigger woman there who was doing washing and I helped her one time and they [soldiers] began calling me 'Nig' in fun and they reenlisted me under that name."[19]

One scout claimed that his name was Willeto, but there was no record of such a person and the name was definitely not Navajo. Agency records proved unhelpful, yet there were many of the older scouts who recognized him and knew that he had served with the military. Franks had to make the final decision: "Jake Segundo, one of the reliable Indians, and Willie, another, were closely questioned and told me there was no such scout. The Indians were all sure that this claimant was one of the Indian officers, and it is my opinion that claimant is identical with the scout Guerito Chiquito."[20] The army at the time of enlistment had hoped to skirt the issue of name and language problems by issuing a small metal disk with a number on it. Each scout had his own number and was sometimes referred to by it. For example, Atcitty Spahe (Atsidiílbáhá—The Gray Silver Man) was number 88, and that became his name. The scouts, for the most part, did not remember their number, but for the white men, this was an important aspect of the administrative written record.

## Of Wives and Women

Stacher tracked not only who had been a scout, but also who had been a scout's wife, since they were also eligible for a pension. At this time, arranged and polygynous marriages were often practiced. The government encouraged agents to prevent or discourage this type of bonding, but the old ways persisted. One question raised was which wife should receive a pension and at what point was a divorce in effect, since there were no official marriage or annulment documents to refer to. Again, oral testimony of friends, relatives, and acquaintances came into play, with the older scouts often testifying for or against a female claimant. As with the men, there were some women who submitted false claims, calling forth an investigation and a reconstructed history of a scout. The women demanded as much research as the men.

Take for instance Ahkadozbah (Ákájoozbaa'—One Who Has Fought for Something) who had married scout Frank Taylor. Her relationship with Frank began when she was thirteen years old, joining her mother, Ahkidesbah (Ák'ideezbaa—One Who Hunted after Something), in wedlock to the same man. "Frank Taylor considered me and my mother as his wives, and treated us on an equal basis during all of the time that we lived with him as his wives. We lived in the same hogan as a family unit until the time of his death."[21] When their husband died, the younger woman filed a claim for his pension, which her mother agreed to because the daughter would live longer. However, to the government the rules were clear:

> Plural wives or widows have never been recognized in the administration of the pension laws, the provisions as concerns marital rights being throughout, with reference to monogamous marriages, necessarily subject to the general rule of law denying the validity of any marriage undertaken during the subsistence of a prior marriage of either party. . . . Pension is not a property right, but is a gratuity, conditioned wholly by federal law. That law, in applying state or tribal marriage laws, does so only within the framework of federal policy. A plural marriage—of an Indian, a Mormon, or a Turk—is contrary to our system of marital law. Our pension laws and other federal laws do not contemplate plural marriage.[22]

Application denied.

Another denial came in the case of Zonne (Zhoonii—Beautiful), who claimed that she had been married to Jose Torres, a deceased scout who left behind a certificate of discharge following his service. Zonne presented it to Stacher, alleging she had been married to the scout, that she had a right to the pension, and that Torres had actually served under the different name of Etcitty (Atsidi—Silversmith). Circumstances surrounding the scout's activities seemed to be confirmed. However, when Etcitty died and Zonne pursued receiving the payments, questions arose. After a brief investigation, Stacher learned that Etcitty was really Torres's brother, he had never served as a scout but had obtained the certificate from Torres while he was still alive, and Zonne had lied and had never been married to Torres. "She is a very ignorant old woman, totally blind, and stated that she thought because she had the certificate she was entitled to a pension."[23]

Children were also eligible for part of a deceased scout's pension once their mother had died. There were also spin-offs concerning children that were unanticipated. For instance, a woman named Nosglinthapah lied to Stacher and denied that she had married Fred Attiski (Atsésk'eh—Hip) according to Navajo custom after the death of her husband, scout Charley

No. 4. She continued to collect the pension even though she was no longer eligible. Catching her in the lie, Stacher withdrew the payments but also withdrew her two children and put them in an Indian boarding school. The daughter, a fourteen-year-old, was also "married" to Fred as a second wife for two years. Both Fred and Nosglinthapah were caught in lies. They hid out in the canyon to avoid interrogation, understood that in the eyes of the government the daughter was too young for wedlock, and knew that their days of living off Charley No. 4's money had now ended.[24]

Older children had other issues. Joe Smith, the son of an unidentified scout, wrote to Stacher when he learned his father had received an increase in his pension. The letter, reproduced here without any corrections in spelling and punctuation, gives a taste of how at least one family viewed the scout's pension.

Dear Sir, I am going drop you a few lines while I have a spare time I just want to know Mr. Stacher how much my father got again this time when he gets his pay again. I just want to know how much he get we never had seen not a cent but we don't know what he did with that. He should spent it on some thing that's worth while some old scouts buy sheep that their paying, but our father has not bought one yet and never helps his children that are in need. That one daughter of his that had a large family of small children not fit to go to school yet she's got 2 in school at Fort Wingate. This family is need in help but he never helps them out. Ever since he gets pay. So we just wish that he could buy some sheep that will help us in the future, but he is spenting it carelessly. He's staying with that is my father his daughter and son that's all he stay with, but we don't know what he buys and he got a debt in every trading store too and we wish this to be stop too. For we want sheep instead of candy and so forth, although he never buys us any thing yet I just want to ask you about this. do the old scouts spent their money in carelessly and never helps their children out with that? I thought his payment was to help his children with and besides he gives money to those that are not in need those that are well off. What do you this [think] about this. Now. He could not listen to us if we tell him. He is in need him self so he got to buy sheep, instead of cans stuff and sweet stuff. This all, yours truly, Joe Smith, Good Bye

Stacher's reply was to the point, noting that the scout's pension had been increased by ten dollars per month, that the money was his to determine how it should be spent, that he was getting older and so more dependent upon what the government paid, and that he could help others as he saw fit.[25]

The issue of trade and trading posts brought another wrinkle of concern. The reservation at this time had stores run primarily by Anglos who were monitored and controlled through regulations dictated by the federal government. They were the hub of incoming and outgoing commerce, the main connection to the dominant society, the focal point of activity for a reservation community, and the means of communicating through postal service with individuals. Barter for wool took place in the spring, and the fall brought barter for lambs and seasonal crops such as piñon nuts, with woven blankets, silver, and rugs coming in all year round. These were the staples of the trade with food, hardware, and every other item the Navajos wanted from the Anglo world going across the post's counters in the other direction. Much of this followed a pattern of ebb and flow, and so traders extended credit throughout the year to the customers who paid their bills and did not overextend their buying power. Pawning items such as silverwork, blankets, and other crafts that could be sold in the Anglo economy was another means of ensuring payment of debt. The scouts had an additional form of collateral—their monthly government pension checks. The trader could expect an inflow of cash on a regular basis and so extended more credit because of the greater guarantee of payment, often withholding part of the check until bills were paid. This later became a big issue, one that altered the entire barter system, but in the 1920s the goods and payments flowed smoothly with only occasional bumps.

The scouts, as part of this large economic system, borrowed against their monthly pension, which caused the agent to find himself in the middle of a controversy between trader and customer. This was the case with As Kan Nas Bah (Ákánaasbaa'—One Who Went to War) and C. F. Gorman. It seems the old woman came to the trader, requesting a little credit to be held against her incoming pension check. She received her goods, but did future shopping elsewhere and went directly to the Crown Point Agency to secure her monthly payment. Gorman wanted Stacher's help in making the Navajos responsible and made a suggestion:

When they have a just debt, they should pay it, so we ask you to send the next two checks to us and we will get her to pay us what she owes. If she gets the checks here, she will not have the nerve to deny that she owes us, and so will pay her bill. If you will do this for us, we will guarantee that you will not be bothered by us for any more such bills. We should have known better, but felt sorry for the old woman. We think her smart aleck son is at the bottom of the matter as he is too mean to live.[26]

The agent, even if he wanted to, could not officially do it without the permission of the individual receiving the pension money. No doubt there were those who might sympathize with the traders and put pressure on the Navajo clientele to pay what was due, but the government frowned upon any type of intervention.

Nevertheless, letters from traders poured into the agency asking for debt relief for impoverished scout families. Trader E. I. Bailey at Two Wells Trading Post sought reimbursement for food he had given to a couple while they were sick and for the burial clothing and coffins he provided after they died. As a central figure in the community, it was hard for him not to do these things. If he was stingy with assistance, people would start boycotting his post and seek other stores at which to trade. Still, the over $300 the couple owed for goods and services rendered was not to be taken lightly. He contacted another trader who received the old scout's check to see if he would help cover the cost. It is doubtful that any payment was given. Other pensioners made a practice of intentionally borrowing over the amount of a check, accruing more debt than the post could absorb. One man "howled around here [Coyote Canyon Trading Post] all winter" wanting the agent to send his check there. Little wonder—he owed three times the amount of the check.[27]

Still, Stacher was not above working with the traders as long as he knew it was approved by the recipient and in the best interest of that pensioner. When J. M. Bailes contacted the agent about a customer at the Toh-Tli-Kai (Tó Łigai—White River Trading Post), a Navajo woman named "Aston Nez" (Asdzáán Nez—Tall Woman), Stacher did what he thought best. The elder had spent most of her pension check but had $300 remaining. Six months previous many of the trader's customers had pawned a lot of their personal items amounting to $2,800 for goods. Now they were trying to sell Tall Woman their sheep for cash but only $600 worth of pawn had been redeemed. Bailes feared that if they got her money, they would leave the pawn where it was, spend it on items in town, and be destitute the next winter when times were hard and the economy was slow. He offered to buy sheep for Tall Woman and sell them to her at cost, in order to encourage his other customers to pay what they owed and redeem their possessions. All Stacher would have to do is send Bailes her pension check amounting to $300. He made the transfer to her Individual Indian Money account, allowing the trader to go through with the transaction. At

*This 1926 photograph of C. R. Franks (left) and S. F. Stacher (right), seated in the front row, surrounded by Navajo scouts applying for pensions, provides a snapshot in time and a footnote to history. Finally recognized for their soldiering in the United States military, each man was eligible for an Indian Wars medal that testified of this service to the country. Many proudly donned their medal for special occasions. (Courtesy of National Anthropological Archives, Smithsonian Institution, NAA INV.02277400)*

the end of his letter, Bailes illustrated another aspect of the trading business when he wrote, "Sam Nelson, an old blind scout, wants to trade his pension check with me. Do you know how much he owes Mr. Westbrook at Mariano Lake?" Traders on the reservation kept informed about their competitors' status and also about what type of credit risk might be sauntering into the post's bullpen.[28]

As the old scouts and their wives died, so did the understanding of their way of life. The days of scouting and the Apache campaigns faded into increasing oblivion, as did the lives of the scouts. Stacher, founder of the Crown Point Agency and Boarding School in 1912 watched its demise in 1935, then was transferred to work in the Indian Land Department until mandatory retirement in 1940. He died on August 28, 1952. While mention is made of his many accomplishments working with and for Indian people, little is said of his dogged determination to assist the scouts in receiving pensions. For many outsiders, it was an administrative duty, with few realizing the impact it had on hundreds of Navajos connected to soldiering for their country. Time smoothed over that story, making their service an increasingly smaller footnote in history.

Twelve years after Stacher's death, one of the last repercussions from his work surfaced in 1964. Ason-Ka-Na-Bah (Asdzáán Kánaabaah—A Woman Going to War), widow of scout John, needed to have her pension file updated. The Navajo Tribe had no census information on her, but it did have a military file on her husband with his three original discharges on parchment paper, a carbon copy of her application for benefits, and carbon copies of correspondence dated in 1931. Jack White, a trader at the Larry Lee Trading Post in Gallup, New Mexico, spoke fluent Navajo and was very familiar with this woman. After noting she signed everything with a thumbprint, he described her, saying:

> She is not a Navajo [further research indicated she was a Comanche married to a scout], nor does she speak the language. She has a beak-like nose, brilliant black eyes and looks like an eagle. I have no idea how old she is, but she must be well over 90. She is very stooped and wrinkled. She is about the oldest Indian woman I know of who still gets around. . . . She has many living descendants, some of whom I have known personally and practically all my life. It is my understanding that she had twelve children or at least twelve children who survived.[29]

Eddie Lee, from the same trading post a few months earlier, added to the picture of this old matriarch. She came to the store twice a month to spend her seventy-five-dollar check on supplies. He described her as a slender, snow-white-haired lady who was "as ornery as ever." He explained that "he did not mean to say that she was malicious, but he felt the old timers are quite independent and enjoy giving traders and the younger folks much devilment."[30] As one of the last of that breed, she had earned the right to have some fun.

One final aspect of the Navajo scouts applying for a pension was the testimony they left behind as Stacher, Franks, and other government employees interviewed them. The goal was to verify the applicant's service and place that experience in a context with other scouts and recorded historical facts. There was not much of an attempt to move beyond these points, and so the rich personal involvement that is often found in Apache scout testimony is missing. There were, however, glimpses of the scouts' activities that reveal what life was like in that closing era. The preservation of some of this detail serves as a reminder of just how difficult their task was and how it appeared to those Navajo scouts. What follows are a handful of excerpts from testimony rendered by these men as they recalled those days of conflict.

Vicente Baca remembered:

> We were out with the white troops. The interpreter had a nickname and was called "Burro." I was first sergeant of this troop and Jose Chaves was the second sergeant. . . . On this campaign we went to the Apache country, where Mescalero now is; we were scouts for the white soldiers all the time. There was a small skirmish while we were there. The white captain sent me and [three other scouts] after a man riding up a draw. We went to the top of a hill and the Apaches opened fire on us. Mariana Begay got off his horse and the Apaches shot and killed it while wounding my horse in the shoulder. That was all the trouble we had that time except we captured some horses belonging to the Apaches and took them into camp and the captain sent us back with these horses where we found them and we turned them loose with the exception of one horse to replace the one that had been killed. We went south from there to where a station had been arranged and we scouted there all summer and back to Fort Wingate.[31]

One wonders why the officer had the scouts return the Apache horses to the men they were chasing.

The next account contains a more startling omission: Why did the scouts commit murder? Hosteen Cly, a.k.a. Barbon Segundo, during the

Victorio campaign went to the field with fifteen scouts, eventually ending up in the Silver City, New Mexico, region for five months.

> From there we were after Indians and went into the Magdalena Mountains. On this trip there were seven Navajo scouts. We captured three men and three women, all Apaches. The men made their escape but we killed the three squaws. There was a baby among them and it was not killed, but was wounded in the heel. We then returned to Fort Bayard and was there for a time. We were there for two months then we again went back to Ojo Caliente where Apaches were reported, and we found Apaches there and we drove them towards San Carlos reservation where there was another fort or army post. The soldiers who were stationed at San Carlos captured and took charge of the Apaches and we then returned to Fort Wingate where we were discharged.[32]

The Magdalena Mountains was the site of another skirmish. Coneho went with eight other Navajo scouts and two white officers to join three companies at Fort Grant before traveling to the Mescalero reservation.

> These troops were white troops and I was with the first company. We entered a canyon where the Apaches were on top and fired on us and this time we lost two Navajos. The sergeant, Sam, was killed, shot through the abdomen. He was shot twice while a second Navajo was shot through the chest and killed. There was one white soldier killed at the same time. They also killed some horses belonging to the soldiers. There were two officers and myself who hid behind a rock while the firing was going on, and while I was looking out, they fired at me and the bullet struck the rock close to my head and splintered. I was not hit directly, but part of the bullet glanced off and struck me on the left knee and I have the scar. I was sent to the hospital they had prepared where they treated my leg wound. I was discharged after I was well and returned to this country. I was in this service about six months.[33]

Not all injuries were a direct result of enemy contact. Stacher recorded what happened to Martine after he enlisted around 1881. A month after joining, he, with two other scouts and two white soldiers, went in pursuit of two deserters from Fort Wingate. They followed the defectors to Gallup. Stacher noted:

They tracked them this far, but that in crossing the railroad track, the deponent's [Martine's] horse caught one foot between the ties and in the struggle to get free, the deponent was thrown from his horse and the bone of his right leg was broken below the hip. He was taken to the hospital at Fort Wingate, where he was given surgical and other medical attention until he recovered. When he was able to leave the hospital, he received what was due him, was dismissed, and given honorable discharge papers, which he later gave to his father-in-law for safe-keeping. This man buried them in a box, but died without anyone knowing where the papers were underground and so the papers were never recovered.[34]

Thus, there were a number of casualties before this story ended, but fortunately, Martine received his pension in spite of the lost documents.

The aphorism "the job is not over until the paperwork is done," aptly describes the Stacher years. Due to his dedication in pursuing pensions for the scouts and his assembling a record of their service, many Navajo men and women received what had been earned during those difficult years following Fort Sumner, the Apache wars, and reservation duty as the dominant society moved on to other concerns. The Navajo scouts, along with their cousins the Apache scouts, proved to be of inestimable value in working with the military when their services were needed. The land, its people, and historical circumstance came together at a time that demanded unique skills and conditioning to bring hostilities to an end. While some may question the practice of turning a people against their own relatives or those of the same ethnic group, the results were effective, and perhaps even more humane by shortening the conflict and subsequent suffering. The Apache wars, in particular, give a harsh reminder of just how brutal conflict can be. Sending many of the vanquished to Florida—even those Apache scouts who had served so faithfully—was a fittingly symbolic conclusion to the harsh, traitorous events that preceded it.

Yet out of these difficult times, those Navajos and Apaches who scouted for the bluecoats created a record of heroism and service of which they can be proud. A difficult time with its difficult tasks brought forth the bravery and determination necessary to complete the job in a challenging environment. Trained from their youth, those men who served as scouts became some of the most formidable light infantry the United States and perhaps the world has ever placed in the field. Those who served as Navajo scouts can be proud of their accomplishments and the legacy they left behind.

# NOTES

## Introduction: Picking Up the Trail

1. Thomas W. Dunlay, *Wolves for the Blue Soldiers, Indian Scouts and Auxiliaries with the United States Army, 1860–90* (Lincoln: University of Nebraska Press, 1982).

2. Grenville Goodwin, *Western Apache Raiding and Warfare*, ed. Keith H. Basso (Tucson: University of Arizona Press, 1971); Charles F. Lummis, *General Crook and the Apache Wars* (Flagstaff, AZ: Northland Press, 1966); John C. Cremony, *Life Among the Apaches* (Alexandria, VA: Time Life Books, 1868, 1981); Charles B. Gatewood, *Lt. Charles Gatewood and His Apache Wars Memoirs*, ed. Louis Kraft (Lincoln: University of Nebraska Press, 2005).

3. Eve Ball, *In the Days of Victorio: Recollections of a Warm Spring Apache* (Tucson: University of Arizona Press, 1970); Eve Ball, *Indeh: An Apache Odyssey* (Provo, UT: Brigham Young University Press, 1980).

4. Robert Christie Collman, "Navajo Scouts, 1873–1895: An Integration of Various Cultural Interpretations of Events" (master's thesis, Franconia College, Franconia, NH, 1975); John Lewis Taylor, *Navajo Scouts during the Apache Wars* (Charleston, SC: History Press, 2019).

5. For some excellent examples of the U.S. military working against the Apaches, see Donald E. Worcester, *The Apaches: Eagles of the Southwest* (Norman: University of Oklahoma Press, 1979); James L. Haley, *Apaches: A History and Culture Portrait* (Norman: University of Oklahoma, 1981, 1997); Daniel L. Thrapp, *The Conquest of Apacheria* (Norman: University of Oklahoma Press, 1973).

6. Samuel Sandoval, presentation, Eighteenth Annual Language Heritage Conference, Monument Valley, UT, April 13, 2012.

# Chapter 1: Athabaskan Origins and Conflict

1. Deni J. Seymour, *From the Land of Ever Winter to the American Southwest: Athapaskan Migrations, Mobility, and Ethnogenesis* (Salt Lake City: University of Utah, 2012) (hereafter cited as *FLEW*).

2. Keren Rice, "Linguistic Evidence Regarding the Apachean Migration," in *FLEW*, 254.

3. Harry Hoijer, "The Chronology of the Athapaskan Languages," *International Journal of American Linguistics* 22 (October 1956): 219–32.

4. Sally Rice, cited in Keren Rice, "Linguistic Evidence," in *FLEW*, 263.

5. Blake De Pastino, "Utah Cave Full of Children's Moccasins Sheds Light on Little-Known Ancient Culture," *Western Digs*, November 17, 2014, http://westerndigs.org/utah-cave-full-of-childrens-moccasins-sheds-light-on-little-known-ancient-culture/.

6. Deni J. Seymour, "'Big Trips' and Historic Apache Movement and Interaction," in *FLEW*, 401.

7. Deni J. Seymour, "Platform Cache Encampments: Implications for Mobility Strategies and the Earliest Ancestral Apaches," *Journal of Field Archaeology* (February 2014): 161–72.

8. Alan D. Reed and Jonathan C. Horn, "Early Navajo Occupation of the American Southwest: Reexamination of the Dinétah Phase," *Kiva* 55, no. 4 (Fall 1990): 297.

9. Douglas D. Dykeman and Paul Roebuck, "Navajo Emergence in Dinétah, Social Imaginary and Archaeology," in *FLEW*, 151–52.

10. There are many excellent versions of the creation story and beginnings of Navajo culture including the emergence and the events surrounding Changing Woman, Monster Slayer, and Born for Water. Here I have included, in alphabetical order, some of the most readily available examples. This information is equally relevant for both this and the next chapter. Stanley A. Fishler, *In the Beginning: A Navaho Creation Myth*, Anthropological Paper no. 13 (Salt Lake City: University of Utah, 1953); Pliny Earle Goddard, "Navajo Texts," in *Anthropological Papers of the American Museum of Natural History*, vol. 34, part 1 (New York: American Museum of Natural History, 1933), 127–79; Berard Haile, *The Upward Moving and Emergence Way: The Gishin Biyé Version* (Lincoln: University of Nebraska Press, 1981); Jerrold E. Levy, *In the Beginning: The Navajo Genesis* (Berkeley: University of California Press, 1998); Washington Matthews, *Navaho Legends* (Salt Lake City: University of Utah Press, 1897, 1994); Don Mose Jr., *The Legend of the Navajo Hero Twins* (Blanding,

UT: San Juan School District, 2009); Franc Johnson Newcomb, *Navaho Folk Tales* (Albuquerque: University of New Mexico Press, 1967, 1990); Aileen O'Bryan, *Navaho Indian Myths* (New York: Dover Publications, 1956, 1993); Mary C. Wheelwright, *Navajo Creation Myth: The Story of the Emergence by Hasteen Klah* (Santa Fe: Museum of Navajo Ceremonial Art, 1942); Leland C. Wyman, *Blessingway: With Three Versions of the Myth Recorded and Translated by Father Berard Haile, O.F.M.* (Tucson: University of Arizona Press, 1970); and Paul G. Zolbrod, *Diné bahane': The Navajo Creation Story* (Albuquerque: University of New Mexico Press, 1984).

11. Perry Robinson, interview with author, October 14, 2017.

12. John Holiday and Robert S. McPherson, *A Navajo Legacy: The Life and Teachings of John Holiday* (Norman: University of Oklahoma Press, 2005), 264–65.

13. O'Bryan, *Navaho Indian Myths*, 181–85.

14. O'Bryan, *Navaho Indian Myths*, 181–85.

15. O'Bryan, *Navaho Indian Myths*, 181–85.

16. O'Bryan, *Navaho Indian Myths*, 181–85.

17. Charles B. Gatewood, *Lt. Charles Gatewood and His Apache War Memoirs*, ed. Louis Kraft (Lincoln: University of Nebraska Press, 2005), 19–20.

18. Gatewood, *Lt. Charles Gatewood*, 20.

19. Washington Matthews, "The Gentile System of the Navajo Indians," *Journal of American Folklore* 3, no. 9 (April–June 1890): 110.

20. Matthews, "Gentile System," 110.

21. Matthews, "Gentile System," 93, 95, 99.

22. J. Lee Correll, *Through White Men's Eyes: A Contribution to Navajo History*, vol. 1 (Window Rock, AZ: Navajo Heritage Center, 1979), 31 (hereafter cited as *TWME*). This six-volume series comprises primary source documents concerning Navajo history.

23. Frank D. Reeve, "Navaho-Spanish Diplomacy, 1770–1790," *New Mexico Historical Review* 35, no. 3 (Summer 1960): 232.

24. *TWME*, vol. 1, 31.

25. *TWME*, vol. 1, 87.

26. *TWME*, vol. 1, 83, 87–88.

27. *TWME*, vol. 1, 89, 93, 108, 110.

28. *TWME*, vol. 1, 271.

29. *TWME*, vol. 1, 290, 324.

30. *TWME*, vol. 1, 332.

31. *TWME*, vol. 2, 66, 86–87.

32. *TWME*, vol. 2, 106, 309.

33. *TWME*, vol. 2, 267, 310.

34. James L. Haley, *Apaches: A History and Cultural Portrait* (Norman: University of Oklahoma Press, 1997), 242.

35. *TWME*, vol. 2, 412, 441–42.

36. *TWME*, vol. 5, 33.

37. *TWME*, vol. 5, 65.

38. *TWME*, vol. 5, 254.

39. *TWME*, vol. 5, 285.

40. See L. R. Bailey, *The Long Walk: A History of the Navajo Wars, 1846–68* (Pasadena, CA: Westernlore Publications, 1978); Peter Iverson, *Diné, A History of the Navajos* (Albuquerque: University of New Mexico Press, 2002); Broderick H. Johnson, ed., *Navajo Stories of the Long Walk Period* (Tsaile, AZ: Navajo Community College Press, 1973); Lawrence Kelly, *Navajo Roundup: Selected Correspondence of Kit Carson's Expedition against the Navajo, 1863–1865* (Boulder, CO: Pruett, 1970); Gerald Thompson, *The Army and the Navajo: The Bosque Redondo Reservation Experiment, 1863–1868* (Tucson: University of Arizona Press, 1982).

# Chapter 2: Navajo, Apache, and U.S. Military Approaches, 1870–1886

1. W. W. Hill, *Navaho Warfare*, Yale University Publications in Anthropology, no. 5 (New Haven, CT: Yale University Press, 1936).

2. There are a number of different versions of the story of the Navajo Twins and their journey to their father. Among the most accessible are Don Mose, *The Legend of the Navajo Hero Twins* (Blanding, UT: San Juan School District Media Center, 2009); Paul G. Zolbrod, *Diné bahane': The Navajo Creation Story* (Albuquerque: University of New Mexico Press, 1984); Washington Matthews, *Navaho Legends* (Salt Lake City: University of Utah Press, 1897, 1994); Aileen O'Bryan, *Navaho Indian Myths* (New York: Dover Publications, 1956, 1993); and Berard Haile, *The Upward Moving and Emergence Way: The Gishin Biyé Version* (Lincoln: University of Nebraska Press, 1981).

3. Berard Haile, *Origin Legend of the Navaho Enemy Way: Text and Translation*, Yale University Press Publications in Anthropology, no. 17 (New Haven, CT: Yale University Press, 1938).

4. Haile, *Origin Legend*, 8.

5. Haile, *Origin Legend*, 9.

6. Haile, *Origin Legend*, 282.

7. Hill, *Navaho Warfare*, 12.

8. Hill, *Navaho Warfare*, 13.

9. Hill, *Navaho Warfare*, 14.

10. Hill, *Navaho Warfare*.

11. Tiana Bighorse and Noel Bennett, *Bighorse the Warrior* (Tucson: University of Arizona Press, 1994), 18.

12. Franciscan Fathers, *An Ethnologic Dictionary of the Navaho Language* (Saint Michaels, AZ: Saint Michaels Press, 1910, 1968), 366.

13. Harry Walters, conversation with author, January 16, 2012.

14. For two excellent, detailed accounts see Haile, *Origin Legend*, and Franciscan Fathers, *The Navajo War Dance* (Saint Michaels, AZ: Saint Michaels Press, 1946).

15. Franciscan Fathers, *Navajo War Dance*, 295.

16. Robert N. Watt, *Apache Tactics, 1830–86* (Long Island, NY: Osprey, 2012); Grenville Goodwin, *Western Apache Raiding and Warfare*, ed. Keith H. Basso (Tucson: University of Arizona Press, 1983).

17. For a brief synopsis of this story, see James L. Haley, *Apaches: A History and Culture Portrait* (Norman: University of Oklahoma Press, 1997), 19–23.

18. Morris E. Opler, *Apache Odyssey: A Journey between Two Worlds* (Lincoln: University of Nebraska Press, 2002), 299–300.

19. Goodwin, *Western Apache Raiding*, 270–75.

20. Eve Ball with Nora Henn and Lynda Sanchez, *Indeh: An Apache Odyssey* (Provo, UT: Brigham Young University Press, 1980), 62.

21. Opler, *Apache Odyssey*, 41–46.

22. Morris Edward Opler and Harry Hoijer, "The Raid and Warpath Language of the Chiricahua Apache," *American Anthropologist* vol. 42, no. 4 (December 1940): 617–22; S. M. Barrett, ed., *Geronimo: His Own Story* (New York: Ballantine Books, 1970), 165–66.

23. Sherry Robinson, *Apache Voices: Their Stories of Survival as Told to Eve Ball* (Albuquerque: University of New Mexico Press, 2000), 101–2.

24. Robinson, *Apache Voices*, 166.

25. Robinson, *Apache Voices*, 102.

26. Morris E. Opler and Harry Hoijer, "The Raid and Warpath Language of the Chiricahua Apache," *American Anthropologist* 42, no. 4 (December 1940): 627–34.

27. Haley, *Apaches*, 118.

28. Robinson, *Apache Voices*, 194.

29. Haley, *Apaches*, 119.

30. Goodwin, *Western Apache Raiding*, 247–49.

31. Goodwin, *Western Apache Raiding*, 259–60.

32. Opler, *Apache Odyssey*, 70–71.

33. Guy Gugliotta, "New Estimate Raises Civil War Death Toll," *New York Times*, April 2, 2012, https://nytimes.com/2012/04/03/science/civil-war-toll-up-by-20-percent-in-new-estimate.html. This article evaluates a study by professor J. David Hacker, a quantitative historian who has mined new digital sources for more accurate information.

34. Robert M. Utley, *Frontier Regulars: The United States Army and the Indian, 1866–1891* (New York: Macmillan, 1973), 14–15.

35. Utley, *Frontier Regulars*, 16–18.

36. Douglas C. McChristian, *The U.S. Army in the West, 1870–1880: Uniforms, Weapons, and Equipment* (Norman: University of Oklahoma Press, 1995), 33–34.

37. Utley, *Frontier Regulars*, 17.

38. Utley, *Frontier Regulars*, 24.

39. Duane A. Smith, *A Time for Peace: Fort Lewis, Colorado, 1878–1891* (Boulder: University of Colorado, 2006), 71–72.

40. Utley, *Frontier Regulars*, 24.

41. Utley, *Frontier Regulars*, 20.

42. McChristian, *U.S. Army in the West*, 112–16.

43. McChristian, *U.S. Army in the West*, 117–20.

44. Don Rickey Jr., *Forty Miles a Day on Beans and Hay: The Enlisted Soldier Fighting in the Indian Wars* (Norman: University of Oklahoma Press, 1963), 104.

45. Richard Allan Fox Jr., *Archaeology, History, and Custer's Last Battle: The Little Big Horn Reexamined* (Norman: University of Oklahoma Press, 1993), 40–46.

46. Fox, *Archaeology, History, and Custer's Last Battle*, 102.

## Chapter 3: Genesis of the Navajo Scouts

1. Sherry Robinson, *Apache Voices: Their Stories of Survival as Told to Eve Ball* (Albuquerque: University of New Mexico Press, 2000), 166.

2. Robinson, *Apache Voices*, 165–67.

3. Clarence B. Chrisman, "After the Apaches, 1885–1886," in *Indian War Veterans: Memories of Army Life and Campaigns in the West, 1864–1898*, ed. Jerome Greene (El Dorado, CA: Savas Beatie, 2011), 344–51.

4. Robert M. Utley, "A Chained Dog: Military Strategy on the Western Frontier," *The American West Magazine* 10, no. 4 (July 1973): 18.

5. Utley, "Chained Dog," 19.

6. Robert W. Frazer, *Forts of the West: Military Forts and Presidios and Posts Commonly Called Forts West of the Mississippi River to 1898* (Norman: University of Oklahoma Press, 1972), 108–9; "History of Fort Wingate Depot, Forts Fauntleroy, and Lyon," government publication, 1970.

7. Richard Red Hawk, "Spies, Guides, and Indian Scouts," *True West* 19 (May 1987): 14–19.

8. Frank Apache, interview with Tom Ration, February 1969, Tape 352, no. 3, University of New Mexico CSWR American Indian Oral History Navajo Transcripts, Albuquerque, NM, p. 19.

9. Apache, interview, 20–21.

10. J. Lee Correll, *Through White Men's Eyes: A Contribution to Navajo History*, vol. 5 (Window Rock, AZ: Navajo Heritage Center, 1979), 353.

11. Correll, *Through White Men's Eyes*, 362.

12. Okah L. Jones Jr., "The Origins of the Navajo Indian Police, 1872–1873," *Arizona and the West* 8, no. 3 (Autumn 1966): 228.

13. William Redwood Price to James H. Miller, May 6, 1871; Miller to Price, May 7, 1871, U.S. Army District of New Mexico, Letters Received, Sept. 1865–August 1890, Record Group 393, Roll 14 (this archive is hereafter cited as NM-Letters Received, RG 393).

14. Price to Assistant Adjutant General, District of New Mexico, May 19, 1871, NM-Letters Received, RG 393.

15. Miller to Price, May 27, 1871, NM-Letters Received, RG 393.

16. Robert Christie Collman, "Navajo Scouts, 1873–1895: An Integration of Various Cultural Interpretations of Events," master's thesis, Franconia College, Franconia, NH, May 1975, 19.

17. Anna Price, cited by editor Keith H. Basso in Grenville Goodwin, *Western Apache Raiding and Warfare* (Tucson: University of Arizona Press, 1971), 34–38.

18. Jones, "Origins of the Navajo Indian Police," 231.

19. Jones, "Origins of the Navajo Indian Police," 233–34.

20. Jones, "Origins of the Navajo Indian Police," 236.

21. Robert M. Utley, *Frontier Regulars: The United States Army and the Indian, 1866–1890* (New York: Macmillan, 1973), 50.

22. John Lewis Taylor, *Navajo Scouts during the Apache Wars* (Charleston, SC: History Press, 2019), 16.

23. Utley, *Frontier Regulars*, 17.

24. Thomas W. Dunlay, *Wolves for the Blue Soldiers, Indian Scouts and Auxiliaries with the United States Army, 1860–90* (Lincoln: University of Nebraska Press, 1982), 94.

25. Utley, "Chained Dog," 21.

26. Utley, "Chained Dog," 24.

27. Utley, "Chained Dog."

## Chapter 4: The Apache Wars, 1873–1886

1. Donald E. Worcester, *The Apaches: Eagles of the Southwest* (Norman: University of Oklahoma Press, 1979); James L. Haley, *Apaches: A History and Culture Portrait* (Norman: University of Oklahoma, 1981, 1997); Daniel L. Thrapp, *The Conquest of Apacheria* (Norman: University of Oklahoma Press, 1973).

2. See Paul Andrew Hutton, *The Apache Wars* (New York: Crown Publishing, 2016); Edward H. Spicer, *Cycles of Conquest: The Impact of Spain, Mexico, and the United States on the Indians of the Southwest, 1533–1960* (Tucson: University of Arizona Press, 1962); Angie Debo, *Geronimo: The Man, the Time, His Place in History* (Norman: University of Oklahoma, 1976); Dan L. Thrapp, *Al Sieber: Chief of Scouts* (Norman: University of Oklahoma Press, 1964); Dan L. Thrapp, *Victorio and the Mimbres Apaches* (Norman: University of Oklahoma Press, 1974); Dan L. Thrapp, *Juh: An Incredible Indian* (El Paso: Texas Western Press, 1973); Louis Kraft, *Gatewood and Geronimo* (Albuquerque: University of New Mexico Press, 2000); Edwin R. Sweeney, *From Cochise to Geronimo: The Chiricahua Apaches, 1874–1886* (Norman: University of Oklahoma Press, 2010); Kendall D. Gott, *In Search of an Elusive Enemy: The Victorio Campaign* (Fort Leavenworth, KS: Combat Studies Institute Press, 2002); and Kathleen P. Chamberlain, *Victorio: Apache Warrior and Chief* (Norman: University of Oklahoma Press, 2007).

3. See William H. Leckie, *The Buffalo Soldiers: A Narrative of the Negro Cavalry in the West* (Norman: University of Oklahoma Press, 1967); Charles River Editors, *Buffalo Soldiers: The History and Legacy of the Black Soldiers Who Fought in the U.S. Army during the Indian Wars* (Las Vegas, NV: Charles River Publishing, 2021); Monroe Lee Billington, *New Mexico's Buffalo Soldiers, 1866–1900* (Niwot, CO: University Press of Colorado, 1991); and Charles L. Kenner, *Buffalo Soldiers and Officers of the Ninth Cavalry, 1867–1898* (Norman: University of Oklahoma Press, 1999).

4. John Keegan, *The Face of Battle: A Study of Agincourt, Waterloo, and the Somme* (New York: Viking Press, 1976).

5. Eve Ball, *In the Days of Victorio: Recollections of a Warm Springs Apache* (Tucson: University of Arizona Press, 1970, 1997), 113.

6. Palmer Valor, cited by editor Keith H. Basso in Grenville Goodwin, *Western Apache Raiding and Warfare* (Tucson: University of Arizona Press, 1971), 51.

7. S. M. Barrett, ed., *Geronimo: His Own Story* (New York: Ballantine Books, 1970), 6; Jason Betzinez with W. S. Nye, *I Fought with Geronimo* (New York: Bonanza Books, 1959), 6; Britton Davis, *The Truth about Geronimo* (Lincoln: University of Nebraska Press, 1929, 1976), 153.

8. Betzinez, *I Fought with Geronimo*, 28.

9. Ball, *In the Days of Victorio*, 17–18.

10. John C. Cremony, *Life among the Apaches* (Alexandria, VA: Time Life Books, 1868, 1981), 188–89.

11. Ball, *In the Days of Victorio*, 4.

12. Eve Ball, *Indeh: An Apache Odyssey* (Provo, UT: Brigham Young University Press, 1980), 32, 102.

13. Davis, *Truth about Geronimo*, 168.

14. Ball, *In the Days of Victorio*, 74.

15. Betzinez, *I Fought with Geronimo*, 57–58.

16. Barrett, *Geronimo*, 150; Ball, *In the Days of Victorio*, 179.

17. Cremony, *Life among the Apaches*, 161–64.

18. Charles Gatewood, cited in Haley, *Apaches*, 323.

19. Ball, *In the Days of Victorio*, 19–20.

20. Betzinez, *I Fought with Geronimo*, 86.

21. Betzinez, *I Fought with Geronimo*, 13.

22. Cremony, *Life among the Apaches*, 156–57.

23. Wolfkiller, cited in Louisa Wade Wetherill (recorder) and Harvey Leake (editor), *Wolfkiller: Wisdom from a Nineteenth-Century Navajo Shepherd* (Salt Lake City: Gibbs Smith, 2007), 67.

24. Davis, *Truth about Geronimo*, 219.

25. Ball, *In the Days of Victorio*, 13, 103; Goodwin, *Western Apache Raiding and Warfare*, 198.

26. Ball, *In the Days of Victorio*, 177.

27. Ball, *In the Days of Victorio*, 16.

28. John Rope, cited by editor Keith H. Basso in Goodwin, *Western Apache Raiding and Warfare*, 153.

29. Ball, *In the Days of Victorio*, 15.

30. Ball, *In the Days of Victorio*, 11.

31. Rope, cited in Goodwin, *Western Apache Raiding and Warfare*, 148.

32. See Alexander H. Leighton and Dorothea C. Leighton, *Gregorio, the Hand-Trembler: A Psychological Personality Study of a Navaho Indian*, Reports of the Ramah Project, no. 1 (Cambridge, MA: Peabody Museum

of American Archaeology and Ethnology, Harvard University, 1949); see also Robert S. McPherson, *Dinéjí Na'nitin: Navajo Traditional Teachings and History* (Boulder: University Press of Colorado, 2012), 13–43.

33. Betzinez, *I Fought with Geronimo*, 113–15.

34. Davis, *Truth about Geronimo*, 82–83.

35. Cremony, *Life among the Apaches*, 189–90.

36. Ball, *In the Days of Victorio*, 13.

37. Cremony, *Life among the Apaches*, 87.

38. Cremony, *Life among the Apaches*, 290–91.

39. Davis, *Truth about Geronimo*, 153.

40. Cremony, *Life among the Apaches*, 36–37.

41. Ball, *In the Days of Victorio*, 75.

42. Betzinez, *I Fought with Geronimo*, 85; Mrs. Andrew Stanley, cited by editor Keith H. Basso in Goodwin, *Western Apache Raiding and Warfare*, 210.

43. Charles B. Gatewood, *Lt. Charles Gatewood and His Apache War Memoirs*, edited by Louis Kraft (Lincoln: University of Nebraska Press, 2005), 27.

44. Ball, *In the Days of Victorio*, 152–53.

45. Cremony, *Life among the Apaches*, 282.

46. Betzinez, *I Fought with Geronimo*, 57.

47. Betzinez, *I Fought with Geronimo*, 53.

## Chapter 5: Tactics and Techniques

1. Britton Davis, *The Truth about Geronimo* (Lincoln: University of Nebraska Press, 1929, 1976), 166.

2. John Rope, cited by editor Keith H. Basso in Grenville Goodwin, *Western Apache Raiding and Warfare* (Tucson: University of Arizona Press, 1971), 103–4.

3. Davis, *Truth about Geronimo*, 38.

4. Davis, *Truth about Geronimo*, 38–39.

5. George Crook to Philip Sheridan, March 31, 1886, cited in Davis, *Truth about Geronimo*, 215.

6. Jason Betzinez with W. S. Nye, *I Fought with Geronimo* (New York: Bonanza Books, 1959), 111.

7. Betzinez, *I Fought with Geronimo*, 91.

8. Davis, *Truth about Geronimo*, 172–73.

9. Eve Ball, *In the Days of Victorio: Recollections of a Warm Springs Apache* (Tucson: University of Arizona Press, 1970, 1997), 134.

10. John C. Cremony, *Life among the Apaches* (Alexandria, VA: Time Life Books, 1868, 1981), 140.

11. Ball, *In the Days of Victorio*, 81.

12. Goodwin, *Western Apache Raiding and Warfare*, 199–200.

13. Charles R. Lummis, *General Crook and the Apache Wars* (Flagstaff, AZ: Northland Press, 1985), 19.

14. Palmer Valor, cited by editor Keith H. Basso in Goodwin, *Western Apache Raiding and Warfare*, 47.

15. Davis, *Truth about Geronimo*, 178–79.

16. Cremony, *Life among the Apaches*, 183–86.

17. Lummis, *General Crook and the Apache Wars*, 82–83.

18. Lummis, *General Crook and the Apache Wars*, 85.

19. Davis, *Truth about Geronimo*, 189.

20. Center of Military History, *American Military History* (Washington, D.C.: Center of Military History, United States Army, 1969, 1989), 6–7.

21. Palmer Valor, cited by editor Keith H. Basso in Grenville Goodwin, *Western Apache Raiding and Warfare* (Tucson: University of Arizona Press, 1971), 47–51.

22. Valor, cited by Basso in Goodwin, *Western Apache Raiding*, 48–49.

23. Robert N. Watt, *Apache Tactics, 1830–86* (Long Island, NY: Osprey, 2012), 46–51.

24. Eve Ball, *In the Days of Victorio: Recollections of a Warm Springs Apache* (Tucson: University of Arizona Press, 1970, 1997), 83–85.

25. Watt, *Apache Tactics*, 23–44.

26. Kendall D. Gott, *In Search of an Elusive Enemy: The Victorio Campaign* (Fort Leavenworth, KS: Combat Studies Institute Press, 2002), 20–21.

27. Vincintie Begay, cited in Robert C. Collman, "Navajo Scouts, 1873–1895," master's thesis, Franconia College, Franconia, NH, 1975, p. 23.

28. Jake Segundo, cited in Collman, "Navajo Scouts," 56.

29. Watt, *Apache Tactics*, 53.

30. S. M. Barrett, ed., *Geronimo: His Own Story* (New York: Ballantine Books, 1970), 124.

31. Betzinez, *I Fought with Geronimo*, 68–70.

32. Lummis, *General Crook and the Apache Wars*, 21.

## Chapter 6: Finding, Fixing, and Fighting the Enemy

1. John Malone, "On the Trail of Geronimo," cited in Robert W. Young and William Morgan, *Navajo Historical Selections* (Lawrence, KS: Bureau of Indian Affairs, 1954), 41–47.

2. Tizwin is a type of beer made from corn that is soaked and allowed to expand before being ground into a mash that is then boiled and strained. The resulting liquid is sweetened by adding mesquite flour or saguaro syrup to assist in the fermentation. It must be drunk shortly after it is made; otherwise, it quickly sours.

3. Malone, "On the Trail of Geronimo," 41–47.

4. Big Hat Charley or Black Horse, Case No. 1564756, June 6, 1927, Record Group 75, National Archives, Washington, D.C.

5. John Rope, cited by editor Keith H. Basso in Grenville Goodwin, *Western Apache Raiding and Warfare* (Tucson: University of Arizona Press, 1971), 93–185.

6. Rope, cited by Basso in Goodwin, *Western Apache Raiding*, 133–34.

7. Rope, cited by Basso in Goodwin, *Western Apache Raiding*, 118.

8. Rope, cited by Basso in Goodwin, *Western Apache Raiding*, 147–48.

9. Rope, cited by Basso in Goodwin, *Western Apache Raiding*, 123–24.

10. Rope, cited by Basso in Goodwin, *Western Apache Raiding*, 156–63.

11. Rope, cited by Basso in Goodwin, *Western Apache Raiding*, 169.

12. Rope, cited by Basso in Goodwin, *Western Apache Raiding*, 184–85.

## Chapter 7: Closing Perspectives on the Apache Wars

1. Charles R. Lummis, *General Crook and the Apache Wars* (Flagstaff, AZ: Northland Press, 1985), 19–20.

2. General George Crook, cited in Paul Andrew Hutton, *Soldiers West: Biographies from the Military Frontier* (Lincoln: University of Nebraska Press, 1989), 6.

3. Eve Ball, *In the Days of Victorio: Recollections of a Warm Springs Apache* (Tucson: University of Arizona Press, 1970, 1997), 181.

4. Ball, *In the Days of Victorio*, 32–33.

5. Ball, *In the Days of Victorio*, 156.

6. Ball, *In the Days of Victorio*, 80–81.

7. Charles B. Gatewood, cited in James L. Haley, *Apaches: A History and Culture Portrait* (Norman: University of Oklahoma Press, 1997), 321–22.

8. Eugene Chihuahua, quoted in Eve Ball, *Indeh: An Apache Odyssey* (Provo, UT: Brigham Young University Press, 1980), 48–49.

9. Charles B. Gatewood, *Lt. Charles Gatewood and His Apache War Memoirs*, ed. Louis Kraft (Lincoln: University of Nebraska Press, 2005), 19–20.

10. Jason Betzinez with W. S. Nye, *I Fought with Geronimo* (New York: Bonanza Books, 1959), 92.

11. William R. Price, Major, 8th Cavalry to Asst. Adj. General, Dept. of Missouri, July 30, 1873, Record Group 94 (Washington, D.C.: National Archives).

12. Britton Davis, *The Truth about Geronimo* (Lincoln: University of Nebraska Press, 1929, 1976), 74.

13. John C. Cremony, *Life among the Apaches* (Alexandria, VA: Time Life Books, 1868, 1981), 215.

14. Muster Rolls (excerpts), Navajo Scouts, 9th Cavalry, United States Army, May 19, 1876–October 31, 1911, Record Group 93, National Archives, Washington, D.C.

15. John Lewis Taylor, *Navajo Scouts during the Apache Wars* (Charleston, SC: History Press, 2019), 80–89.

16. Bernard James Byrne, *A Frontier Surgeon: Life in Colorado in the Eighties* (New York: Exposition Press, 1935, 1962): 153–54.

17. Frances Gillmor and Louisa Wade Wetherill, *Traders to the Navajos: The Wetherills of Kayenta* (Boston: Houghton Mifflin, 1934).

18. Henry L. Mitchell to Galen Eastman, February 15, 1880, Letters Received—New Mexico, Record Group 75, National Archives, Washington, D.C.

19. J. Carpenter to Carl Schurz, February 28, 1880, Record Group 75, Letters Received—New Mexico.

20. Mitchell to Eastman, February 27, 1880, Letters Received—New Mexico.

21. Galen Eastman to Commissioner of Indian Affairs, March 8, 1880, Letters Received—New Mexico.

22. Captain F. T. Bennett to Acting Assistant Adjutant General of New Mexico, March 22, 1880, Letters Received—New Mexico.

23. See Robert S. McPherson, *Fighting in Canyon Country: Native American Conflict, 500 AD to the 1920s* (self-published, 2021), for a more detailed account of this and the previous Mitchell incident.

24. Dennis M. Riordan to Commissioner of Indian Affairs, April 19, 1884, Letters Received—New Mexico.

25. "Report of Pete," May 4, 1884, Letters Received—New Mexico, Record Group 75, National Archives, Washington, D.C.

26. Riordan to Commissioner of Indian Affairs, April 22, 1884, Letters Received—New Mexico.

27. "Report of Sam-Boo-ko-di," April 19, 1884, Letters Received—New Mexico.

28. Ten nai tsosi (Diné Ts'ósí—Slim Man) "Story," given to Dennis M. Riordan, May 5, 1884, Letters Received—New Mexico, Record Group 75, Washington, D.C.

29. John H. Bowman to Commissioner of Indian Affairs, July 3, 1884, Letters Received—New Mexico.

30. L. P. Bradley to Adjutant General, Dept. of the Missouri, June 27, 1884, Letters Received—AGO.

31. Bowman to Commissioner of Indian Affairs (CIA), July 11, 1884, Letters Received—New Mexico.

32. Bowman to CIA, July 12, 1884, Letters Received—New Mexico.

33. Bowman to CIA, July 19, 1884, Letters Received—New Mexico.

34. Bowman to CIA, July 12, 1884, Letters Received—New Mexico.

35. S. E. Marshall to CIA, August 22, 1884, Letters Received—New Mexico.

36. H. P. Kingsbury to Post Adjutant, September 1, 1884, Letters Received—AGO.

37. Tiana Bighorse with Noel Bennett, ed., *Bighorse the Warrior* (Tucson: University of Arizona Press, 1990), 62.

38. Kingsbury to Post Adjutant, September 1, 1884, Letters Received—AGO.

39. Kingsbury to Post Adjutant, September 1, 1884, Letters Received—AGO.

40. Kingsbury to Post Adjutant, September 1, 1884, Letters Received—AGO.

41. For a more complete history of William Shelton and the Shiprock Agency see Robert S. McPherson, *Traders, Agents, and Weavers: Developing the Northern Navajo Region* (Norman: University of Oklahoma Press, 2020).

42. Shelton to Commissioner, September 18, 1907, in *Report on Employment of United States Soldiers in Arresting By-a-lil-le and other Navajo Indians*, 60th Congress, 1st sess., May 25, 1908, p. 12 (hereafter cited as *ABONI*); Adjutant General to Commanding General, Department of Colorado, October 15, 1907, *ABONI*, 13–14.

43. J. Lee Correll, *Bai-a-lil-le: Medicine Man or Witch?* (Window Rock, AZ: Navajo Historical Publications, Biographical Series #3, 1970), 20.

44. Unless otherwise noted, the information concerning the movement and attack on Ba'álílee's camp is taken from Captain Harry O. Williard's

report to the Adjutant General, Headquarters Department Colorado, October 30, 1907, *ABONI*, 14–20.

45. This phonetically spelled name is untranslatable and does not sound like a Navajo word.

46. Isabel Lee, interview with author, February 13, 1991.

47. Williard to the Adjutant General, October 30, 1907, *ABONI*, 16.

48. Ba'álílee's Wife Testimony, April 22, 1908, U.S., Congress, Senate, *Testimony Regarding Trouble on Navajo Reservation*, 60th Congress, 2nd sess., March 3, 1909, pp. 19–20 (hereafter cited as *TRTNR*); J. A. Heffernan Testimony, April 22, 1908, *TRTNR*, 32.

49. George H. Hunter to Adjutant General, Department of the Colorado, August 26, 1908, Record Group 393, Black Mountain Expeditionary Report (Washington, D.C.: National Archives, 1908).

## Chapter 8: Troop L and the Navajo Police

1. Clifford P. Coppersmith, "Indians in the Army: Professional Advocacy and the Regularization of Indian Military Service," *Military History of the West* 26, no. 2 (Fall 1996): 159–85; Eric Feaver, "Indian Soldiers, 1891–95: An Experiment on the Closing Frontier," *Prologue* (Summer 1975): 108–18; R. Eli Paul, ed., *Sign Talker: Hugh Lenox Scott Remembers Indian Country* (Norman: University of Oklahoma Press, 2016); Michael L. Tate, "Soldiers of the Line: Apache Companies in the U.S. Army, 1891–1897," *Arizona and the West* 16, no. 4 (Winter 1974): 343–64; Michael L. Tate, "From Scout to Doughboy: The National Debate over Integrating American Indians into the Military, 1891–1918," *Western Historical Quarterly* 17, no. 4 (October 1986): 417–37; W. Bruce White, "The American Indian as Soldier, 1890–1919," *Canadian Review of American Studies* 8, no. 1 (Spring 1976): 15–25.

2. John M. Schofield to Secretary of War, December 8, 1890, Record Group 94, National Archives, Washington, D.C.

3. C. B. Hoppin to Adjutant General, U.S. Army, December 26, 1891, Record Group 94, National Archives, Washington, D.C.

4. John M. Schofield, "Memorandum," March 6, 1891, Headquarters of the Army, Record Group 94, National Archives, Washington, D.C.

5. General Orders No. 28, Adjutant General's Office, Headquarters of the Army, March 9, 1891, Record Group 94, National Archives, Washington, D.C.

6. Tate, "Soldiers of the Line," 349.

7. Adjutant General to Commanding General, Headquarters of the Army, May 7, 1891, Record Group 94, National Archives, Washington, D.C.

8. R. B. Wallace to Assistant Adjutant General, April 12, 1891, Record Group 94 National Archives, Washington, D.C.

9. C. B. Hoppin to Adjutant General U.S. Army, July 22, 1891, Record Group 94, National Archives, Washington, D.C.

10. Troop L Muster Roll, 2nd Cavalry Regiment, August 31, 1891–December 31, 1894, Record Group 94, National Archives, Washington, D.C.

11. Theodore Schwan to Adjutant General, Washington, D.C., December 31, 1891, Record Group 94, National Archives, Washington, D.C.

12. Schwan to Adjutant General, Washington, D.C., December 31, 1891, Record Group 94.

13. Schwan to Adjutant General, Washington, D.C., December 31, 1891, Record Group 94.

14. Schwan to Adjutant General, Washington, D.C., December 31, 1891, Record Group 94.

15. G. G. Huntt to Adjutant General of the Army, November 14, 1893, Record Group 94, National Archives, Washington, D.C.

16. Thomas J. Lewis to Adjutant General of the Army, March 23, 1894, Inspection Report L Troop, 2nd Cavalry, Record Group 94, National Archives, Washington, D.C.

17. Lewis to Adjutant General, March 23, 1894.

18. John M. Schofield, Report of the Secretary of War, 1893–94, House of Representatives, Exec. Docs. 2nd sess., 53d Congress, 68.

19. Schofield, Report of the Secretary of War, 68.

20. A. M'D M'Cook, Report of Brig. Gen. M'D. M'Cook, Headquarters Department of the Colorado, September 1, 1894, Report of the Secretary of War, 1893–94, House of Representatives, Exec. Docs. 2nd sess., 53d Congress, 141.

21. Commander, 2nd U.S. Cavalry to Adjutant General of the Army, March 23, 1894, Record Group 94, National Archives, Washington, D.C.

22. Major Adam Chaffee to Adjutant General, Department of Colorado, May 1, 1894, Record Group 75, National Archives, Washington, D.C.

23. Commander, 2nd U.S. Cavalry to Adjutant General of the Army, March 23, 1894.

24. Hoppin to Regimental Adjutant, 2nd Cavalry, October 17, 1894, Record Group 94, National Archives, Washington, D.C.

25. Coppersmith, "Indians in the Army," 180.

26. D. M. Riordan to Commissioner of Indian Affairs, August 14, 1883, *Reports of the Commissioner of Indian Affairs* (Washington, D.C.: Government Printing Office, 1883), 121.

27. David L. Shipley to Commissioner of Indian Affairs, August 31, 1891, *Report of the Commissioner of Indian Affairs* (Washington, D.C.: Government Printing Office, 1891), 310.

28. Alfred W. Yazzie, *Navajo Police* (Rough Rock, AZ: Navajo Curriculum Center, Rough Rock Demonstration School, 1980), 19–20.

29. Charlie Mitchell, cited in John Lewis Taylor, *Navajo Scouts during the Apache Wars* (Charleston, SC: History Press, 2019), 80.

30. Roswell T. Nelson, interview with Frank McNitt, October 31, 1957, Frank McNitt Collection, Two Grey Hills folder, State Records Center and Archives, Santa Fe, New Mexico; "Indian Strikes Down Wife of Trader in Attempted Robbery," *Farmington Times Hustler*, September 30, 1927, p. 1; "Navajo Who Committed Assault Is Captured," *Farmington Times Hustler*, October 7, 1927, p. 1; Albert H. Kneale, *Indian Agent* (Caldwell, ID: Caxton Printers, 1950), 365–68.

31. "Indian Strikes Down Wife," 1.

32. Kneale, *Indian Agent*, 367.

33. John Daw, interview with David Brugge and Bernadine Whitegoat, December 10, 1960, Doris Duke #782, Doris Duke Oral History Project, Special Collections, Marriott Library, University of Utah, Salt Lake City, Utah.

34. This version of events comes from Gladwell Richardson, *Navajo Trader* (Tucson: University of Arizona Press, 1986), 49–57. Another version that exonerates John Wetherill may be found in Frank McNitt, *The Indian Traders* (Norman: University of Oklahoma Press, 1962), 271–72. The Richardson version is used here because of its firsthand nature and the perspective it gives on John Daw.

35. Richardson, *Navajo Trader*, 53–54.

36. Richardson, *Navajo Trader*, 55.

37. Tillman Hadley, "Saga of the Indian Tracker," *True Detective* 31, no. 5 (February 1939): 17–19, 116–19. All quotes and information are derived from this source.

38. Hadley, "Saga of the Indian Tracker," 116.

39. Hadley, "Saga of the Indian Tracker," 119.

40. Leo W. Banks, "John Daw, the Navajos' 'Big Policeman,'" *Arizona Highways* 79, no. 2 (February 2003): 14–17.

## Chapter 9: S. F. Stacher and the Eastern Navajo Agency Experience

1. Agent Samuel F. Stacher to Governor A. T. Hannett, February 15, 1926, Record Group 75, National Archives, Washington, D.C.

2. "An Act to Amend the Indian War Pension Act of March 4, 1917," H.R. 1501, 2d Sess., 68th Congress, February 17, 1925, pp. 1–3; Bill, H.R. 11798, 2d Sess., 68th Congress, January 20, 1925, pp. 1–5; Stacher to Commissioner of Indian Affairs, December 7, 1924, Record Group 75, National Archives, Washington, D.C.

3. Marianito, Case No. 20649, October 8, 1925, Record Group 75, National Archives, Washington, D.C.

4. Julio Francisco or Hola, Case No. 20546, October 5, 1925, Record Group 75, National Archives, Washington, D.C.

5. C. R. Franks to Commissioner of Pensions, November 10, 1925, Record Group, National Archives, Washington, D.C.

6. Memorandum, S.E. Division, I.S.O. 19486, Vicente Baca, January 10, 1927, Crown Point, New Mexico, Record Group 75, National Archives, Washington, D.C.

7. Franks to Commissioner of Pensions, "Casa Miri," I.S.O. 17840, November 4, 1925, Indian Scouts 1885–86, Record Group 75, National Archives, Washington, D.C.

8. Franks to Commissioner of Pensions, "Casa Miri," November 4, 1925.

9. Franks to Commissioner of Pensions, "Casa Miri," November 4, 1925.

10. Franks to Commissioner of Pensions concerning Jake Segundo, Case No. 19222, January 9, 1926, Record Group, National Archives, Washington, D.C.

11. Inspector S. L. Hoover, Field Report on Kiddespah vs. Aheyibah, contesting widows of Jose Chavez, April 24, 1932, Record Group 75, National Archives, Washington, D.C.

12. Stacher Statement on Mamuzza Case, No. 12548, October 5, 1926, Record Group 75, National Archives, Washington, D.C.

13. Stacher to Major Kemp, August 3, 1932, Record Group 75, National Archives, Washington, D.C.

14. Jake or Delgadito Carrizozo, Case No. 12544, June 15, 1927, Record Group 75, National Archives, Washington, D.C.

15. See Gladys A. Reichard, *Social Life of the Navajo Indians* (New York: Columbia University Press, 1928), 96–107.

16. Black Horse or Big Hat Charley, Case No. 1564756, June 6, 1927, Record Group 75, National Archives, Washington, D.C.

17. Hosteen Cly, Narbon or Barbon Segundo, Case No. 20659, April 27, 1929, Record Group 75, National Archives, Washington, D.C.

18. Hola, Case No. 20546, October 5, 1925; Mosto, Mose, or Tom Brown, Case No. 20656, October 7, 1925; Nakaii or Nalga, Case No. 1612729, April 16, 1929; Jake Segundo, Case No. 20530, June 7, 1928, Record Group 75, National Archives, Washington, D.C.

19. Nod-do-he, Nashdui, Louis, Nig, Case No. 21084, December 5, 1928, Record Group 75, National Archives, Washington, D.C.

20. Franks to Commissioner of Pensions, July 1, 1962, Record Group 75, National Archives, Washington, D.C.

21. Frank Taylor, Case No. XC–2,580,878, April 6, 1944, Record Group 75, National Archives, Washington, D.C.

22. Frank Taylor case, April 6, 1944.

23. Zonne, Case No. 17578, January 28, 1927, Record Group 75, National Archives, Washington, D.C.

24. Nosglinthapah, Case No. 17323, October 15, 1925, Record Group 75, National Archives, Washington, D.C.

25. Stacher to Joe Smith, September 18, 1931, Record Group 75, National Archives, Washington, D.C.

26. C. F. Gorman to Stacher, January 31, 1927, Record Group 75, National Archives, Washington, D.C.

27. E. I. Bailey to Olin C. Walker, October 16, 1936; Mike Kirk to Stacher, September 21, 1931; George W. Lee to Stacher, May 28, 1929, Record Group 75, National Archives, Washington, D.C.

28. J. M. Bailes to Stacher, July 25, 1932; Stacher to John G. Hunter, August 4, 1932, Record Group 75, National Archives, Washington, D.C.

29. Jack White, interview with Hal Houston, January 24, 1964, Record Group 75, National Archives, Washington, D.C.

30. Report of Field Examination about John, Claim No. XC 2 636 432, November 8, 1963, Record Group 75, National Archives, Washington, D.C.

31. Vicente Baca Statement, January 27, 1927, Record Group 75, National Archives, Washington, D.C.

32. Hosteen Cly or Barbon Segundo, Case 20659, April 27, 1929, Record Group 75, National Archives, Washington, D.C.

33. Coneho, Case No. 20708, February 10, 1926, Record Group 75, National Archives, Washington, D.C.

34. Martine, Case No. 1645695, February 24, 1930, Record Group 75, National Archives, Washington, D.C.

# INDEX

*Italic page numbers correspond to images.*